Praise for *Learning from the Bumps in the Road*

"The title of this book tells it all! The four authors describe the typical bumps in the road that workers in the field of early care and education encounter daily, throughout their careers. The 'insights' from the title refer to increasingly deep understandings of inevitably complex events and relationships in the field, and they are offered on every single page of this book, exquisitely presented for adults who must accomplish complex tasks, plans, and interactions and provide leadership for the benefit of our young children on a day-to-day basis. And, yes, the authors provide the richest store of insights I have ever encountered in a single book during my fifty years of reading and studying in this field. Every page addresses the kinds of bumps everyone whose work involves young children and their families must face throughout their careers, and all four authors share their insights in diverse, enlightening, helpful, and provocative ways."

Lilian G. Katz, PhD, professor emerita at the University of Illinois

"*Learning from the Bumps in the Road* is a unique and great read: at once stimulating and great fun. Having four authors discuss their often quite different perspectives on central topics in today's early childhood education discourse encourages readers to also find their own voices on these same topics. It is a very thought-provoking experience to come across ideas with which you agree, with which you disagree, and which provoke you. I especially and highly recommend *Learning from the Bumps in the Road* to leaders in early childhood education who like to push the boundaries of their thinking on pressing, important issues in our field."

Louise Derman-Sparks, international speaker, coauthor of *Anti-Bias Education for Young Children and Ourselves* and *What If All the Kids Are White? Anti-Bias Multicultural Education with Young Children and Families*, and former member of the National Association for the Education of Young Children (NAEYC) governing board

"Often we speak only of our triumphs, put our best selves forward, and focus on our strengths. Inside, most of us have the tendency to be very hard on ourselves; we dwell on our mistakes, weaknesses, and perceived deficiencies. Strength and growth come from flipping these behaviors. We need to think well enough of ourselves and make self-talk positive. And with each other, we need to fearlessly share the challenges and struggles as well as celebrate the successes. We talk about being authentic with children, and we know how to do this. These authors become our mentors as their stories and strategies help us become more authentic with one another and within ourselves. This ability to be real will change our behavior and our practice. We could have no better mentors than Holly Elissa, Janet, Luis, and Debra."

Bonnie Neugebauer, founder and executive editor of *Exchange* magazine and founder and director of program development at the World Forum Foundation

"This book is a joy and an adventure—I invite you to enjoy it as much as I have. You will learn much during your journey and be better prepared for and informed about helping young children and families meet the challenges of early childhood and beyond."

Mark Ginsberg, PhD, dean and professor of the College of Education and Human Development at George Mason University

"This book is an invitation to be on a journey of self-discovery with four of the field's visionary leaders. Along the way, you'll get to know yourself as an educator, leader, mentor, advocate, and world citizen. It's all here. The authors skillfully weave a rich tapestry of theory, practice, research, and wisdom with life experience, practical tools, and perspectives grounded in the lives of the children, families, and communities that call our programs home. They have saved each of us a place at the table—join them!"

Claire Chang, associate vice president of grants and program at Minnesota Philanthropy Partners

Learning from the Bumps in the Road

Also from Redleaf Press

Learning to Lead: Effective Leadership Skills for Teachers of Young Children, second edition, by Debra Ren-Etta Sullivan

Managing Legal Risks in Early Childhood Programs: How to Prevent Flare-Ups from Becoming Lawsuits by Holly Elissa Bruno, with Tom Copeland (copublished by Teachers College Press)

Learning FROM THE Bumps IN THE Road

.... **Insights from Early Childhood Leaders**

Holly Elissa Bruno, MA, JD

Janet Gonzalez-Mena, MA

Luis Antonio Hernandez, MA

Debra Ren-Etta Sullivan, EdD

Redleaf Press®
www.redleafpress.org
800-423-8309

Published by Redleaf Press
10 Yorkton Court
St. Paul, MN 55117
www.redleafpress.org

First edition 2013
Cover design by Jim Handrigan
Background photograph on front cover by Jim Handrigan
Photograph of Holly Elissa Bruno by Corey Fitzgerald; photograph of Janet Gonzalez-Mena
  by Frank Gonzalez-Mena; photograph of Luis Antonio Hernandez courtesy of the author;
  photograph of Debra Ren-Etta Sullivan by Bob Hereford
Interior design by Percolator
Typeset in ITC Stone Serif and Trade Gothic
Printed in the United States of America
20 19 18 17 16 15 14 13   1 2 3 4 5 6 7 8

Library of Congress Cataloging-in-Publication Data
Bruno, Holly Elissa.
   Learning from the bumps in the road : insights from early childhood leaders /
 Holly Elissa Bruno, MA, JD, Janet Gonzalez-Mena, MA, Luis Antonio Hernandez,
 MA, and Debra Ren-Etta Sullivan, EdD.
     pages cm
   Includes bibliographical references and index.
   ISBN 978-1-60554-206-5 (pbk. : alk. paper)
   ISBN 978-1-60554-260-7 (e-book)
   1. Early childhood education—Administration. 2. Educational leadership.
 I. Gonzalez-Mena, Janet. II. Hernandez, Luis Antonio. III. Sullivan, Debra Ren-Etta.
 IV. Title.
 LB2822.6.B783 2013
 372.21—dc23
                             2012050787

Printed on 30 percent postconsumer waste paper

*To those who work with children in classrooms every day and the people—
the leaders—who make that work an experience of wonderful development
and learning for the entire community of learners. When you hit your next
bump in the road, may your landing be soft and your laughter abundant.*

Contents

Holly Elissa Bruno

In the Beginning

Talk about bumps. At the annual National Association for the Education of Young Children (NAEYC) conference at the Jacob K. Javits Convention Center in New York City back in 2002, an inspiration was shaken into me as I jockeyed for balance on a bumpy and rainy nighttime tuk-tuk (bike-cab) ride back to my hotel: invite inspiring, savvy, and insightful colleagues to present with me at the next conference! Now that would be fun! Plus, I would learn along with the participants. Why not just do it?

Images of three presenters appeared before my eyes: Luis Antonio Hernandez (that man is crazy like a fox), Janet Gonzalez-Mena (gentle, wise, lives and breathes diversity), and Dr. Debra Ren-Etta Sullivan (always offers eye-popping, one-of-a-kind "takes" on issues). Maybe it was no accident that we each hailed from opposite corners of the country: Miami (Luis), Boston (Holly Elissa), San Francisco (Janet), and Seattle (Debra).

As one person after another said, "Great idea! Let's do it!" I knew our gang of four mavericks was meant to be. Look out, NAEYC!

Holly Elissa Bruno, Janet Gonzalez-Mena,
Luis Antonio Hernandez, and Debra Ren-Etta Sullivan

Organic Planning

Who knew that by agreeing to agree we had already hit our first bump? Even though NAEYC had supplied us with a topic (which is reflected in the chapters that follow, along with other topics from conferences over the years), we had no clue where to begin. Or, more honestly, we all knew where we as individuals wanted to begin. You know how this goes. Whenever you agree to partner with another person, as soon as the honeymoon fades, the questions start flying:

"What are you going to do?"

"It depends, what are *you* going to do?"

"Do you have a PowerPoint presentation?"

"How much time do we each have?"

"I have a great activity for the closing, so can you do the opening?"

"I can do the opening, but I think you should go first."

"Okay, but what are you going to do?"

"It depends, what are *you* going to do?"

"I'll let you know."

Twice a year now for over ten years, we always hit this same bump: Who will do what? When? Me? Are you kidding?

Not entirely by accident, in our process we each have reflected one of the themes of this book: Every bump is an invitation to grow, or to trip up. Every bump is an opportunity to learn, or to resist changing. Every bump, especially the unwelcome ones, can be a curious gift, waiting to be unwrapped. Are you ready to join us on the journey? Let's do some *Learning from the Bumps in the Road*.

About This Book

In this book, we write about twelve key topics we have presented on over these last ten years. However, we share our messages in a different way because this is—well—a book.

In planning this book, we decided to divide the presentations we've done so that we each took the lead on three chapters. After we wrote the beginnings of our chapters, we each responded to one another's thoughts. Our editor, Kyra Ostendorf, used a complicated spreadsheet to keep track of who had which chapters at any given moment. We took turns responding first to one another's introductions, and we continued from there, adding our thoughts in response to what was written before our turn with each chapter. This method allowed us to offer thoughtful contributions while remaining true to our individual perspectives on the topic.

The result is that for each chapter you will read a long introduction from one of us, followed by a few pages from a second author, a few pages from a third author, and a few pages from the remaining author. Then, each chapter concludes with a summary and three reflective questions written by the same author who wrote the introduction. To help you know who wrote what, our names appear before each of our contributions.

The Lineup (A Sum of Our Parts)

As Holly Elissa wrote in the beginning of the preface, we each bring our own area of expertise and life experience to our work together, both as presenters at the NAEYC conferences and as authors writing this book. You can read more about us at the end of the book, but for now know that we each care deeply about young children and about the people in our field who dedicate their life's work to caring for and teaching children and partnering with their families to make a difference.

Our Hopes for the Book

This book is an invitation to civil discourse. You will see that we do not always agree and that we value those disagreements because they help us better understand the world. With that said, we want you to use this book however it best fits your needs. We encourage you to read it and discuss it with fellow students, colleagues, or members of a discussion group at your local Association for the Education of Young Children (AEYC)—there's a lot in this book to support your professional development. Make the most of the learning by discussing the chapters with colleagues in similar work environments *and* with people experiencing something different. In other words, think outside the box and engage in discussion with people who will further challenge your thinking and practices. We hope as you read this book that you will respect the different points of view we share and that it will help you respect your colleagues' opinions as well.

Learning is a lifelong adventure, and we hope that this book contributes to yours. Remember, learning should be joyful. The discussion we start in this book should never be over. Thank you for joining us on the journey.

Acknowledgments

I give my heartfelt thanks to Janet for her gentle strength, Debra for her lightning-quick intellect, Luis for his joyful heart, and David Heath and Kyra Ostendorf for believing in us.

I am grateful also to Marina Colonas, Wendy Dunning Carter, Sue Baldwin, Elizabeth Kendall, Arthur B. LaFrance, Sr. Madeline Birmingham, Dr. Michael Gonta, Dr. Alicia Smith, Dr. Kay Albrecht, Lily and Nick Bruno-Hymoff, and Richard Harrison—as well as my fellow twelve-step travelers for reminding me of all things beautiful and true.

Holly Elissa Bruno

. . . .

To the folk in the early childhood education (ECE) field who negotiated the bumps to help eradicate the "babysitter" label and turn us into the professionals we are!

To Kyra Ostendorf and David Heath for their vision, encouragement, support, and push to get us to write this book.

To my fellow copresenters/coauthors who make everything we do together interesting, fun, and educational.

Janet Gonzalez-Mena

. . . .

To my fantastic family, teachers, and mentors who unknowingly provided direction, guidance, and a sense of joy for all that is ahead.

To all the teachers, students, and families I've met throughout my career, a sincere thank-you for keeping me humble and real.

To my dear book colleagues for providing encouragement, support, and an occasional kick in making this creation possible.

To all the readers and users of this book for keeping the passion and joy in early learning alive and interesting.

Luis Antonio Hernandez

. . . .

To all of the children who continue to inspire me to work diligently on their behalf, especially children of color, children learning English, and children from low-income communities who need the most leadership from as many grown-ups as possible.

To Luis, Holly Elissa, and Janet, who have introduced me to a rich spectrum of ideas and practices around leaders and leadership and how much we all have to contribute to the profession.

To our fantastic Redleaf team: Kyra Ostendorf for accepting my "permission to nag" with much grace and diplomacy and David Heath for "herding cats" to get us all together to keep us focused on the vision.

To my family and friends, who have provided me with countless stories to share about what leadership in the making looks like.

Many thanks to you all.

Debra Ren-Etta Sullivan

. . . .

1

Our Way to Sincerity

Affirming Civility and Tolerance in Our Daily Work

Janet Gonzalez-Mena

A friend of mine named Marcus Lopez, a Chicano and an activist, worked long and hard for equity and social justice. Marcus would often say, "Remember, it's nice to be nice." I can still hear his voice in my head even though he died five years ago. I think his little expression was a way of affirming civility. He *was* nice *and* he also stood up to injustice. It sounds like a contradiction, but it isn't.

Dancing with conflict is another expression that sounds like two things that don't go together. Who likes conflict? Well, maybe some people do, but I don't, and most of the people I know don't either. Conflict seems like war—or at least seems to lead to war. Personally, I much prefer peace. So think about the phrase *dancing with conflict*. The idea of dancing with something you don't like sounds strange, but it's all in your attitude. If you have a conflict with another person, imagine dancing with them because you are partners in something, even if it's something you might regard as negative. Thinking of an argument like a dance changes the image. And changing the image gives you power! So let me transfer this theme of conflict and civility to early childhood education. I'm dedicated to the idea that diversity, equity, and social justice must always be part of the picture.

Here's a story to illustrate what I want to focus on: I was at a conference waiting for a session to start. I found myself standing next to a woman I hadn't met before, so I introduced myself. She introduced herself in turn.

As she said her name, I looked at her name tag and saw that it read "Ana." I remarked that she had only one *n* in her first name. Well! That little remark brought a flood of feelings to her face. "Yes, one *n*," she said and paused. Then she launched into an emotional story. She told me that when she started kindergarten she already knew how to write her name. She proudly showed her teacher. The teacher said, "Oh, honey, Anna has two *n*'s," and he added the second one for her.

Ana went home that day and told her mother that her name was spelled wrong. Her mother was angry and insisted that the spelling was correct. "It was your grandmother's name," she assured Ana. "Your Croatian grand-mother. That's the proper spelling." Ana got tears in her eyes as she contin-ued to tell me her story. "I was caught between my teacher and my mother. Who was right? I had to decide at that moment." She paused, sighed, and then said, "I decided my teacher was right, so I spelled my name with two *n*'s until I was thirteen years old. Then one day I suddenly said to myself, "It's *my* name and I will spell it the way I want!" At this point she stood taller and her voice was loud and clear.

I've never forgotten that story. And I often wonder how many children in our early childhood programs feel forced to make a decision between who is right—their family or their teacher. I have an image of a child standing between two powerful adults facing him. He turns to one and his back faces the other. If he turns around, he still faces one and turns his back on the other. The child is caught in the middle. I like to change that image to the adults standing side by side when they face the child—a team—and nobody is in opposition. They all work together.

These are the kinds of conflicts—diversity versus early childhood educa-tion (ECE)—that I'm most interested in. My goal is to change the phrase to diversity *and* ECE. As a profession we have standards, regulations, best practices, research, and other guiding principles that tell us what's right for children. We also need to have room for families to tell us what's right for their children even though those things may not fit with what we know and believe. When we discover conflict, are we able to dance with it instead of trying to convince the other person or party that we are right and they are wrong or instead of stepping down and giving up? Can we create a dance that doesn't involve us trying to win by pulling power plays or losing by just giving in? Can we be nice and still work toward resolution that is just? The answer is yes!

Maybe one day when I get this all figured out and I am good at dancing with conflict, I won't have to keep talking about it. In the meantime, let me introduce you to another person, besides Marcus, who has helped me along this path. Her name is Isaura Barrera. The first thing Isaura taught me was to envision cultural bumps rather than conflicts. This was helpful because I could picture speed bumps. Luckily, when we drive, there are signs that speed bumps are ahead so we can slow down and not hit them so hard that we break an axle. That's true of cultural bumps too—once you recognize they exist, you can learn to watch for them, slow down, and negotiate them successfully. I was starting to use an approach that could work with the kinds of conflicts that occur between teachers and families (and sometimes among staff or between staff and administration). I should add that these conflicts can occur within families as well. I know that from my experience living in a cross-cultural family.

Then Isaura introduced me to the term *third space.* I already understood the concept, but I didn't have terminology to talk about it. Isaura helped me see that a third space perspective involves moving from dualistic (two spaces) thinking to holistic (third space) thinking in the face of what seems to be a contradiction or paradox. For example, say I am a teacher and I disagree with something a parent is doing with her child; it's possible that I have a blind spot.

Let me stop and talk about blind spots for a minute. Another friend of mine has tunnel vision. One day I was trying to understand what tunnel vision means, so I said to him, "I guess it's like looking through two toilet paper tubes and the rest of what you see is black." He laughed and said, "Janet, what I see out of the sides of my eyes is just what you see out of the back of your head. It has nothing to do with being black." I was surprised. I never thought about that before. There's nothing to give us a clue that a blind spot exists. I have discovered that it's easy to have a blind spot when it comes to understanding what parents do with their children. I think of examples I have encountered: toilet training a baby earlier than I agree with, spoon-feeding a child long after he should be able to do it himself, babying a preschooler who is fully capable of many things the parent is still doing for him. If I have a blind spot and don't realize it, I am likely to consider our differing views to be a problem. In that case, what do I do?

By now, I've learned what to do—not that I always do it—but looking back, I can analyze where I went wrong and do better next time. First, I must change the word *problem* to *bump.* It may be a cultural bump or just a regular one. That doesn't really matter. The important thing is to suspend judgment and seek to understand the parent's perspective on the matter. I have to put aside ideas about determining the one right way. This doesn't mean that all ways are fine (Rogoff 2003), but it does mean that I need to open up my mind and remind myself that there is always more to learn. Phillips and Cooper (1992) write about how child-rearing practices have patterns of meaning that are shared by and embodied in the lifestyles of a larger group. It is important for me to see the patterns that are involved in my way as well as patterns behind the other person's practice.

Isaura's first book, written with Robert M. Corso (Barrera and Corso 2003), provides some additional insight into the concept of third space. A third space perspective does not resolve the issue; rather, it changes the arena within which that situation is addressed by increasing the probability of respectful, responsive, and reciprocal interactions. To get to third space, I have to do three things:

1. Believe that it exists.

2. Accept that there are multiple realities.

3. Dialogue with the person instead of arguing.

I use the well-known advice of thirteenth-century Persian poet Rumi to move my thinking from argument to dialogue. He said, "Out beyond ideas of wrongdoing and rightdoing, there is a field. I'll meet you there." If I go out to the field with the person whose practice I'm questioning and we talk about our views, we may be able to see a reality that is bigger than both of us. We may even be able to move from *my* way and *your* way to *our* way as we figure out what to do about our differences in this situation with this child in this program. If we do all that, we've reached third space.

Sue B. Bredekamp and Carol C. Copple, in the revised edition of *Developmentally Appropriate Practice in Early Childhood Programs*, explained third space thinking without calling it that. They said, "Some critical reactions to NAEYC's (1987) position statement on developmentally appropriate practice reflect a recurring tendency in the American discourse on education: the polarizing into *either/or* choices of many questions that are more fruitfully seen as *both/and*" (Bredekamp and Copple 1997, 23). They are writing about dualistic thinking, where contrasting ideas are seen as dichotomous. If it's right, it can't be wrong; if it's bad, it can't be good. If it's blue, it can't be yellow. When you move into holistic thinking from dualistic thinking, you don't separate things into opposites. You can also see that when blue and yellow come together they make green! Blue keeps its blueness and yellow keeps its yellowness, and together they make something new altogether. Green is an example of third space.

Stephen R. Covey writes about what he calls *synergy* in the foreword to a book called *Crucial Conversations*, which has excellent strategies for getting to third space. According to Covey (2002, x), synergy makes for "a better decision, better relationship, better decision-making process, and increased commitment to implement decisions made." He talks about how synergy transforms people and relationships and creates an entirely new level of bonding, producing what Buddhism calls the *middle way*. This is not a compromise; it's not meeting halfway between two opposites. Instead, it's "a higher middle way, like the apex of a triangle" (Covey 2002, x). When you produce something with another person that is truly creative, it's one of the most powerful forms of bonding there is.

Initially, I needed something more concrete than visualization to actually get to third space, so I came up with a system. I never could remember the steps of other people's problem-solving approaches, so I made up my own. Although it looks like it, mine isn't a series of steps; it is more holistic. I call it RERUN. The first *R* stands for reflect. Reflection is important, and there are two aspects to reflection: self-reflection and active listening. Self-reflection allows you to become aware of what's going on inside yourself—in your guts and in your head. Ask yourself why this issue is a challenge for you. How much do you understand about where you are coming from and what's really going on inside you? The other aspect of reflection—active listening— involves communicating with the other person. Active listening is about reflecting back what you hear the other person saying—not just the words, but the meaning and the feelings behind them. You can't have a judgmental tone, or it won't work. When reflecting back what you pick up from the other person, you encourage more talk. Best of all, it helps avoid getting into an argument with the person. Arguing won't take you to third space.

The *E* stands for explain. When you have really listened to the other person and are beginning to understand a point of view that isn't yours, then you can explain your point of view. Don't start with this and don't do it too soon. Listening is a very important part of communication. If you forget that, just remember that we have two ears and only one mouth, so we are meant to listen twice as much as we talk. Also remember that *listen* and *silent* have the same letters. Seek first to understand before being understood.

The second *R* stands for reason. You should be clear about your reason for what you believe in. You should also encourage the other person to explain her reason. Be gentle about this, but remember that it's important to get down to the reasons.

The *U* stands for understand. Obviously, understanding is key to success. It may take more than one discussion—it might take many discussions! Having a relationship with the person you don't see eye to eye with will help in this process. Do work continually on building the relationship. Start early and keep at it. Keep going back to Reflect, Explain, and Reason at any point when understanding is weak or nonexistent.

Finally, the *N* stands for negotiate. It's not the kind of negotiation you do when you're buying a house or a car. It's the kind that has you talking together to see how you can come to an agreement about what to do about this child in this family who is part of this program. If one of you has to give in, it's not a third space solution.

Everything I've said so far depends on sincerity and authenticity. You have to be yourself, to show genuine feelings. You can't pretend or deceive. You have to be honest—with yourself and with the other person. And while you are doing all this, remember that it's nice to be nice! To summarize, here are six suggestions to help early childhood educators be sensitive and responsive (Gonzalez-Mena 1992):

1. **Know what each parent in your program wants for his or her child.** Find out families' goals. What are their caregiving practices? What concerns do they have about their child? Encourage parents to talk about all of this, to ask questions, and to be honest with you about their dreams for their children.

2. **Be clear about your own values and goals.** Know what you believe about children and your goals for them. Have a bottom line, but leave space above it to be flexible. When you are clear, you are less likely to present a defensive stance in the face of disagreements.

3. **Build relationships.** Relationships enhance your chances for successfully negotiating cultural bumps. Be patient. Building relationships takes time, but with them you'll enhance communication and understanding. You will communicate better if you have a relationship, and you'll have a better relationship if you learn to communicate effectively!

4. **Become an effective cross-cultural communicator.** It is possible to learn these communication skills. What is your communication style? Learn about communication styles that are different from your own. What you think a person means may not be what he or she really means. Do not make assumptions. Listen carefully. Ask for clarification. Find ways to test for understanding.

5. **Use a problem-solving rather than a power approach to conflicts.** Be flexible— negotiate when possible. Look at your willingness to share power. Are you dealing with a control issue?

6. **Commit yourself to education.** Educate yourself and your families. Sometimes lack of information or understanding of each other's perspectives is what keeps a conflict going.

Holly Elissa Bruno

Making Nice

Hey, Janet, your mention of the word *nice*, especially when you said your colleague was both nice and a fierce advocate, got me pumped. Why? The answer is simple: niceness can be a cover for conflict-avoidance, for going along to get along, and for pretending to be just fine when we are unhappy, sad, or just plain angry. This phenomenon is what my colleague Luis-Vicente Reyes calls "the hegemony of niceness": the command to be nice is so strong that anyone perceived of as not nice is in danger of ostracism. I had to look up the word *hegemony*. Hegemony is defined by *Merriam-Webster's Dictionary* as "preponderant influence or authority over others."

For us in ECE, Luis-Vicente Reyes's words mean that the pressure to be nice is so dominant that if anyone speaks up, speaks out without prettifying her words, especially if she confronts someone, is cruising for a bruising. "Make nice" means "don't rock the boat." Sure, some aspects of making nice are worthy, like being kind, accepting, forgiving, and upbeat. Those other aspects, like inauthenticity and sugarcoating? Not so much. How can we make a difference if we don't rock someone's boat?

Want evidence for the hegemony of niceness? Consider this data:

- Eighty percent of early childhood leaders are conflict-avoidant (Bruno 2007).

- Seventy percent of women take things personally and get their feelings hurt (Myers et al. 1998).

- More than half of early childhood professionals say they regularly experience gossip, negativity, and backbiting at work (Bruno 2007).

By demanding niceness over directness, we end up with early childhood settings where conflicts are dealt with indirectly, usually through gossip or backbiting. Gossip allows us to release our anger and surround ourselves with supporters while never facing the person who offended us directly. What are we modeling for our children?

In the *New York Times* (December 11, 2005), Alexandra Starr reported that even four-year-old girls are forming exclusive cliques. Or, as I heard a preschooler say to another preschooler, "I'm not going to play with Madison for a hundred years, are you?" You can bet your paycheck that Madison will feel the sting of being rejected by her classmates even though Madison's offense was to be from a different culture, socioeconomic class, or have a different personality style. What if instead we modeled for our children the ability to name, address, and work through our differences? The desire to affirm and nurture often trumps the deeper need for the tough love of confronting misdeeds and injustices. Niceness frees us from facing the tough things: confrontation is a prickly thing. We all know that smiling and being nurturing, selfless, and supportive help us fit in. We also know that confronting and showing anger are tickets to ostracism. Who would choose pain?

Act Like a Lady

Okay, so I confess this is personal. I have gotten myself into all kinds of maelstroms for speaking out. Even my own father accused me of speaking like a CEO. He meant I was too forceful for a woman. He raised me to act like a lady; a lady in her white gloves would never rock the boat. Ladies who don't have something nice to say don't say anything at all. Ladies don't get angry, or sweat for that matter. Ladies smile when their feelings are hurt. Ladies also wear high heel shoes that hurt their feet and, at one time, had their feet bound. Ugh! Did "Act like a lady" really mean "Be a good girl and you stand a better chance of moving up in social class"? Were ladies ever told to act like a lady? That seems redundant.

I wonder what the *Oxford English Dictionary* would tell me about the history of the word *nice*. Did *nice* originate with the move from rural life to the cities, creating the necessity to coexist comfortably in groups? Did the command to "be nice" grow popular when young women, in the quest to be upwardly mobile, had to act ladylike? Did *nice* become a gender-coded word warning women to skirt around conflict and smile at their rivals? As soon as I finish writing this, I will research the etymology of that word. Regardless of what I discover, I know already that *nice* is not a pretty word for me. Nice meant that being true to myself was unacceptable. I was a tomboy who climbed trees and took off in the early morning on my bike to unknown places. I wrestled with boys, and when I broke my wrist, I didn't cry or fall apart. I told my parents I needed to get to a doctor. I beat boys in sports. I ran for class president. I challenged my teachers and, as a result, wore a path to the vice principal's office.

"Be nice" was a two-word reminder to pretend I was happy when I wasn't, sweet when the situation had gone sour, or conflict-avoidant when I wanted to confront an interpersonal slight. Being nice went hand-in-hand with acting like a lady. It was synonymous with keeping scrubbed and neat, not offending anyone, not standing out, and above all, keeping your knees together. In my day, acting like a lady meant white gloves, girdles, stockings, and proper little hats and dresses. I was even shown how to sit down on the floor properly, sliding one leg behind my body discreetly. For tea with the dean of the women's college I attended, a basic black sheath dress, white gloves, and a hat with a froth of meshy lace was de rigueur. How much more comfortable we all were in sweats and jeans, poring over our texts, debating with professors over dinner, or talking politics in our dorms.

Acting like a lady had a lot to do with being proper. Both were commands: thou shalt act like a lady or else. Both carried unwritten rules of conduct, including sitting still with a straight back, crossing your legs at the ankle, never the knee, saying please and thank you, never interrupting, and letting a man win in any kind of game or competition. My father stood at the bottom of the stairs every Sunday morning to inspect our attire and determine if we were properly dressed for church. I was not a mean-spirited child. I was, however, passionately curious, wanting to understand the why of things. Curiosity and being proper rarely shook hands. Much of my life consisted of questioning, breaking, and eliminating unnecessary rules.

Janet's point about civility is that we can disagree and still be respectful. We can have differences and still be colleagues. We can cocreate a space where we can resolve our conflicts. Amen! However, if being civil is the same as avoiding conflict, I am one uncivil person. To me, going deeper and addressing the story behind the story is the only way to alleviate the deeper pain. Short-term fixes and pretending to be happy when we are not eventually make us—or me, at least—sick. Is it possible to be nice and confrontational? You bet. Is it possible to have disagreements and still be colleagues? You bet. Is it possible not to like a colleague but to respect her? You bet. All I am saying is give honesty a chance. Give me respect over niceness any day!

Debra Ren-Etta Sullivan

Dancing with Conflict

I was so very moved by the notion of grown-ups making children choose. In Janet's introduction, Ana had to choose who was spelling her name correctly, and unfortunately, this is not uncommon. My sister's name is Johniça with a cédille, a French accent mark, under the *c* in her name. The cédille changes a hard *c* sound (like *k*) into a soft *c* sound (like *s*). The teachers in our school decided that it was too much work (for them) to pronounce my sister's name correctly and to type it, so they dropped the cédille and called her JOHN-nika instead of Jah-NEE-sa. My sister, being a relatively quiet child, went by one name at home and another at school. She's fifty-two, and her school friends still know her by a completely different name than her family knows her. My sister was too polite to correct her teachers after one or two attempts and is too polite to correct her classmates decades later. Besides, what should a child be expected to do when a teacher decides that renaming (or respelling) is in order? Although I think this is a good question for our chapter on power, the correct solution is for teachers to ask the child or the child's family.

You note, Janet, that we need to leave room for families to tell us what's right for their children, even though it might not fit with what we know and believe. I would even go so far as to say we should do this even when it doesn't fit with what we *think* we know and believe. It might become easier to dance with conflict if we can "scooch" over what we know and believe to make room for the fact that there may be more than one right way. Children always find a way to scooch over to make room for one more, and one more, and one more. Diversity can work only if we make room for one more idea, one more belief, one more perspective, one more practice, one more value. Then we can begin the dance with conflict.

Dancing with conflict: when you make conflict a bad thing, you don't consider it to be a good dance partner. Who wants to dance with something bad? But I want to ask, why can't conflict be a good thing? Conflict and disagreement are perfect opportunities to learn something new, something different. I think conflict has been given a bad reputation that makes it too easy to automatically avoid it whenever possible. Conflict is probably a great dancer just waiting for us to step out onto the dance floor. When we do, a whole world of possibilities will unfold before us—something new and different. The big disagreements, misunderstandings, clashing of perspectives in our work with a diversity of families and communities will never be resolved by people who are afraid of learning something new or seeing something different. Besides, new and different aren't going away. That's why we are still struggling over the same realms of diversity today that we've been facing for decades. We expect children to dance with conflict ("How do you think that made her feel?" "How can you share it with him?" "How do you know you don't like it if you haven't even tried it?") but are hesitant to do it ourselves. This is actually quite odd because we all remember being children and being expected to try new things, learn new things, taste new things. I wonder what age you have to be to stop learning or trying something new and different. When are you old enough to begin assuming that everyone sees what you see, believes what you believe, thinks what you think?

The example of green being both blue and yellow and something new is perfect. That perplexity shows up so often for biracial, bilingual, and bicultural people, and so many others who experience a life that combines two or more aspects that others see as conflicting. That perplexity also shows up when we make dichotomous good/bad judgments about differences. We teach children that it's not polite to notice difference. We teach them that they shouldn't notice that someone may be missing a leg or have a darker skin color or speak a second language with an accent, and a variety of other differences that must be bad if we're not supposed to notice them. If it's not polite for a child to ask me why my skin is dark, then it must mean that I'll feel bad about being asked and that my darker skin must be a bad thing. However, since it's not polite to talk about my skin color, there is no way to have a conversation about why someone would think my skin color is considered bad by some. There is some sort of unspoken agreement taking place that seems to leave me at a disadvantage, and it would be rude or impolite for me to talk about it too much.

I once worked with a child care center that was focusing on team building and getting to know more about one another. One of the teachers mentioned that being Canadian, she had a different perspective around one of the topics we were discussing. A coworker turned to her and said, "I don't think of you as Canadian." The teacher reaffirmed that she was, indeed, Canadian and therefore had different perspectives. The coworker simply reiterated that he considered the teacher "one of us." This exchange was interesting to watch (and navigate) because the Canadian teacher wanted to ask about the difference between "us" and "them," but her coworker was now uncomfortable having to talk more about why it was good to be thought of as "one of us" and not Canadian. The dance with conflict was avoided in the interest of maintaining a civil workplace. The hegemony of niceness you mention, Holly Elissa, is clearly something that needs more of our attention. The worst of it is that those who are negatively affected by it also participate in perpetuating it!

We need to talk more about the fear many grown-ups have of emotion, especially anger. "Don't be mad" is a common command, but what do I do if I *am* mad? Am I supposed to feel good about something that makes me mad? Wouldn't that make my niceness fake? Is it better to be fake than to be angry? That leads to what my grandmother calls being "nicety"—the fake nice that is used to cover nasty. Besides, there are some things that should make us angry and mad, should make us want to rock the boat on purpose. Injustice, inequality, discrimination, prejudice, inequity, and oppression all live in that boat. If we don't rock it, we'll never tip it over. If our silence is required in order to maintain civility and niceness, we have to remember that silence equals acceptance, agreement, and condoning of something we claim isn't right.

It's getting to that third space again. People avoid third because it's hard. It requires work, the work of actually listening and understanding, considering another perspective—maybe not even changing your mind, but just understanding and considering. It's much easier just to make a difficult topic or different belief, viewpoint, language, value, and so on wrong or bad and then create rules around niceness and civility that prohibit us or inhibit us from talking with each other. The hegemony of niceness is so bad that we can't talk about some things *even when we are clear that we want to!* I once worked for an organization that had conversations about race and social justice as a key feature of its mission. We were in the process of hiring a new teacher and had really narrowed it down to one who was bilingual in Spanish and English. Below is an intriguing conversation that ensued between me and another teacher who was new to the organization.

> *Me:* I think we should hire Mr. Y because he's bilingual in Spanish and English, and we need that.
>
> *Her:* If we hire him just because he's bilingual, we'll be tokenizing him.
>
> *Me:* He would only be a token if we don't hire anyone else who's bilingual. Our plan is not to hire just one bilingual person. And, he's Latino, and we're committed to increasing racial diversity.
>
> *Her:* Well now you've made it about race so we can't talk about it.
>
> *Me:* Why not? I'm here. You're here. It's part of our work to face such things head-on.
>
> *Her:* You're right. I don't know why I said that. I'm just more used to *not* talking about it.

We need to be very careful about passing on our unproductive processes to children. We teach them that uncomfortable conversations are not polite, are not safe, and that pretending to be nice is better than engaging in conflict or difference. We want them to have emotional intelligence, and then we teach them to ignore unpleasant emotions. When children disagree, we sometimes tell them just to be nice and play nice or just hug and make up. We make children say I'm sorry to someone they've wronged or injured even when we know a child really isn't sorry. The sad part is that the wronged or injured child *also* knows the other child isn't really sorry. One child learns that pretending to be sorry is acceptable and another child learns to hold in true emotions and accept a fake one. And so the hegemony of niceness begins and another generation has to struggle to dance with conflict.

Luis Antonio Hernandez

Affirming Our Actions

I want to start with the roots behind the phrase *affirming civility*. To affirm is to assert or to dedicate oneself to a position deemed important and valued. Civility is a foundation of respect that prevails when one considers the circumstances of others. By linking these terms, we define the behaviors and manners we learned in our young years and strive to enact every day. We've also learned social protocols—niceness, silence, passivity—that help us get along and, to a degree, be a civilized and well-adjusted people. Our wonderful colleagues— Janet, Holly, and Debra—have provided great stories and anecdotes from their personal and professional experiences on those learned behaviors, many directly related to our world of ECE. With affirming civility in mind, real-life lessons can come from sources far from our professional experiences. At this point, I want to extend that conversation by sharing the dynamics of tragedy, resiliency, and tension from a recent natural disaster.

In the fall of 2012, Superstorm Sandy devastated towns and neighborhoods along the coast of New Jersey and coastal areas of New York City. People in this region were not used to or prepared for the consequences of such a powerful storm that occurred as evening approached, right as the seas reached high tide during a full moon. Over a hundred people died in the region, seaside towns were destroyed, piers and boardwalks were ripped away, tunnels were flooded, transportation systems were shut down, and homes were destroyed by wind and water. Hundreds of thousands of people were without power for weeks, making life miserable as cold weather set in. A major disaster disrupts and upends society with incredible consequences to the economy, the environment, and most importantly, the lives of people.

As it happens with many disasters, people responded with open hearts. People donated money, collected food items and clothing, and volunteered to help with whatever was needed. Right after such disasters there are extraordinary acts of support and assistance with neighbors helping neighbors, with promises for a quick recovery, and with the satisfaction that good is being done. Full of the best intentions, a feel-good atmosphere prevails. For a short time, gaps and divisions are put aside for the benefit of all. As the first hours of recovery become days, weeks, and even months, the reality of the situation hits the people on the ground—the residents and volunteers. It is the realization that the conditions in which people lived before the storm have been deplorable for decades, that poverty is a reality to millions, and that it can exist in our own backyard.

During the aftermath of Sandy, the result was a palpable tension and mistrust pointing to unspoken divisions. According to a story by Sarah Maslin Nir (*New York Times*, November 16, 2012), right after the storm, tensions became apparent and slowly began to simmer. For the storm not only uprooted lives, but it also exposed undercurrents of the divide between the "haves" and "have not's": those with electrical power and those without, those with working cell phones and those without, those with hot meals and those without, those with safe drinking water and those without. The divide not only accentuated economic disparities, but it also centered on racial, ethnic, and cultural life and even on geographic location—an example of how the chaos of a disaster unmasks the reality of divergent realities, of lives barely connected.

As in the aftermath of Katrina in New Orleans, the resulting devastation of Sandy left many without the basics of life: shelter, food, water, warmth. Thousands of volunteers, mostly white and upper income, poured into the areas most affected, all having the best intention to help. In Brooklyn the volunteers encountered people who were stranded in pockets of poverty living completely different lives: a foreign experience compared to their well-to-do neighborhoods of Manhattan. A cultural clash of mostly privileged people meeting face-to-face with mostly poor brown and black people was the result. The tensions centered on perceived assumptions and stereotypes; well-meaning help turned into words and actions perceived as condescending, arrogant, and plainly ignorant. The mistrust also came from the local residents in the form of resentments and old biases of those who could assist during this time of need. Local residents, who managed the worst of the storm during the first few days, relied on their own resources, friendships, and community networks.

All of a sudden these local "strangers" descended on the neighborhood like they were visiting a zoo. It did not help that strangers came to these neighborhoods and snapped photos, a deplorable version of disaster tourism. Some locals were outraged and humiliated when the volunteers assumed that the locals had not eaten or bathed or been in contact with the rest of the world in days. The perceived attitudes ("You must be ready for a hot shower") were insulting to people who had a sense of pride and dignity in keeping themselves and their families relatively safe and intact. A disaster is not defined as people being completely helpless, incapable, ignorant, or in desperation. As for the volunteers, it was a reality check for their own purposes in helping without the mantel of saving or preaching or satisfying residual guilt about being better off. For at the end of the day and at the end of the devastation, volunteers returned to their privileged sectors and the locals returned to neighborhoods forever changed. Although much of the help was genuinely appreciated, and volunteers could feel satisfaction in having made concrete contributions, opportunities for common understanding and true community building were not possible this time.

In a world where a disaster changes lives forever, it is certain that people will be there for each other. Creating and sustaining meaningful interactions and exchanges with one another can have positive lessons for all, with or without a storm. We can start by affirming the reason for the action—and acknowledging the urgency of the situation—and that the action upholds individual values and principles of helping others. The hardest part is maintaining a sense of civility in difficult situations: having a high standard of respect for others without assumptions, value judgments, or arrogance. For respect builds trust among people; it makes us humble and creates the space—that third space—where both parties can coexist for common good and the affirmation of human dignity. Civility is beyond being nice, playing by the rules, and acting accordingly. It defines approaches to face the world—or a storm—with a heart that asserts respect and trust. Genuine civility, indeed, is hard work.

Summary..

Janet Gonzalez-Mena

Reading what my coauthors had to say brought home to me how words trigger feelings and some words have different meanings depending on personal experience. *Nice* is one of those words. I started with Marcus and his "It's nice to be nice," and look where it took us! I certainly understand Holly Elissa's strong reaction and the hegemony of nice in ECE. Being nice is often a way of getting along, smiling, and being quite dishonest. But Marcus was never like that. He was the last person you would expect to be giving advice using the word *nice*. I should have painted a picture of him, because his words contrasted with his appearance. He was a dark-skinned, hefty, tough-looking Chicano with long hair and a beard. He must have looked scary to some people until they talked to him. He was a fierce advocate for civil rights, and at the same time he displayed civility. He didn't use that word, but I think that's what he meant when he used the word *nice*. He danced with conflict and—as Debra said—used the dance as a way to expand his knowledge.

Debra also wrote about equity and social justice, which Marcus dealt with his whole life. He was civil, but it was clear from the day I met him that he never let anybody run all over him. *Civility*—another word with different meanings for different people. It took us a long time to get back to civility in this chapter. Thanks to Luis, who brought the chapter full circle and ended with great examples of civility. He also left a lovely third space image, "where both parties can coexist for common good and the affirmation of human dignity." To me the affirmation of human dignity is the goal of promoting equity and social justice.

Discussion Questions ....

1. What images, feelings, and memories come up for you when you hear or read the word *nice*? What does the word *civility* mean to you?

2. It may be easy to see how Luis's example of people helping people during disasters relates to affirming civility. Can you see how working toward equity and social justice can also be about affirming civility?

3. How can a person stand up for what he or she believes in yet remain civil?

References ....

Barrera, Isaura, and Robert M. Corso. 2003. *Skilled Dialogue: Strategies for Responding to Cultural Diversity in Early Childhood*. Baltimore, MD: Brookes.

Bredekamp, Sue, and Carol Copple, eds. 1997. *Developmentally Appropriate Practice in Early Childhood Programs*. Rev. ed. Washington, DC: National Association for Education of Young Children.

Bruno, Holly Elissa. 2007. "Gossip-Free Zones." *Young Children* (September): 26–33.

Covey, Stephen R. 2002. Foreword to *Crucial Conversations: Tools for Talking When Stakes Are High*, by Kerry Patterson, Joseph Grenny, Ron McMillan, and Al Switzler, xi–xiv. New York: McGraw-Hill.

Gonzalez-Mena, Janet. 1992. "Taking a Culturally Sensitive Approach in Infant-Toddler Programs." *Young Children* 47 (2): 4–9.

Myers, Isabel Briggs, Mary H. McCaulley, Naomi L. Quenk, and Allen L. Hammer. 1998. *MBTI Manual: A Guide to the Development and Use of the Myers-Briggs Type Indicator.* 3rd ed. Palo Alto, CA: Consulting Psychologists Press.

Phillips, Carol Brunson, and Renatta Cooper. 1992. "Cultural Dimensions of Feeding Relationships." *Zero to Three* 12 (5): 10–13.

Rogoff, Barbara. 2003. *The Cultural Nature of Human Development.* New York: Oxford University Press.

Power Imbalances
Unwritten but Binding Social Contracts

Holly Elissa Bruno

If I tell you "That goes without saying," I expect you know exactly what I am *not* saying. I assume you and I agree, so nothing further needs to be stated. We both go about our business as usual. For example, getting to work on time is a rule that goes without saying. However, I may be in that 45 percent of people in the United States who have a relaxed attitude toward timeliness (Myers et al. 1998). To me, what goes without saying is if my work day starts at 9:00, I'll arrive around 9:15 or 9:30 and work an extra 15 minutes or half hour at the end of the day.

What goes without saying can turn into a mess of misunderstandings. If we fail to talk through our differences and come to an agreement, our relationships can tumble into a tangle of poison ivy. Making the assumption that other people are just like us, especially when our cultures differ, can cause deep misunderstandings. How do we keep the road clear in organizations when so much goes without saying? What can the leader, in particular, do to prevent a poison ivy takeover?

You Know What They Say about Assumptions

Does it go without saying that the director has the power in her organization? Having the title of director should carry weight, right? Not if the organization requires a new director to pay her dues first, or a resentful teacher, passed over for the director position, is determined to kneecap the director. Not if the prior or founding leader was so powerful that the staff cannot envision anyone else filling the original leader's shoes. In those cases, and others you likely have faced, the person who should have power does not. If the new director acts as if she has buy-in from her staff, her unfounded assumption will trip her up. Power can be illusive in organizations.

Making assumptions about power (for example, who has the power) is something we do naturally. In fact, our brains are hardwired to make quick judgments about people and situations. Once we make those judgments, we tend to believe them. Before we stop to think it through, our assumptions become reality, at least in our own mind.

Imagine our surprise when we crash unwittingly into another person's contradictory assumption! Have you ever passionately believed in an idea only to find that other people couldn't care less or thought you were off your rocker? Or, have you expected teachers to understand that greeting each family member or keeping the staff lounge sparkling goes without saying? Assumptions, especially when unstated or unexamined, can put us in a world of hurt and muddle the power dynamics in an organization. You know what assumptions make out of you and me (I assume!). Can you identify the assumptions made by each of the people in director Chandronne's case that follows?

Case study. Chandronne, thrilled about the board's naming her director of Children's Haven Child Care, is aflutter with creative ideas for change. Having most recently served as lead teacher at the local YWCA's preschool, Chandronne assumes she needs to build alliances with teachers who share her passion. Chandronne meets individually with teachers Tsu and Mandi Anne. Both teachers nod and smile, agreeing that a warm and friendly parent lounge is precisely what the program needs. Expecting Tsu and Mandi Anne to have her back, Chandronne buoyantly introduces her parent lounge idea at the next staff meeting. Instead of showing interest, the entire staff stares in weary silence, prompted by long-term teacher Alice, who condescendingly shoots Chandronne "the look." Limited in vision by her assumptions, what land mines has Chandronne failed to anticipate? As her coach, what would you advise her to do differently?

An Expectation Is a Resentment Waiting to Happen

Not only does each of us have our own expectations, but organizations, teams, and other individuals have expectations that might conflict with our own.

When I think I have the ability to read the mind of another person, I set myself up for failure. The only way I can know what another person needs and expects is to ask that person. And even then, if I ask, not everyone is able or willing to say what's on her mind. Teachers Tsu and Mandi Anne likely knew Chandronne's idea would fall flat. They knew that Alice, passed over for the directorship, is gunning for Chandronne. However, Tsu and Mandi Anne also know that crossing Alice is dangerous. So the teachers smile and nod instead of warning Chandronne about who holds the real power in the organization.

Steps to Evaluating Assumptions

Being an effective leader requires "battle-hardened confidence," notes author Adam Bryant (2011, 12). Battle-hardened confidence results from getting back up when we have been sucker punched, learning from our failures, and moving on. A leader with battle-hardened confidence knows to do the following:

- Articulate, examine, and challenge assumptions.

- Accept that no one is a mind reader.

- Invite others to share what's on their minds.

- Model for others that honesty, especially if it is risky, will be respected without retaliation.

- Take what others say with a grain of salt because they might tell you what they think you need to hear rather than the truth.

- Be willing to step up and take a risk to do the right thing.

Chandronne, for example, might have probed the board who hired her for information about the organizational climate: How does the staff feel about her being named director? Were any insiders considered for the position? If so, how did that insider respond when she didn't get the job? What expectations, written or unwritten, were established by the prior director? What expectations does the board have for Chandronne?

Chandronne also might have stepped back to ask herself why she made the assumption that Tsu and Mandi Anne were the opinion influencers on the staff. Just because Tsu and Mandi Anne have garnered excellent evaluations over the years does not mean they hold sway with other teachers. In fact, some other teachers may resent Tsu and Mandi Anne for setting too high a standard. Opinion influencers become powerful for different reasons, not just their success in the organization. An opinion influencer's power may derive from her family's position in the community or her longevity as a staff member. An opinion leader may gain power from his close relationship with board members. A program bully like Alice, who intimidates others, uses power negatively to influence others' opinions.

Filling the Founder's Shoes: Expectations for Leaders Who Follow an Organization's Founder

Chandronne might also have investigated Children's Haven's history of dealing with change. If she had, she would have found she was stepping into leadership after the beloved founder was fired. More often, the founder retires and the organization likely expects the new director to be a clone of the founder and use the same leadership style. After all, the founder not only defined the organization through her vision and style, but she also set expectations about how staff would be treated, how tasks would be delegated (or not), and whether consequences for inappropriate behaviors were enforced, if confronted at all.

This particular unspoken organizational power dynamic occurs when the original leader's impact was so great, employees expect subsequent leaders to behave the same way as the founder. Employees who have experienced only the founder's brand of leadership can assume no one else can fill the shoes of the prior leader. To learn more about how this dynamic affects organizations and leaders in particular, listen to my podcast interview "Filling the Shoes of the Founder" (McLaughlin and Offutt 2012) with Thomas McLaughlin, coauthor of *Moving beyond Founder's Syndrome to Nonprofit Success*, and Dr. Sue Offutt, executive director of McCormick Center for Early Childhood Leadership. Sue, who replaced Dr. Paula Jorde Bloom, a giant in our field, speaks firsthand about how she dealt successfully with expectations that could have boxed her in or defeated her but didn't. Based on my discussion with Sue, here are some steps a new leader can take:

- Meet individually with each staff member in advance to get their hopes and concerns about change out on the table.

- Develop and implement a plan with the founder for an overt and well-thought-out transition.

- Continually check in with staff about how the transition is or is not working.

- Revise strategies and approaches as often as necessary.

- Call upon a support network outside the organization for infusions of optimism or for a reality check.

Sue's insights identify this underlying principle: acknowledge, clarify, and address assumptions about power as transparently as you can. Her successful strategy is the opposite of the goes-without-saying approach. Would Sue's aboveboard leadership style work in your organization?

Acknowledge, Clarify, and Address Assumptions about Power as Transparently as Possible

As savvy leaders, we hone our skills of checking assumptions—our own as well as individuals' and an entire organization's assumptions. Realizing that assumptions can be our downfall, we dive deeper for something elemental: the truth. Even, and perhaps especially, when the truth is painful to face, we know we have to face it squarely or be haunted by it.

Chandronne may have been shaken to learn that teacher Alice is invested in Chandronne's downfall. However, failure to see and act on that knowledge would surely have caused Chandronne more pain and perhaps cost her the job. Leadership, after all, is courage to do the right thing regardless of pressure to take the easy path. Robert Frost (1915) had it right when he wrote, "The best way out is always through."

Unwritten Contracts Bind Us as Much as Written Contracts

Because unwritten assumptions are similar to written contracts, let's step back to examine whether unwritten assumptions have as much or more impact as written contracts. Written contracts carry the force of law; that is, parties to the contract can sue in a court of law to enforce the contract. For example, if you sign a contract of employment, you can use that document in a court to determine the terms (expectations) of your employment. Similarly, your employer can hold you accountable to that contract. If you or your employer fails to meet the expectations established by that contract, a rupture—and often a lawsuit—ensues. The contract gives you and your employer that right.

Some verbal contracts can also be enforced in a court of law. If the parties rely to their detriment on an agreed-upon expectation, those parties feel wronged and expect to have the wrong corrected. In other words, the person who reneged on the agreement should somehow compensate the person wronged for failing to live up to expectations. The original legal term for this expectation is *promissory estoppel*. Your verbal promise binds you: You are as good as your word. If we shake hands and you promise to pay me five hundred dollars for my used bedroom set, and you don't pay up, I can take you to small-claims court.

What Contracts Have You Signed?

How do you know when a contract is binding? To be legitimate in a court of law, a written or unwritten contract must consist of these elements:

- **Offer.** What one person will transfer to another person. For example, goods such as a car or refrigerator or a service such as drum lessons or child care.

- **Acceptance.** The other person's agreement to take that offer.

- **Consideration.** Some form of compensation, usually monetary, that will be paid by the person who receives the goods or services.

For instance, the bank *offers* you a mortgage at 3.5 percent interest, which you *accept*. The *consideration* is the payment you make to get the benefit of entering into this agreement. Consideration must be given for a contract to be valid. Have you ever wondered why a grandson has to pay his grandmother $1 to purchase her used Chevy Impala? That's because some kind of consideration must pass for the sale contract to be legitimate. The bottom line with legal contracts is that they establish boundaries, rules, and consequences for human interactions. Do social contracts serve the same function?

Social Contracts: The Total Package of Unwritten Rules

Social contracts are unwritten, and often unspoken or *tacit*, agreements that govern our interactions in groups. Social contracts are those it-goes-without-saying agreements we forge with one another, often without awareness that we are making a contract. You know what happens when dogs meet. They sniff each other out, assessing which dog has more power. After that, the contract is set for dominance and submission. Are human beings that much different? We forge and follow social contracts virtually every time we interact with another human being or group. Usually we don't call these interactions contracts, but they have the same effect. Tacitly we agree that certain behaviors are acceptable and others are not. Failure to live up to the agreement leads to discomfort, censure, or ostracism.

When you drive through a fast-food take-out window, you and the salesperson tacitly agree you will promptly pay for the food you ordered. You will have the money or credit card ready. The salesperson will provide you with your food and drink, packaged to stay cool or hot, along with napkins and utensils. Both of you agree your transaction will be completed in less than three minutes so you get out of the way for the next customer. Contracts for take-out window behavior are not posted anywhere, yet we all know what's expected and act accordingly. What happens if you get chatty with the salesperson and exceed your three minutes? You get dirty looks. Horns blare. What happens if the salesperson gets your order wrong? You hand it back and expect her to get it right. If she doesn't, you can tell her how unhappy you are, demand your money back, or speak with her manager.

In the workplace, a social contract among team members is rarely spelled out. How do you know what being a team member means? Easy: You observe the behaviors of people on the team. Do teachers greet each other with a welcoming smile or keep their heads down and bullet into their classrooms? Do team members pay it forward and look out for one another without being asked? Or do you hear people complain, "That's not in my job description," and "Why should I have to do all the work?"

However you enter an organization's social contract, you are expected to honor that contract if you want to keep your job. Here's how the contract works:

- **An offer is made.** If you want to work here successfully, you will behave in certain ways.

- **Acceptance follows.** You tacitly agree to fit into the norms.

- **Consideration occurs.** You pay by forfeiting behaviors that would rock the boat.

In everyday practice, social contracts can be just as compelling as written contracts that can be enforced in court. No one wants to be ostracized. Think about it: What unspoken ground rules are you expected to follow in your organization? What happens when someone bends or breaks that social contract? Would you say your organization makes a social contract with each new employee?

Workplace Drama: When the Social Contract Is Violated

Social contracts may not be enforceable in a court of law; however, they get enforced swiftly in the workplace. When we meet another person's expectations, comfort (for the other person, at least) ensues. When we fail to live up to another person's expectations, discomfort (both for us and the other person) ensues. Unless expectations are articulated, shared, and negotiated, we are likely to disappoint or offend others. How many times have you heard a teacher say, "I just can't work with her. You have to reassign me"? In the majority of those cases, the teachers failed to share expectations and negotiate (and continuously renegotiate) their relationship. Consider how you would coach Chandronne to handle the complexity of hidden expectations in her workplace:

While infant teacher Mandi Anne would like to support new director Chandronne, Mandi Anne fears toddler teacher Alice's vindictiveness. Mandi Anne has witnessed Alice isolate or grind down teachers who don't side with her. Mandi Anne wishes she had more courage, but as a sensitive person, she can't bear the thought of being ostracized. Preschool teacher Tsu wants to quietly do her job, help children and families, and avoid conflict. Her parents taught her to be humble, agreeable, and dedicated to the community, not to seek personal gain. Board chair Milagros, an attorney, is all about high standards. She pushed for Chandronne to be hired because Milagros pictures Chandronne as being a lot like her: hardworking and rigorous. Milagros wants the program to be accredited within the year.

Board treasurer Reginald, an accountant, can't understand why he let himself be talked into working with all these women. This program needs to be run more like a profit-making business! The founding director, Delora, had to be fired for putting the program in the red. If Chandronne can't corral unruly staff members, Chandronne will get a pink slip too. Former director Delora is hurt and angry. Children's Haven is her baby, the organization she gave her heart and soul to founding. So what if the program was in the red? Delora could never bring herself to terminate families who couldn't pay tuition. Manipulated by Alice, Delora holds out hope that if Chandronne fails, Delora will be rehired.

Chandronne has just completed her master's degree in administration and is eager to use insights from her course work to transform Children's Haven into a Reggio-inspired program where children and families thrive. She tends to see the world through rose-colored glasses and would rather lead by inspiring others than confronting them. All of these expectations knit together into the fabric of Children's Haven's unwritten social contract.

Transitioning from Drama to Transparency

Can a director hope to replace such drama with honest, aboveboard conversations and ground rules? Are we powerless over this unspoken world and at the mercy of unseen booby traps? Have you had success keeping work relationships clear, dynamic, and perhaps even joyful? As the twelve-step saying goes, "Progress not perfection." Chandronne may never cocreate a fully transparent workplace, but she can eliminate unnecessary conflicts, soothe wounded spirits, and open a lot of windows. Let's look at steps to defuse bombs and forge more enlightened contracts.

Transparency Replaces Unstated Social Contracts

Despite the discomfort of the last staff meeting when her new idea flopped, Chandronne is determined to bounce back and deal with the underlying issues. Her first step is to meet with each individual staff member to listen to her hopes and concerns and to answer questions. She demonstrates through her behavior as well as her words that she is committed to cocreating with them a happier work environment. When underlying issues arise at these meetings—as with Alice's resentment—Chandronne listens closely and speaks honestly about her concern; together, they must find ways for Alice to use her strengths and lose her bullying tactics. Chandronne finds opportunities for Alice to participate in the local resource and referral agency's emergent leader program. Chandronne also confronts Alice when she hears Alice bad-mouthing another teacher. Chandronne lets Alice know her future is in her own hands: perform well and have a future or behave inappropriately and be asked to leave.

In your experience, do you think Alice will change for the better or attempt to persist in her clandestine manipulations? For a five-step process for holding resistant staff accountable, see my book *What You Need to Lead an Early Childhood Program: Emotional Intelligence in Practice.*

Turning Unwritten Expectations into Healthy, New Organizational Ground Rules

Consider this scenario and think about what you would do if you were Chandronne: The rest of the staff closely watches the dynamics between Chandronne and Alice. Chandronne utilizes her board members' expertise as well as the local directors' network to support her in becoming more adept at holding the line with difficult staff members. She also gets parent and community contributions to take her staff off-site for a team-building retreat. Here are some exercises she implements with her staff to turn the organization around:

Exercise 1: Identify unwritten rules and productive ground rules. In preparation for the retreat, Chandronne devotes ten minutes of a staff meeting to this exercise. She invites each staff member to do the following anonymously:

- List at least three unwritten expectations the individual feels the program requires of the employees.

- Place a plus sign (+) in front of the expectations the individual agrees with and a minus sign (–) in front of the expectations she disagrees with or finds troublesome.

- Create one ground rule the individual would like everyone to follow to make the workplace a happy environment.

As Chandronne collates and compiles everyone's statements, she uses that information to design a retreat that will address underlying concerns while simultaneously uplifting staff morale. The morning of the retreat is dedicated to Myers-Briggs Type Indicator training, wherein each staff member learns about her own preferences as well as pointers on how to communicate with people who push her buttons. After the initial session (or an alternate team-building session), Chandronne moves on to exercise 2 (below). She invites staff members to use insights they gained from the morning session to make the afternoon equally successful.

Exercise 2: Create team ground rules. Give each staff member the collated results from the prior staff meeting (exercise 1), then assign them to small groups to complete the following tasks:

- Identify one unwritten rule they agree must be eliminated.

- Identify one unwritten rule they would like honored and put into writing as a team ground rule.

- Identify one new additional written ground rule they believe will make the workplace happier.

Chandronne asks each small group to list on three separate flip chart pages their responses to each of the prompts. After each group reports on what they decided, Chandronne facilitates a discussion about what ground rules would make working together better. The groups work together to come to an agreement on what to eliminate, what to put into writing, and what new ground rule to write.

Exercise 3: Practice using team ground rules. Chandronne knows that agreeing to ground rules and practicing them are two different things. She learned in one of her courses that only a small number of teachers readily embrace change and that twice as many believe, "If it ain't broke, don't fix it." She wants her team members to experience real-life situations in advance. That way they will be better prepared to deal with these challenges and will hopefully internalize the new ground rules. With this in mind, Chandronne asks her team, again in small groups, to resolve the issues in two employee-focused case studies by applying their new ground rules.

Ming Mei

Ming Mei has just been hired as a floater. She works well with children of all ages; however, she appears to be shy and is reluctant to share her suggestions or observations with teachers. Ming Mei is also new to the community and unfamiliar with free resources available to teachers. She has the potential to become a creative teacher and a valuable team member. What are three implementable steps the team could take and one step each individual could take to help Ming Mei blossom at the program? How will our new ground rules offer guidance in identifying these steps?

Exercise 4: Create a conflict resolution process. For this case study, Chandronne asks small groups to serve as coaches to these team teachers with a deep, unresolved conflict.

Javier and Jolena

Team teachers Javier and Jolena appear to be opposites. Javier prefers structured lesson plans and organized activities and is impatient with surprises. Jolena is a firecracker, a laugh-a-minute emergent-curriculum practitioner who feels constricted by predictability. Neither teacher is comfortable with conflict, so they avoid talking through their differences. Just this morning, Javier was upset that Jolena totally dropped the lesson plan when the children spotted a rainbow outside the window. Jolena felt Javier pressured her to end the animated discussion of the rainbow before the children were ready. Children don't miss the tension between the teachers. As peers, how would you help these teachers build on one another's strengths and establish ground rules for working through their differences?

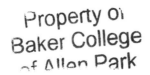

Exercise 5: Implement a debriefing process. Throughout the retreat day, Chardonne has carefully selected different team members to capture in writing the important outcomes of the team-building session and afternoon exercises. At the end of the day, each of these scribes presents a summary of team agreements and ground rules. The entire group discusses how they feel about moving forward with the ground rules. Chandronne also announces a follow-up retreat in six months—with volunteer massage therapists as a bonus—to evaluate team progress and make changes as needed.

Exercise 6: Close with affirmations. As a closing exercise, Chardonne gathers the team into a circle for the affirmations exercise. She invites each team member in turn to state two things: something she will take away from the retreat that will help her when she returns to work and one thing she has come to appreciate about the person to her left. This exercise concludes when each team member has shared her takeaway and her affirmation of the teammate to her left. The team member to Chandronne's right shares what she appreciates about Chandronne.

How do you think this retreat design would work? What other ways do you recommend to unite disconnected individuals into a functional team?

Living Ground Rules Decrease Power Struggles

Living ground rules, like living documents, keep changing. This year your team may need a ground rule that only one person at a time is to speak when an issue is raised. Once that ground rule turns into an everyday practice, a new ground rule may be needed; for example, no conflict will go unresolved for more than one week before the team members involved meet to discuss the conflict.

Does Chandronne's organization still have unwritten rules? Of course, human nature is human nature. Clarity of vision and honest self-assessment are always evolving. However, has the minefield been cleared? Yes. Have expectations gotten clearer? Yes. Are conflicts still occurring? Of course. All in all are the staff happier? You bet. Those constraining unwritten rules that blocked honest interactions have been replaced with processes for working things through. As Chandronne reminds everyone, especially herself: progress not perfection.

Luis Antonio Hernandez

How Our Actions Impact Children

Our friend and colleague Holly Elissa has covered the waterfront, the seashore, and the mountains on this thorough piece on issues of power dynamics and imbalances so typical in a number of early childhood workplaces. And much like other public, private, and corporate settings, power dynamics and imbalances define how an individual or a dedicated group can begin to shift and change circumstances that are ultimately damaging to the organization and the people within. For those of us in early childhood education, this is a major concern and an ethical dilemma since the damage can directly impact young children's lives and well-being. Indeed, the attitudes and behaviors of adults—both consciously and unconsciously—have an effect on the children. While children may not be aware of the power plays of adults, they can sense when adults are not happy or in the mood to play with them. A power imbalance ultimately does impact the essence of our work: the temperaments, moods, and lives of children.

With children on the forefront of any power dynamic, what corrections can we make? Holly Elissa provides a number of ideas and strategies on how to move individuals and organizations forward. As much as we tell folk to leave their drama in the parking lot, it naturally seeps into daily exchanges in classrooms and centers. Although I may tell someone that if the atmosphere in the workplace is unbearable, it is time to pack up and go, not everyone has that choice. And even though there are many good attempts to remedy poisonous atmospheres, it is disingenuous to create solutions and ground rules when there will be no meaningful support, follow-up, or consistency with potential solutions. It all becomes lip service, and the problems continue, staff become cynical, and trust is permanently broken. Who needs to work in such a place?

In this discussion of power dynamics, ECE leaders need to return to—and revisit regularly—the vision and mission of their organization. These guiding principles provide the foundation for the work we do; they are like the United States Constitution for the organization. Policies and procedures also ensure the smooth daily operation of any program—from broken toilets to personnel disputes. Most importantly, the clear direction set by the leadership starts with respectful relationships and clear communication, be it with single individuals or the entire team. Key to this dynamic is to continuously refresh the spirit of the team—praising, encouraging, guiding, and moving forward. From a leadership perspective, try and use a variety of administrative tools, such as those suggested by Holly Elissa, that can best maintain a focused and united team. Whatever advice or recommendation you garner from these readings, know that they are based on a life of work experiences within or outside organizations. Each case is unique in its circumstances, most are acquired as we go, and the best are the blood, sweat, and tears learned from our mistakes and missteps. Every leader will discover what works best for her by experimenting and applying strategies to balance elements of power in the organization.

It is rare to find an ECE director with an MBA—a mark of administrative excellence—running a center, which can then claim smooth daily operations. Even with that esteemed degree, it is only through daily and ever-changing experience that strategies for balancing power become applicable and real. Many factors—a few particular to our profession—challenge power dynamics in a center: a primarily low-paid female workforce, a profession still demanding respect and recognition, and positions that increasingly demand more and more academic credentials. Other pressures that make work challenging include outside forces, such as financial pressures on families, economic downturns, lack of public support and funding, shortsighted ECE polices, and greater outcome accountability. No wonder tensions and imbalances abound in many programs. In recognizing how these many factors pose difficult challenges, visionary ECE leadership must pursue a vision of importance and excellence based on merit, purpose, and joy. Regardless of the power dynamics, which will continue to exist in every organization, it is key to move forward in developing a healthy learning community for everyone— the children, their families, and the team—that makes it all possible.

Debra Ren-Etta Sullivan

How Oppression, Dominance, and Privilege Impact Learning Communities

I decided to focus my part of this power imbalance conversation around issues of oppression, dominance, and privilege and the impact they have on our learning communities. Power has always been an interesting topic in the world of early childhood education. Do we have it? Do we not? Are we just afraid to own it? Do we want to keep it but hope others won't notice it? And if oppression, dominance, and privilege are added to a conversation about power, the discomfort level increases rapidly. However, leadership requires that even uncomfortable topics be addressed, and we do ourselves and others a disservice when we ignore our areas of power and our role in addressing oppression, dominance, and privilege.

Oppression is prolonged cruel or unjust treatment or control over a group of people that holds them back or holds them down. Sometimes this is done in the form of a law (as was the case with women's right to vote), and sometimes it is done as a "common" practice (the early practice of not hiring women of childbearing age). Dominance is having power and influence over others to the extent that if two elements are in conflict, the more dominant one is likely to win or prevail. For example, English is the dominant language in most of our work settings and will likely prevail even when another language is gaining in usage. Privilege is a special right, advantage, or immunity granted or available to one group of people and not another. It can be a special advantage that you work toward (such as socioeconomic status), that you are born with (such as country of origin), or that can come and go as a matter of circumstance or with time (such as physical ability or age).

I'm going to address the areas listed below. There are many more, however, so even though I'm starting with these, further exploration and learning about power, privilege, dominance, and oppression should be a key focus of any leadership development plan.

- Age
- Citizenship
- Employment
- Gender
- Language
- Legal authority

- Physical ability
- Race
- Religion
- Sexual orientation
- Socioeconomic status

Age. We don't always think of age as a tool of power, but it is. For example, grown-ups have power over children. We make multiple decisions daily that impact their world and their experience of their world. Being a grown-up is an area of privilege and dominance, and we must always be vigilant about how we use this status as power over children, power with children, and power for children. To a three-year-old, even a teenager is a grown-up with power. On the other hand, the seventeen-year-old may feel quite oppressed by the rules, regulations, and barriers imposed by older adults. At the other end of the spectrum are senior citizens who find their lives and circumstances in the hands (and power) of those who are middle-aged. What age group are you in right now? Who has more power or less power than you based on your age?

Citizenship. People who are citizens of the country in which they live and work have more privilege than those who are not. The United States has been a dynamic, ever-changing country that includes people who were born here, those who came of their own free will, those who were brought here against their will, and those who came seeking refuge. In our work with children and their families and communities, a vital part of addressing the power imbalance is to acknowledge that not all of us share the same experiences. Refugee and immigrant children and families will not have the same experiences in our learning communities as children and families who were born here. Their citizenship status can affect so many areas of their daily lives in ways that many of us never even give a second thought to. What do you need to know about the effects of citizenship on the children, families, and communities you serve?

Employment. It seems almost a given that those who are employed have more power and privilege than those who are not, but we need to be aware of what happens to those who are underemployed. Many of us work with families that are considered working poor because their incomes do not always cover their basic needs. The cost of quality child care is high, and for some families, paying for it almost equals the monthly income they earn. In addition, we continue to battle for worthy wages for those who care for and educate the children of these same families. If you are regularly employed, how can you use this power and privilege to make quality early learning settings affordable for families and ensure that the teachers who serve families have income worthy of the importance of this work?

Gender. This is always a complicated topic in early childhood. On the one hand, men tend to have more power, privilege, and dominance in the world at large, but they are a small minority in the field of early childhood education. It can be challenging for women to recognize their power in one area when they do not have it in another. The fact is, however, women dominate our profession, and we have a leadership obligation to pay attention to this area of privilege and how it may be used to oppress the role of men in the field. At the same time, we must remain attentive to our work with young children and how gender roles and biases are addressed. How do you fight gender oppression in society at large while ensuring that you don't perpetuate it in a female-dominated profession?

Language. Yes, English is the dominant language in the United States, and yes, it is the language we use to conduct the vast majority of our work. And, yes, if English is your first language, you have a privilege that can influence power dynamics and perceptions of dominance in your work with children and families. Like age, language is a topic to approach with consideration and openness. Not all of the children and families we work with speak English as their first language. This does not mean that my workplace will stop doing business in English. It does, however, mean that I need to be aware that I may have the upper hand when communicating with someone whose first language is not English. How often do you put yourself in environments where English is not the dominant language?

Legal authority. This one can be a little tricky to grasp. What I'm talking about here is what happens when you have the authority to say yea or nay to something that impacts another's well-being. Two examples in early childhood education are licensing and accreditation. If you have authority to approve or veto something, you have the power to make critical decisions about who can move forward. Are there rules and regulations in place that require you to always say yea to one group or cultural practice and nay to another?

Physical ability. Those of us who define ourselves as able-bodied are only temporarily so. It is the path of any living organism to eventually break down. Age, accidents, genetics, diseases, and so on all influence the nature and degree of our physical abilities. Leadership in this area must go beyond helping a blind person cross the street (a worthy deed) to lobbying for crosswalk signals and curb cuts that don't rely on sight. Is your environment accessible and comfortable for a multitude of physical abilities?

Race. This is an obvious and long-standing area for rich discussions of power, oppression, dominance, and privilege and also the one where many experience the most discomfort. Regardless of the present circumstances regarding race and skin color in the United States, we need to have ways to discuss and address racial oppression. Racial prejudice and discrimination do exist, and we must be prepared to support the children and families who experience them. Sometimes we say we don't see race or skin color, only people. This does not change the fact that others among us do see it, and leaders have a responsibility to understand the experiences of others. How willing are you to have a conversation with someone about the realities of their experiences and your role in changing that?

Religion. I like to watch a History Channel program called *How the States Got Their Shapes*. One episode talked about our "backing and forthing" around religion and government. Christianity is still the dominant belief system in the United States even though other religions continue to grow. And although we want separation of church and state, our currency says to the whole world "In God We Trust." But this just brushes the surface. Seeing someone wearing a crucifix, a yarmulke, or a hijab causes some to make certain assumptions and decisions about the person. And finding out that a person is atheist or agnostic creates equal discomfort for some. In what ways do you ensure that the children and families you serve do not face oppression, prejudice, or discrimination in your learning environment due to their religious or nonreligious beliefs?

Sexual orientation. This is another area of great divide and great coalescence. Heterosexual people have more privileges and face fewer acts of discrimination than those who do not identify as heterosexual. For example, heterosexual couples do not have to think twice about the validity or legality of their marriages and relationships or how people may treat them in front of their children. The ability to not have to think about something is a privilege, and children pay close attention to how others treat or feel about their parents. In what ways do you provide a learning environment where children feel their gay, lesbian, or transgender parents are welcome, involved, and included?

Socioeconomic status. This is not the same as employment, mentioned earlier. You can be unemployed and still meet your family's needs without concern if you have access to lots of financial resources. Those who are generationally poor have less power and privilege than those who are generationally middle class or rich. Access to money makes a difference. When we ignore that, we create financial expectations for families that they may not be able to achieve or even consider. In what ways do you offer families financial literacy skills they can use to improve their socioeconomic status?

In all of these areas, as well as in the ones I didn't cover, our task is to identify when we might be perpetuating oppression or dominance through our privilege and power or by upholding oppressive practices, policies, and procedures in the workplace. Moreover, our task is to act when others need us to use our power and privilege to advocate for them. We all hold some place of power and privilege at certain times. To deny that, to ignore it, is to deprive ourselves and others the opportunity to assess power imbalances and to make changes toward enhanced equity and inclusion. Power imbalances created by oppression, dominance, and privilege are like weather-related disasters: we did not create the problem, but we are all affected by it—and it affects some more than others. If we use power and privilege constructively, we can pool our resources and address larger social problems.

Chandronne, Tsu, Mandi Anne, Alice, Reginald, Delora, Milagros, Ming Mei, Javier, and Jolena in Holly Elissa's case studies all have some power and privilege, enough to influence outcomes in their environments. How should they use their resources, and in what ways should they each attend to how their actions may influence oppression and dominance? In what ways, as Luis points out, do these varying degrees of power dynamics and power imbalances affect their organization's vision and mission, and at what point do individuals need to decide that it's time for them to leave because of the policy and procedures of their organizations? Luis is right: power dynamics exist in every organization. Your task is to decide what you will do about that for the sake of developing a healthy learning community for children, their families, and the team.

Janet Gonzalez-Mena

Finding Your Personal Power

If I were still working in an organization, I would find Holly Elissa's introduction and Luis's advice extremely useful. But I'm not in an organization these days. A few years back I retired from college teaching and became a self-employed writer, speaker, and trainer. I also have to say that I'm not an organizational person and never have been, although I found a wonderful sense of community in the volunteer organization I joined back in the 1960s for low-income Spanish-speaking families and their children. I started helping out in the preschool, worked my way up to assistant teacher, and eventually became a preschool teacher in that program. By that time the program had federal funds. Quite a bit later, I became the child care director in a different organization. That was a hard job! As the new boss, I met with the very situation that Chandronne was in. I look back on myself as an innocent lamb walking into a slaughterhouse. I had a master's degree in human development but little administrative experience. Too bad I didn't have this chapter to read before I took that job.

Debra's perspective on the theme of power and equity issues is exactly what has been consuming me for half my life now, ever since I discovered myself as a white person. I always just thought of myself as regular—just a person. But that was before I learned how oppression, power, and privilege operate. I first began to understand it when the feminist movement helped me understand patriarchy. Before that I had just accepted the fact that I was a woman in a man's world. The word *oppression* wasn't even part of my vocabulary. I remember how lots of us women called ourselves girls in those days. Nobody ever called white men boys. That term was reserved for African American men. At the time it was easy for me, a white woman in California, to understand how demeaning that term was. It took the feminist movement for me to see that, though not equally demeaning, it was definitely a putdown that we called ourselves girls and didn't protest when white men called us that.

Debra covered the subject of isms and brought into view the other side of the picture: power and privilege. She did such a good job that I want to turn to issues related to power from a slightly different perspective. I want to focus on one-on-one interactions.

Personal Power and Nondefensive Interactions

I'll start with some definitions. First, a question: What is power? In my experience many people equate power with control and domination. If you have read this far, I'm sure you have a broader perspective. Dominating power, or controlling people, is not really power. That's oppression! For me, the true meaning of *power* relates to what some call *personal power*. Personal power can be thought of as the ability to be who you truly are. I took Latin in high school and learned then how helpful it can be to go back to the Latin root of words we use every day. The word *power* comes from a Latin root meaning "to be able." Ability is not oppression!

Interactions Involving Domination

Domination has to do with winning and losing. Some say this is human nature; I disagree. It's what dogs do when they sniff each other, as Holly Elissa described earlier. If the sniffing by itself doesn't establish dominance, the dogs then fight. The dog on top is the winner. People who usually feel powerless are apt to put themselves immediately in the underdog position when interacting with someone who tends to dominate, so there is no fight. Sometimes a person who feels powerless becomes a dominator when interacting with someone weaker than herself—a child, for example. By doing that she shows that she has bought into the domination system of interaction.

The domination system in humans is learned; it's not natural. Institutions support the domination system. No one is born a top dog or underdog. We are born into the system and learn our roles. As Debra points out, groups targeted for bias on the basis of race, culture, gender, age, class, ability, or sexual orientation—to name just seven reasons why some people target others—struggle for legitimate power more than those who enjoy the privileges that society automatically gives them. When people from targeted groups internalize their oppression, their chances of having power in their interactions are even slighter.

It may help to explain what internalized oppression is. To make it really clear, we have to go back to slavery. A few slave masters couldn't possibly control large numbers of slaves without showing them every day and in every way that they were inferior to the masters. Of course, not all the slaves internalized their oppressors' opinions of them, but those who rejected their subordinate status and fought back suffered extreme punishment. It was definitely safer to go along with the program, and for a lot of people that included accepting themselves as inferior. That's an extreme example, but internalized oppression can occur in any group that has been oppressed for any length of time. Of course, some parents raise their children to reject internalized oppression and to refuse to submit to domination. That kind of teaching can really work; however, though some people may stand up to individual dominators, institutionalized biases keep them from achieving legitimate power with those who control the institutions.

Tapping into Personal Power

The personal power that everybody has—that is, the ability to be who we really are—is something we are born with and keep all our lives. When personal power is acknowledged and nourished from infancy on, people grow up able to show who they really are. Some people lose touch with their personal power, especially when oppression becomes internalized and the messages of the oppressor guide the person from inside. Standing up to sexism and to racism are two examples. Standing up to homophobia by working to enact laws that allow same-sex marriages or dismantle ones that forbid it is another example of rejecting internalized oppression in order to be who you really are.

Moving Away from Battlegrounds and Dogfights

When people are not in touch with their personal power and are faced with a threat, they usually get defensive. They play the dominator's game by either rising to meet the threat head-on or by putting up a protective shield so the spear of the dominator can't poke them where they are vulnerable. In either case, communication is blocked and an authentic interaction is difficult to achieve. Someone who is in touch with personal power realizes that her non-defensive response will make all the difference. She tries to have a human-to-human interaction and open the doors of communication.

You may ask, how can personal power win out over a strong opponent? It's not about winning or losing or being opponents, it's about moving from a win-lose battle to a conversation in which each person is heard. It's not about being a top dog but is about being a human. It takes skill to be who you are in the face of a dominator, but those skills can be learned. They can be learned early! And if they can be learned, they can be taught.

So think about yourself. You can be a model for young children when you begin to look at your own interactions. How often do you use your personal power to move from a battle to a conversation? Conversely, how often do you have a knee-jerk defensive reaction to something that puts you in a fight-or-flight mode? Most of us fall into patterns of reactions depending on the stimulus. We can change our behavior by remembering that between the stimulus and the response lies a gap. In that gap lies the freedom to choose a response. When we are in touch with our personal power, and we remember the gap is there, we can see a bigger picture and choose from alternative responses. We can change patterns. We can move from win/lose battles to creating new realities for ourselves and others. That's power!

Summary

Holly Elissa Bruno

Power, like religion, politics, sex, or money, can be a prickly topic. Courage from that deep place within is needed to acknowledge, name, and face power inequities. Avoidance is easier. Who wants to be the messenger of change, especially when messengers get shot? Even if we can't abide unfair power dynamics in our relationships or organization, why should we rock the boat? If we keep our heads down, hide out in our classrooms or offices, we can mostly sidestep those unpleasant organizational power struggles. The risks of promoting change are high. Almost nobody says "yippee skippee" to changing her ways.

Isn't it just easier to go along to get along? Even if the answer is yes, the question remains—what are we modeling for the children? Children don't miss a thing! They know when adults don't like each other. Children know if we let someone bully us. Children feel our anxiety. Children learn from what we do even more than they learn from what we say.

Perhaps another adage—from historian Laurel Thatcher Ulrich—will help us stand up to unjust power dynamics: "Well-behaved women seldom make history." Would I prefer to take a stand and fail or not take a stand and buckle under to injustice? As Luis, Deb, and Janet have each said in his or her own way: Take a stand to right a wrong. Assure our children that power can be used to make a difference. Adults can be the grown-ups in the building.

Discussion Questions ....

1. What power do you have at work and in your personal life? How do you use that power? What goes without saying in your workplace? What messages are children getting from these unwritten rules of conduct? Would you change or add anything to those unwritten rules?

2. When someone at work hurts your feelings or does something offensive, what options do you have? Which of these options has the greatest likelihood of addressing (or resolving) the underlying issue?

3. Take a look back on your day. Can you describe a time today when you modeled for children how to use personal power to make a difference? How did the children respond? If you ask them what they learned by watching you in that moment, what might they say?

References ....

Bryant, Adam. 2011. *The Corner Office: Indispensable and Unexpected Lessons from CEOs on How to Lead and Succeed.* New York: Times Books.

Frost, Robert. 1915. "A Servant to Servants." In *North of Boston.* New York: Henry Holt.

McLaughlin, Tom, and Susan Offutt. 2012. "Filling the Shoes of the Founder." Podcast interview by Holly Elissa Bruno. *Heart to Heart Conversations on Leadership*, July 18. http://bamradionetwork.com/index .php?option=com_content&view=article&id=868:leadr&catid=69 :infobamradionetworkcom&Itemid=144.

Myers, Isabel Briggs, Mary H. McCaulley, Naomi L. Quenk, and Allen L. Hammer. 1998. *MBTI Manual: A Guide to the Development and Use of the Myers-Briggs Type Indicator.* 3rd ed. Palo Alto, CA: Consulting Psychologists Press.

3

Creating the Village
Building Relationships That Support Children

Debra Ren-Etta Sullivan

There is an African proverb that says it takes a village to raise a child. The challenge is, what does it take to create a village? In a real village, every grown-up has a valued, understood role in the education, health, welfare, growth, and development of the children who live there. Every grown-up knows this and every child takes it for granted. In early childhood care and education, we are still working to create that village for children—working on truly understanding and valuing each of our roles in raising children in the United States. Creating the village in early childhood care and education happens when you create processes, interactions, and activities that help turn a group of people into a team that is effective and efficient at meeting the needs of the children and families you serve.

You can create that village by creating new relationships between children, parents or guardians, other family members, teachers, and the community. In fact, we each help create a village everywhere we go; however, we may not be giving the process intentional thought. Everywhere we go, we bring our most important values, perspectives, communication styles, interpersonal interactions, and a host of other factors that serve as the foundation for how we want our village to function. Knowing what you want your village to look like is an important first step. The reality, however, is that we come together with others, so we have to carefully blend individual preferences, desires, values, and so on to create a cohesive environment for children. Each of us needs to know what we bring to and want for the village, *and* we need to understand how our differences can work together.

Creating Your Village

Not all villages are alike, and not everyone envisions the same thing when they picture their villages. Imagine your perfect village, the one you would create if you were in charge. How big is it?

Some prefer small, intimate communities where everyone knows everyone else. Deep relationships can be formed because there are fewer people to get to know. There may be less diversity, but there may be more shared values and goals. The pace of life may be slower, with time to stop and smell the roses or stop and speak with friends and neighbors. It may not be very efficient, but it is very inclusive. For others, the village may look more like a city with lots of people who may not even meet one another, let alone know one another. In a large village, it is more likely that the population will be diverse in many ways, including how key values are prioritized. There may be fewer shared values, but with different values taking center stage, there may be more opportunities for creative problem solving and innovation. The pace in a larger village may be quite fast with everyone working more independently, which may be less inclusive but more efficient. Then there is the village that is neither small nor large. Those who like a medium-size village are looking for a mix. They want to build deep relationships with a select number while leaving open the possibility of meeting new people or going someplace where no one knows them. They want to move goals and objectives forward with a community of like-minded people while leaving open the possibility of meeting others from different cultures who have new ideas, new perspectives, and new solutions. This village may not be as diverse as the large village, but it won't be as homogenous as the small village. There may be more opportunities for people to change the pace of their lives—going back and forth between slower and faster.

The size of your village will deeply influence how the people in it interact with one another, so it is helpful to understand why you prefer large or small or somewhere in between. My own preference is somewhere in between. I love lots of diversity—many races, cultures, languages, religions, values, viewpoints, you name it. Within all that diversity, however, I like having a community of family, friends, acquaintances, and colleagues who share a common vision or mission in life. For me, the very large village seems exciting and adventurous and ever-changing, but I could only go there for vacations. Living there would leave me feeling like I'm trying to accomplish my life mission on my own. The smaller, more intimate village would leave me feeling stifled or stuck—like I couldn't really do something daring or take risks, whether that be a daring, risky action or a daring and risky thought or perspective.

Where is your perfect village located? Is it surrounded by forests and trees? Is it out on the plains? Or are there mountains and hills? Is it surrounded by streams, lakes, and rivers? Is it tropical and lush, or do you prefer the quiet serenity of the desert? I always have a difficult time answering this question for myself because I like many different kinds of locations as long as there are only a few days where there might be extreme heat or extreme cold. I love green, so there would have to be lots of trees, grass, and other plant life. I also love water, so large bodies of it would have to be nearby. Mountains feel majestic to me, but they could be far out in the distance. I don't mind rain, but I couldn't live in a rain forest or somewhere too tropical. Of course, I just described Seattle, which happens to be where I live. This says a lot about me because I'm always striving for balance and trying to reduce extremes. In my role as a leader, I tend to create a village that is alive and organic. I understand, though, that this is possible because there are times when the interactions of those who live in my village look more like rainy, cloudy days. There will be a few times when our relationships might be extremely cold or extremely hot, but for the most part, my village will use these moments as opportunities to achieve balance.

Who gets to live in your village? Who doesn't? Often, when I ask people this question, someone will say everyone gets to live in her village. Then I'll ask if mean people get to live there, or people who don't like children, or people who are selfish and self-centered, or people who lie, cheat, and steal. If everyone gets to live in your village, you'll have to really think about how to treat people you may not like. Most people know when they are not liked, when they are not welcome. On the other hand, most people do not want to make a list of people who can't live in their village—at least not a public list. Secretly, we all have at least a mental list of those with whom we prefer not to associate or with whom we just interact. In my case, I would not be happy if people who lie, cheat, steal, or who harm children try to live in my village. This does not mean that if you tell a lie you'll be exiled, but a generally dishonest person would not be welcome. If you happen to steal a loaf of bread to feed your child, I can be forgiving, but if you steal candy from a baby, you have to leave. Again, it is important for me to know this about myself because this is the environment I'm most likely creating everywhere I go, whether I'm aware of it or not.

How are decisions in the village made? Who makes them? There are lots of ways to make decisions. They can be made by one person, a team of people, or the whole group. Decision making can be based on fact, on priority values, on emotions, or even on the amount of time available to decide. For some, a majority rule is preferred because it is the most efficient way to go. For others, consensus is preferred as the most inclusive way. And, again, there are those who are most comfortable with something in between. I've often spoken with people who claim to want a very inclusive, collaborative, consensual form of decision making in their village—but they want inclusivity to be more efficient. That's a very difficult balance to achieve. Others prefer efficiency but often find that decisions made in a vacuum or by a small group of people leave the implementation vulnerable because those responsible for that implementation were not included in the decision-making process.

I once copresented a workshop on team building. Part of the workshop focused on decision making and the role of inclusion and efficiency. The workshop participants were primarily of African and Asian descent who were challenged by their attempts to create a culturally cohesive environment for the children in their preschools. My copresenter was a Burmese woman. We were a good team because she's an Asian woman who grew up in Botswana, Africa, and I'm an African American woman who grew up with a lot of Asian family members. The workshop participants were surprised to find out that we could appreciate and incorporate both the African and the Asian perspectives around team building, decision making, inclusion, and efficiency.

My copresenter's decision-making experience in Botswana was extremely inclusive. The town made major decisions at annual town hall meetings. Everyone in town was invited and everyone got to have his or her say—no matter how long it took. You could speak for one second or one hour, and everyone who wanted to was given a chance to speak. This tended to drive many of the westerners there crazy because there seemed to be a never-ending stream of input, and no one knew quite how long the meeting would last.

On the other hand, I'm quite familiar with the more Western town hall meeting where everyone has a set amount of time for input (for example, two to five minutes) and the number of people able to provide input at the meeting is limited by the end time of the meeting. This process would have seemed insincere to someone from Botswana because it would seem as if the attempt at inclusiveness was just a gesture.

Our friends, Inclusion and Efficiency, do not always play well together, but there are ways to help them get along. If you want to be as efficient as possible, be very clear that not all voices will be heard and not all input will be sought. I think what offends people most is being asked to provide input that is not really wanted. If you have a good relationship with your team and are very familiar with what they want and need, your efficient (or even solo) decision may be representative because you have their input received over a long period of time together. If you want to be as inclusive as possible, start early. People are also offended if everyone is expected to provide input but they have to provide it right now because of short deadlines. Although endpoints are necessary, try to provide as much time as possible to receive authentic, thoughtful input.

Are there common areas, shared spaces in the village? For some folk, their village needs lots of common and shared spaces to increase the likelihood that people will run into each other and spend time together. Of course, others will want people in their village to have opportunities for replenishing alone time or simply for more privacy. And my favorite—surprise, surprise—is the choice in the middle. The best balance of shared and private space for me is a village that resembles my favorite layout in a house. After age ten, everyone has a small bedroom, maybe just enough room for a single bed, a dresser, and a desk. The kitchen, the dining room, and the living room areas would all be shared space, and they would be large enough to accommodate the whole family plus friends and neighbors. There would be a big yard in the back with grass for lounging and rolling around and a couple of small, private spaces for outdoor getaways. In my perfect village, every family or family group would have their own living spaces, but they would not be large. They would still have all the spaces that describe my favorite house layout, but the village itself would have space large enough for village gatherings, potlucks, meetings, and other group activities.

What is the economic gap, and how would you deal with it in your village? Why and how do these gaps happen? These questions always generate lively discussions because some feel there has to be an economic gap if not everyone is pulling their weight. In other words, those who work harder have access to more financial and monetary resources than those who do not work as hard. However, not everyone has the same idea about the root of the problem and, therefore, the economic gap. Some feel that most people want to work hard but do not have equal access to opportunities that make that happen. They feel that if their village has lots of jobs so that everyone who wants to work can and if *all* jobs provide a good living wage, then most people would work and work hard. And, of course, there are those who envision villages where there is no economic gap because everyone makes the same amount of money and has free access to anything that is determined to be a basic need.

What about the academic achievement gap? Why and how did that happen? Imagine a lake with different villages on either side. In one village people feel that an academic achievement gap is an inevitable consequence of the fact that some are smarter than others and some try harder than others. On the other side of the lake is a village where people think that all children can achieve at high levels if they all have access to excellent schools, excellent teachers, and excellent curricula. Naturally, there is an island in the middle of the lake, and I'll take you there to visit momentarily. There are as many schools of thought around intelligence and academic achievement as there are educational leaders, philosophers, researchers, and advocates. There are just as many schools of thought as to why not everyone excels academically in our country. Intelligence and academic achievement have been linked to a number of factors, such as race, socioeconomic status, gender, age, teacher preparation, parent involvement, culture, values, curricula, educational leadership, monetary support—you name it. As the creator of your perfect village, you need to be very familiar with your own views and beliefs about intelligence, intellectual capacity, and academic achievement. If there is an academic achievement gap in your village, you as the leader of your village should know why it exists, what caused it, and whether it is fixable. If it cannot be changed, you should know why. If it can, you should know how. If there is *not* an academic achievement gap in your village, you should know what was done to eliminate it or why it never had a chance to exist. What factors, circumstances, efforts, and so on allowed you to create a village where all children excel and have access to a great education?

Now let me take you to the island in the middle of the lake. Imagine that the people who live in the island village have decided that academic achievement is a consequence of hard work and inherent intelligence. And they have decided that it is possible to create an educational system where all children excel academically through the intentional collaboration of all the grown-ups in the village. That's my perfect village. No time is wasted arguing about who is to blame for underachievement and unequal access to an excellent education. As the leader of my island village, my role is to create a team of grown-ups who stay focused on our goals: to create the optimal learning environment based on the needs of each and every child and ensuring that all of them—yours, mine, and theirs—have equal access to it. Yes, it is hard work. Yes, we do not all start on equal footing. Yes, meeting the educational needs of each and every child takes time and energy. To me, that is what "every child is valuable" and "every child can learn" look like.

What do people outside of your village think about your village? As you envision your perfect village, you may be quite sure that it's a place where everyone wants to live. I'm always convinced that my village is ideal and that people outside my village are trying to move in. Some may have been planning to visit only for a while, but once they get there, they don't want to leave. I'm also convinced that people who are stuck in other villages are secretly jealous of my village. I know, though, that some people are apprehensive about coming to my village. It really takes a lot of time, communication, reflection, collaboration, interaction, effort, patience, and perseverance to live there, and not everyone is sure that the outcome is worth the input. Some do not think my village is even possible, so why bother?

My village may also be a bit too extroverted for people from other villages. They think they would have to work extra hard to find time alone for self-reflection and recharging—and they would be right. For introverts to thrive in my village, I have to be intentional about making sure they are not forced to assimilate to an extroverted existence. This fits directly with my village accepting all children, too, because introversion is not something that comes on in adulthood. Many children are introverted. So, if I plan to meet the needs of all children in my village, I have to be mindful of the needs, wants, and requirements of children who are not extroverted like me. I think outsiders might also think that my village has too many gray areas. I'm not big on dichotomy: right/wrong, subjective/objective, either/or, yes/no, true/false, fact/feeling. My most common answer to most questions is "it depends" because I have a tendency to want to consider and weigh many options, answers, solutions, perspectives, and values. And I usually reserve the right to change my mind if I receive new input. I'm quite comfortable with this type of ambiguity, flux, and evolving processes, but it doesn't work for everyone. My village does make progress, accomplish goals, meet objectives, solve problems, and come to conclusions, but it takes more time and involves more people.

Your Village, Your Team

The purpose of this whole exercise is to think critically about the kinds of environments you re-create wherever you go. Your values, your interactions with others, the spaces you create and decorate, your approaches to problem solving, your preferences for decision making, your beliefs and perspectives, your values—everything you've envisioned—are all part of you and what you carry with you wherever you go. This is the village, the environment, you want, what you strive for, what you hope to achieve and accomplish. Creating the village is team building. Who lives in your village and who's on your team? Who are the other adults connected to your work? Who are the welcomed ones and who are the people you really don't want there? Keep in mind that these last questions are not always about people you like and don't like. These questions are more about who's part of the team or not—for whatever reason.

As an example, I often use a story from my daughter's preschool from many years ago. There was a cook who prepared the lunches and snacks for the children, and every day my daughter would come home and tell me what the cook had made and how she made everything just right for every child there. My daughter is not a big cheese fan (How did that happen?), and it made her feel so special that the cook would serve her the crusty outside of the mac and cheese instead of the gooey middle. I did professional development at the center for my parent volunteer hours, and the cook was never there. When I'd ask the other staff why she wasn't, they would say the cook didn't need to be there because she isn't a teacher. When I'd ask the cook herself why she never came, she would say she's just the cook, not a teacher. Yet, to my daughter (and probably to the other children as well), the cook was an equally important grown-up in the village that was her preschool. But she wasn't part of the team; she wasn't a recognized member of the village. Are there people in your village who are not part of the team because of their position? Their language? Their religion? Their age? Their education? Their gender? Whatever the reason, there may be those who decide for themselves that they are not part of the team, and there may be those who have just been invisible to you. You haven't ignored them on purpose; you've just never really interacted with them or paid attention to them.

Another factor in the team-building process is that every member of your team is bringing her or his envisioned village to the team. They are most likely doing just what you are doing: trying to re-create their perfect village. Having everyone describe their perfect village is a good way to know what kind of team each person is trying to create. Even if you are the leader, the mayor of the village, you will be a better one if you ensure that the people who live there feel represented, included, and welcomed. If every grown-up has a valued, understood role in the education, health, welfare, growth, and development of the children who live there, then leaderlike actions must come from every director, driver, teacher, assistant, parent, cook, custodian— every single adult. Your leadership task is to know what gift or strength each grown-up brings to the team. What would your village be missing, what would the children be missing if that person were not there? As a leader, you have daily opportunities to talk about your team and talk with your team members. You can be a part of recognizing that everyone is on the team and acknowledging the leadership that takes place on every level in your work setting. You have the opportunity to create the ideal village by building relationships that help children grow, thrive, and excel.

Holly Elissa Bruno

Finding Core Values and Working Principles

Thank you, Debra, for thoughtfully and thoroughly articulating questions and considerations to help us imagine a village where all children, and all community members, can grow and learn.

Five years ago, I asked colleagues around the country to write their own ground rules for such a community, and law professor colleague Art LaFrance suggested several thought-provoking ideas.

He said (quoted in Bruno 2012, 143), "Our community must

1. Have a purpose/function beyond itself.

2. Agree upon a process for inclusion, action, and dissolution before commencement.

3. Have leadership that is time limited.

4. Recognize me as leader for life, and anyone who doesn't like that should get out now!"

I love Art's final ground rule. Tongue-in-cheek as he is, Art knows power is difficult to share. Power dynamics in any village need to be clarified up front to avoid internecine and Machiavellian struggles than can shove a community through the shredder.

Art also wisely mentions a kind of village "prenup" wherein members agree before they enter into the community how they will end the community or at least terminate their involvement in the village. I find it interesting that part of the compact for a community includes envisioning the end of the community. The Sisters of Charity is an example of this. The sisters, in assuming their numbers will dwindle to extinction, have agreed upon how to invest their assets to further their charitable mission after the last sister dies. Communities often do have an ending, but that doesn't change the fact that they can be valuable while they exist. So what can we do to create a community that is supportive and effective for as long as it lasts? What makes an ideal community?

In Search of an Ideal

The creation of ideal communities, sometimes called *utopian* communities, has always fascinated me. What, if anything, endures from utopian villages with alluring names such as Harmony (Indiana), Kaweah (California), Icaria (Illinois), Roycroft (New York), Halcyon and Fountaingrove (California), and Drop City (Kansas), or even Holy City (California) and Fruitlands and Brook Farm (Massachusetts)? What were their visions? What caused some to thrive and others to crumble? What can they teach us today about the village we would like to create to make the world better for children and families?

Whenever we come together to create a village, we bring our complexity, for better and for worse. We need practices that enforce the rules of the village, and yet those practices can become discriminatory and harmful. People with differences, especially those whose "morals" are at issue, are often not tolerated. Sometimes the very people who want to be inclusive end up enforcing exclusivity.

American history includes the rise and fall of many experimental utopian communities. These communities had varying levels of success, but their dreams continue: communities of people wanting to live together in peace, happiness, lifelong learning, and productivity. And doesn't every community grapple with human nature and our perfect imperfectness?

Vision for the Community

One of the most forward-looking, compassionate, and, in fact, spiritual visions for a village today is that of the country of Bhutan in southern Asia. Bhutan doesn't just pay attention to their gross national product, Bhutan pays equal attention to their gross national happiness index. The well-being and contentment of the people is every bit as important as their financial well-being.

Now this sounds like a child care program! Every member's well-being and happiness affects every other member. Everyone works to cocreate a dynamic environment where children, families, and the team are happy, learning, and growing. What ground rules might be the basis for an ideal community like this? We can thank the drafters of NAEYC's (2011) *Code of Ethical Conduct and Statement of Commitment* for establishing a vision: "Respect the dignity, worth, and uniqueness of each individual" (1).

R-E-S-P-E-C-T

That's it: respect. I believe that to build a community, the first of our shared values must be respect for everyone's differences, needs, and contributions. Without respect at the core of our village, we have little chance. The challenge, however, is this: when we beat ourselves up and don't treat ourselves respectfully, can we hope to respect others? My colleague Ann Terrell works in the Milwaukee Public Schools and says she puts her efforts of self-respect toward two things: making appointments with herself and taking responsibility for her own energy (Terrell, Neff, and Flanagan 2012).

When was the last time you showed respect to yourself and not just to others? Self-compassion as well as altruism appear to be essential in our hoped-for village. If we could find practical everyday ways to respect ourselves as well as others, and keep our eyes on that prize when the inevitable conflicts and power struggles emerge, we have a chance at sustaining our village.

Letting Go of Egocentrism

One other dynamic is also essential: melting the ego. Melting the ego is my way of reminding myself to get out of my own way and to get over myself. Melting the ego is necessary when I get that holier than thou conviction that my way is the moral high ground. Explosive face-offs emerge when my right makes you wrong and vice versa. To prevent and address these power struggles, I remind myself to set my ego to the side and remember the bigger hope and goal. This means reminding myself of a few things:

- I am not the center of the universe. It's not (often) about me.

- Success is not measured by my winning or losing.

- Am I thinking about what I can learn from this experience rather than how my will can prevail?

- Will I look back in five, ten, or twenty years and say integrity prevailed over ego?

As Maya Angelou (2012) reminds me, "I've learned that people will forget what you said; people will forget what you did, but people will never forget how you made them feel."

Building the Village

If you were asked to draft ground rules for your ideal village, what would they be? Now imagine all the other people in your community coming together with their ground rules. Do you think you could pull together and draft something enduring, or would you end up with a hodge-podge of watered down, unrealistic, unenforceable rules and values? I believe that if we truly value respect for differences at the heart of our community, we can begin to draft ground rules that will allow our communities to endure.

Creating a village is not just an exercise. It's a reality. Every time I meet another person, work with another person, fall in love with or disagree with another person, a microvillage is created. Therein lies the test: can we come together in the moment and climb to the mountaintop together?

Luis Antonio Hernandez

Real Villages

With all due respect to my colleagues Debra and Holly Elissa, every time I hear "it takes a village" I want to turn around, get on a bus, and run to the biggest urban spot around. This village usually comes with aromas of exotic spices, children skipping and running, women humming songs that put babies to sleep in seconds, and strong men doing hard work under ever blue skies. And don't forget birds up in the trees, clouds in the shapes of bunny rabbits, and a barking dog somewhere in this surreal village green.

My reality-based village is a child care center in a South Bronx housing project, the family child care home in eastern Tennessee, the Head Start program at the bottom of the Grand Canyon, or the church center in suburban Chicago. Many times villages are difficult places; sometimes they are the best places. What makes each of them hum along is the spectrum of relationships between one and all. It is about the drums of humanity beating for connection, identification, and respect in the work of caring for the children and looking out for each other.

Call for Responsibility

Fred Rogers said, "We live in a world in which we need to share responsibility. It's easy to say 'it's not my child, not my community, not my world, not my problem.' Then there are those who see the need and respond. I consider those people my heroes."

I want to take up Mister Rogers's call for responsibility. The word *responsibility* carries the weight of an individual and collective charge to do and respond, all for the sake of a greater good. One can be responsible for the well-being of one's family, for the outcomes of one's work, or for simply following traffic rules. We are, therefore, responsible for others. Debra outlined a number of related outcomes or intentions in her introduction that have a subtext of responsibility in their delivery.

Where to start? I will start with the core values inherent in the notion of responsibility that I bring from my family. As many children do, I saw my mother and father diligently go to work. For them it meant meeting the responsibilities of our home and their life in a new country. Beyond our immediate home, my parents were also helping other family members by sending regular money transfers—family came first, so we always helped relatives in need. My parents also taught my brother and me about our responsibilities at home, from taking out the garbage and cleaning up to our weekend night curfew. Going to school was our primary responsibility, but if we wanted extra money, we needed to find a job. Both of us worked from early on—delivering groceries, recycling bottles and cans, shoveling snow. Working was a responsibility that provided values about work: being pleasant, showing up on time, and opening our first savings accounts. Family teaches values about taking care of oneself, helping each other, and—by extension—seeing the world through the lens of what is important. Most importantly, our grandparents and parents were our role models—much as we are to the next generation—transmitting values that we only later recognize as important and essential in life. The joys, the sacrifices, the determination to do good and move ahead was a path of responsibility for each of us. Our parents are gone now, but my brother and I delight to see the next generation carrying on those core values, all with the care and humor that runs through our family.

My Village

In the village of my mind, we would all get along and be happy. I know it is easier said than done! My expectations for this community began early and have survived through many rough patches of tensions and difficult times. Looking back, I see that my faith in different communities stems from living in a very diverse and difficult neighborhood. We lived in Hell's Kitchen on the west side of Manhattan—the setting for *West Side Story*—where there were certain blocks you did not walk down. There were Irish gangs from the West Side, Puerto Rican gangs from the Bronx, and black gangs from Harlem. And I almost forgot the Italian crew from Little Italy. What a mix, what tensions, what good times. Interestingly, we went to the same schools from elementary to high school. And in school we all got along, sometimes with a few scrapes here and there. But we learned to appreciate, tolerate, and accept each other, resulting in relationships that have lasted a lifetime.

A lesson for me was to not be intimidated by those I didn't know but to make an effort to connect and turn the fear of a stranger into the potential for a friend. Those initial encounters meant friendships based on sports, music, or just hanging out. We are older now, and I wish I'd gotten to know others in my class in a deeper sense. By now all the school cliques and in-groups are forgotten. For me, it was a responsible act to meet others, get to know them, and get along. Although it may seem like a survival strategy, it also gave me a wider world of friends—as an honorary member of every gang!

The Infamous Village

So, how are we going to be part of this infamous village? What are my responsibilities as a member of this community? A compilation of interviews (Bryant 2011) of organizational leaders indicated a sense of curiosity as a key element for any leader. To be curious is to be open to discover, explore, and experiment—to do what comes naturally to a young child. To be curious means one has to be genuinely interested in others, ask questions, inquire deeply for explanations, and be outside one's own world. It is the Margaret Mead approach. As a world famous anthropologist, Dr. Mead lived with a native people to learn from them, never to judge but to observe, ask questions, and appreciate their uniqueness and differences. In being curious, she highlighted the humanity in each of us. For who can say who is more civilized or advanced or better than another human being? And she observed and noted, no matter the size or composition of that human village, children were always central to community life. In her observations, adults all cared for the children and children learned their roles and responsibilities within the group.

Having that curiosity provides a winning strategy, for people are social beings interested in other social beings. An example is when a person is astonished when someone takes the time to ask about their lives in an open manner, without judgment, assumptions, or bias: "Tell me about the religious holidays you celebrate." "Why is it that women in your culture cover their hair?" "What is it like being a teen mom?" Find the anthropologist within you, be respectfully curious about others, and see what you discover about them and about yourself. Even though it is hard work and takes practice, a degree of curiosity provides a fountain of knowledge and information that makes us attuned to the rhythms of our community. We respect individuals, we appreciate and understand differences, and we can truly say, "I know where you're coming from." Trust and respect are the keys for entering the village that Debra has outlined. I encourage and challenge you to enter your new village with a deep sense of responsibility.

Janet Gonzalez-Mena

My Village Experience

I wish I could have recorded the feelings that arose in me as I read about villages from my three friends. This is a hard job—building a whole village, an ideal one at that. I tried to figure out in which parts of my life I lived in a village in its broadest sense: a village that honored and supported children and families. Then I started thinking of taking up Debra's original challenge to design my ideal village, but that thought was overwhelming. Both Luis and Holly Elissa gave me things to think about when it comes to designing a village, but then it came to me: I don't have to design one, I lived in one once—a village made up of diverse grown-ups who had a role in the education, health, welfare, growth, and development of the children who were in the village. This happened in an early care and education program by creating relationships, interactions, and activities that turned parents, teachers, and communities into a team! Here's the story—starting way back when I was a child.

The village I grew up in as a child was segregated. I didn't know that. I must have realized that there were people who didn't look like me and my family, but that they weren't part of my life. They weren't part of the media either—or my education. Those were the Dick and Jane days. Even though I grew up in California, I didn't know any Mexicans. I did know about tacos, though. They were called "Spanish food" and were served in "Spanish restaurants." I probably didn't hear the word *Mexican* until sixth grade when we studied Mexico and South America. I still hadn't met anybody who wasn't a European American like I was.

Fast-forward to 1970 when I met my husband, who was born and raised south of the border in Mexico. He arrived in California as an adult in 1956 with his parents, so by 1970 he was a United States citizen and well acquainted with the language and culture. Plus, by then he had a college degree and a teaching credential. This was a time when there were no teaching jobs in California due to a decline in the number of children. This was also a time of change in California (and across the nation) as oppressed people began to demand equal rights. At the time I met him, my husband had declared himself a Chicano and was attending demonstrations, sit-ins, and even a pray-in or two.

At that time, segregation was still occurring in Northern California. It wasn't legal, but it effectively separated middle-class children and families, who were mostly white, on my side of town from children and families on the other side of town, who were mostly from black and brown low-income families. By that time, I did know Mexicans, partly because I started my career as a volunteer in a preschool for Spanish-speaking children and families.

The staff was divided, half English speakers and half Spanish speakers. The English-speaking teachers were middle-class white women; the Spanish-speaking aides were from the low-income community across town. Status and salaries were higher for teachers than for aides. My soon-to-be husband and I felt that situation wasn't good for the self-concept of the Spanish-speaking children. We came up with a solution. Why not just train Spanish speakers to be preschool teachers? That way they could give the children strong messages about retaining their own language and culture.

It was about that time that we got married and rented an apartment on the other side of town from where I had been living. We then came up with the idea of a new bilingual home-centered preschool. We started with meetings of interested Spanish-speaking families. We discussed the value of a home-centered program where teachers moved with a group of five four-year-olds to the home of each so that every day of the week they were in a different home with a different parent to help the teacher. Thus, parent education became part of the program. The group was enthusiastic and decided on a name right away: La Escuela Cuauhtemoc. (Cuauhtemoc was the last emperor of the Aztecs.) The idea caught on, and we found all kinds of support from both sides of town, including some high-ups in the county office of education.

We started up and operated first on a volunteer basis with four teachers from the Spanish-speaking community. My husband, with his credential, was the director. By that time I had become a preschool teacher, so I was the curriculum expert. We were ready to go to work training the teachers and needed a place to do so. The director of a community center in a low-income community offered us space in the center at no charge. We were delighted for more than one reason. This was during a period of the federal war on poverty, and the federal government was the source of funding for the community center. At that time, there was enormous competition for federal funds, which had created bad feelings between the African American community and the Spanish-speaking community, who were in competition for funding. The director of the community center was an African American man; his reaching out to us and the Spanish-speaking teachers was a huge step toward creating positive relationships between the two communities.

Already we were having an integrated "village experience," and it felt *wonderful*. The low-income community was coming together in a way it hadn't before. We were also integrating with the white community on the other side of town by including two English-speaking families in each group. We all operated on a volunteer basis—doing various kinds of fundraising for essential needs. By that time, the county office of education had taken us under its wing. People there helped us write a grant to apply for federal innovative-education funds. A call came one morning that we had gotten the money and that our application scored higher than any other. We were numero uno! Those were very exciting times! Once we got funded, we were able to rent the space at the community center, which helped us continue our integrative experience as we were trying to work on bringing the two communities—brown and black—together.

It wasn't an ideal village, but it was one where children and their futures were our main focus, and we were supported by a wide range of people and institutions. Looking back, I have to say it was a highlight in my life. The memories came flooding back while I was writing: memories of relationships and team building—the integrating of lives. We were all working together: administrators, teachers, families, volunteers, and the community. We were definitely a village.

Summary . . . .

Debra Ren-Etta Sullivan

The notion of a village and the prospect of creating one brought up a number of important themes. Power was certainly one of them. Yes, power can be quite difficult to share. I found myself thinking that, on some level, there are people who want equity but don't necessarily want everyone to be equal. In any well-functioning community the power dynamics need to be quite clear. There would be no doubt or misunderstanding about who is in charge of Art's village, but when it's unclear or when not everyone agrees, challenges and struggles will arise. Those who want to retain all the power will find themselves confronted by those who refuse to relinquish their power. Maybe this is where the "village prenup" comes into play. The Sisters of Charity example helps us see what continuing a legacy after a community dies out could look like. But what would it look like for a community at its inception to discuss dissolving the community if members are no longer in agreement or in a case of irreconcilable differences? In other words, what would it look like for a community to plan its "divorce" while it is planning its "wedding"? How does a community split apart without going to war?

Another theme that emerged is that of rules and practices that are inclusive and those that are exclusive. As stated earlier, even those who want to be all-inclusive end up having rules or practices regarding those they really don't want to live with. Some may be quite upfront and direct: "Those people" can't live here. Others just make "those people" feel so uncomfortable and unwelcome that they leave. I think love and fear are related to the themes here. Communities built on love may be more welcoming and inclusive than those built on fear. The fear of the unknown—of those who look different, of those who think different, of those who believe different—and fear of "not the same" can lead to the creation of a community that is exclusive by design, even if no one wants to say that out loud. We may also ask about who gets to say that one group is more civilized or advanced or better than another. The truth is some really do believe such differences matter, and that will have an impact on any leadership situation.

A third theme is that sense of curiosity about others. My bachelor's degree was in cultural anthropology, and I think I majored in the field because, like Margaret Mead, I wanted to know more about others. All four of us carry strong aspects of curiosity in our lives, our stories, and our paths. Luis made friends among the Irish, Puerto Rican, African American, and Italian "gangs" at school. I first met Holly Elissa because she always (yes, always) takes time to initiate intriguing, meaningful, friends-forever conversations with perfect strangers. Janet has countless examples of stepping outside of her own community to learn about, advocate for, teach in, and communicate with the Latino communities she encounters. Creating a village—be it a neighborhood, a preschool, an office, a family, or a utopian society—requires a healthy and strong sense of curiosity about others. Yes, it is hard work and takes time to really get to know, understand, and appreciate someone who is not like you, but when children see grown-ups work, struggle, problem solve, and thrive together on their behalf, that's when they learn the most about why it takes a village to raise a child.

Discussion Questions ....

1. What is your ideal village? Define it, describe it, and explain its core beliefs, practices, and values.

2. What are your beliefs about power? Should a few have it? Why or why not? Should a lot have it? Why or why not? Should you have it? Why or why not? We will often find ourselves in challenging situations where it appears that my right makes you wrong or your right makes me wrong. Creating a village requires imagination, openness, traversing new territory, and exploring third space, so instead of either/or, take a look at both/and. What if we're both right? Your first thought may be that we can't both be right, but what if we both really are? What would that look like?

3. Think of a "village" you have very little contact with or knowledge about (for example, another ethnic or racial group, a group belonging to an income level that's different from yours, a group facing discrimination or prejudice that you don't face, a group that speaks a language you don't speak). Find the anthropologist within you to be respectfully curious about others and see what you discover about them and about yourself. What are their core values and beliefs? What do they want most for their children?

References

Angelou, Maya. 2012. Interview by Trisha LaNae'. "A Conversation with Dr. Maya Angelou." *Beautifully Said*, July 4.

Bruno, Holly Elissa. 2012. *What You Need to Lead an Early Childhood Program: Emotional Intelligence in Practice*. Washington, DC: National Association for the Education of Young Children.

Bryant, Adam. 2011. *The Corner Office: Indispensable and Unexpected Lessons from CEOs on How to Lead and Succeed*. New York: Times Books.

NAEYC (National Association for the Education of Young Children). 2011. *Code of Ethical Conduct and Statement of Commitment*. Position statement. www.naeyc.org/files/naeyc/file/positions/Ethics%20Position%20 Statement2011.pdf.

Terrell, Ann, Kristin Neff, and Nancy Flanagan. 2012. "Driving for Ed Leadership: Excellence without Driving Yourself over the Edge." Podcast interview by Holly Elissa Bruno. *Heart to Heart Conversations on Leadership*, September 28. www.bamradionetwork.com/index .php?option=com_content&view=article&id=896:leadr&catid=36 :administrators-channel&Itemid=90.

4

From the Universal to the Uniform

Considering Cultural and Diversity Standards across Our Personal and Professional Connections

Luis Antonio Hernandez

Simply speaking, the word *universal* sounds huge, far out there, beyond the beyond. *Universal* infers people in faraway places sharing some common ground, having parallel experiences, laughing at identical stories. The concept unites us in ways that are always surprising with a hint of awe. We are walking on the same road. We are part of something beyond my corner of the world. It is the light from afar into a tomorrow.

"A smile is the universal welcome." —Max Eastman

Then we come to the term *uniform*. If a smile is universal, is being uniform cause for a frown? The mere image of a uniform can repel some, since it hints at something that reeks too much of the same, unchanging and repetitious. Part of the distaste may lie in the fact that we consider ourselves unique and exceptional, while the term *uniform* boxes us into sameness. We exclaim, "I don't want to be like everyone else!" or "It's important to think outside the box." Yet, we cling to regularity and order in our lives—a schedule, a routine, and a sense of what is expected in just about every turn of daily life. That consistency gives us order and, ultimately, security. We can function because we know what comes next and thereafter. Any break becomes a disruption, an alteration of what is a normal day. No room for smiles here.

"I think people are universal." —Ang Lee

In this delicate dance between universal and uniform forces, leaders in ECE can balance the big picture—the vision—of what is best for children and families and the minute details—policies and procedures—that make a quality program hum on a daily basis. A vision-guided program is attuned to the available resources—the latest research, national and state public policies, and market forces—in positioning a program for excellence. Uniformity is the steady partner in this dance. Uniformity propels a program through good and bad times: it administers and manages its fiscal well-being, it maintains the physical environment, it provides staff with a sense of purpose, and it defines a safe harbor for children and families.

And then we throw in the dynamics of a world that is quickly changing, with new family compositions, new immigrant groups, and new staff characteristics. We have linguistic and cultural diversity, an emerging pluralism in ethnic and racial groups, clear evidence of class differences, and generational gaps ("She has how many tattoos?"). What's a leader to do?

For many, there are ways to connect the global universal concepts—the big ideas—to the nitty gritty of everyday uniformity. One way to connect is to start with the end in mind: meaningful human relationships and interactions. As the strongest principle in early childhood education, relationships are the grease that keeps the universe of people spinning; it is the tool to fine-tune any system. And considering the dynamics of diversity, relationships provide the foundation to support learning, progress, and aspirations. In this ideal version, each person is the catalyst to connect, to interact, and to take action for the greater good.

"Live your life as though your every act were to become a universal law." —Immanuel Kant

What is universal in ECE work? The big picture in our work with children and families can be evident whether one lives in Kenya, Illinois, or Iceland. Here are some of those comprehensive principles that unite ECE leaders across the globe:

- The primary focus is the safety and security of children.

- The essential well-being of every child—health, nutrition, comfort—is key.

- The development and learning process in each child is promoted, encouraged, and supported.

- A natural balance exists in the dynamics of play, early academics, and social-emotional development.

- Families are respected for their strengths and are welcomed as partners in the learning process.

- The cultural environment abounds with music, stories, movement, exploration, and a joyous atmosphere.

- Those working with children are professionals who know the basics of human and child development and are willing to advance their knowledge and skills.

- We recognize that these principles are possible through genuine relationships.

As a universal leader, what else would you add to these collective principles?

As a new or emerging leader in our field, the route to your position likely started in unexpected places. Perhaps you began by volunteering or you decided that accounting was not for you or your first academic interest was in architecture and now you are a preschool teacher. Or, perhaps, you always wanted to work with children and families. Regardless of how you got here, a universal need is a passion and love for the profession. The work is too important to be disregarded or trivialized. Whatever the case, be passionate about the essence, the cause, and the purpose of the profession. Or let work itself gradually and organically become your passion. Falling in love and staying in love with the profession involves a lifetime of study and interest. And the enthusiasm and passion can be contagious to the children, families, and teams we work with.

What is universal is that those who work with children need to have an incredible pack of energy to keep up with those three- and four-year-olds! Besides fortitude and ready smiles, teachers need a charm box of ideas and storytelling skills. They need to be ready to hug a crying child, make sure naptime is a quiet time, run with the children during outdoor time, and basically be on all the time. Once we lose the enthusiasm for the joy of this new generation, once the body lags and tires, it is time for rejuvenation, even time off. Children know when we are not really there.

"Everyone who wants to do good to the human race always ends in universal bullying." —Aldous Huxley

Unfortunately, our efforts to do good sometimes turn into unpleasant experiences for children or their families. An attitude of "This is the way we have always done it and everyone has always liked it," or "I know what is best for every child" can be counterproductive. In addition to typical preschool topics, teachers are also guided and mandated (some will say bound) by a series of expectations for uniformity in their daily work. What should be a smooth cycle starting with a guiding curriculum, engaging and exciting teaching strategies, observing children, assessing and documenting progress, and building partnerships with families turns into reams of documentation and more. These are not a favorite set of work requirements but are understood to be essential in today's world. These work standards are usually established by "experts" that neatly set uniformity across the ECE land; conformity is institutionalized from high up. An example of one such requirement is that four-year-olds need to learn how to get into a line so they can be ready to enter kindergarten. Teachers dutifully follow this mandate on a daily basis, shaping a uniform behavior. A closer look at this mandate had me thinking like a child: Just how long does it take to learn how to get in line? Do I need to do this ten times a day? I want my naptime back! I want to play with blocks!

"The unity of freedom has never relied on uniformity of opinion." —John Fitzgerald Kennedy

While many who work with children do so because they love being with children, they find themselves torn between the innocence of the younger years and the requirements that sometimes turn classrooms of color and joy into gray replicas of a fifth-grade classroom. What happened to early childhood education? Uniformity continues in the daily routines for children and adults from the morning greeting to the afternoon good-byes. It is an entire day that depends on harmony, efficiency, and coordination. But the increasing accountability for the overall purpose or outcomes in children's growth and experience zaps the creative and spontaneous process of the early years. Are children learning? Are teachers teaching?

From the gritty realities of everyday work, how do we stay true to the vision of *big ideas* in our field? Those ideas and concepts serve to inspire and motivate our professional roots. They nourish what we care about. Other visions provide a glimpse of what is possible. And just as importantly, other forces give us an occasional kick in the pants by challenging us and making our heads spin.

A favorite story in challenging conventional uniformity comes from an interview with a teacher on NPR from a number of years ago. This exceptional teacher had been named Teacher of the Year. The interviewer asked, "What is the secret or formula for your success?" The teacher responded that at the end of each year, he would burn all the notes, PowerPoint presentations, copies, and outlines from his classes. The purpose was to start from scratch at the beginning of the academic year with his new students. He saw it as his professional responsibility to stay fresh, to be curious, and to look for new information to upgrade his knowledge and skill base. He saw that his students were motivated by his work, which provided a renewed sense of purpose. Can you imagine you doing that? Can you see teachers burning their fall harvest theme boxes?

While burning old lesson plans may seem a bit risky or plain crazy, it is about wanting our professional horizons to be full of exciting ideas and concepts. The usual first reaction is to be dumbfounded by new concepts. Think of your first introduction to developmentally appropriate practices. Or when your program sweated through the rigorous process for being recognized as a nationally accredited center. From there, you may have discovered green play spaces, the use of appropriate technology in the classroom, brain development research, or the success of an intentional family engagement approach with your program's community. All these concepts and strategies propel us to new professional and personal stages of growth. They are evidence of lifelong learning. And in this garden of universal ideas, divergent learning domains come alive, making the world of the classroom a humming place filled with excitement, laughter, and greater learning.

"America has believed that in differentiation, not in uniformity, lies the path of progress. It acted on this belief; it has advanced human happiness, and it has prospered." —Louis D. Brandeis

The lofty and practical ideals and dreams for our profession are pulled between universal aspirations and meaningless uniformity—an uneasy combination for dreamers and doers. The ideals and dreams uplift and drain the spirit and energy of those working with children, creating a seesaw of uneven proportion. And as leaders, we seek and congeal principles to live and work by. What are some principles to follow? What is uniform in our ECE work?

While the term *uniform* has implications of conformity and homogeneity, it also provides a foundation for everyday harmony:

- All children, as well as adults, need a sense of consistency and normalcy in their daily routines.

- All children need the constant comfort of knowing who is there for them, who their friends are, what their favorite play activities and learning routines are.

- All families need consistent and familiar relationships with teachers who care for their children every day.

- All children and families deserve a sense of respect and trust when staff communicates the purposes in daily experiences.

- A program's formats—lesson plans, routines, activities, curricula, assessments—need to be appropriate for the cultures and languages of all the enrolled children.

- Teachers and other staff must adhere to work standards that constantly keep the place humming.

- Great leaders need to constantly improve and adjust well-proven routines and learning formats.

As an ECE leader, how do you balance the principles of uniformity with the drive to innovate and improve?

While a happy balance between the universal and the uniform may not be easily attainable, many lessons can be gained. A good place to start is with the children we work with every day. Observations of their play, conversations, moods, and explorations can provide clues as to what works and what doesn't. It is the light that guides our practices, redefines the curriculum, and provides rich observations and concrete evidence for assessment purposes. The singular vision of children at play and work is the universal language of the profession. And the world and culture of the children and families come through the front door of our programs.

"What a distressing contrast there is between the radiant intelligence of the child and the feeble mentality of the average adult." —Sigmund Freud

While we are still in the beginning of a new century, diversity and cultural topics continue to lead to vigorous discussions, analyses, suspicions, and even a few tears. The topics are a platform of challenges and opportunities. We need a sensitive space to confront economic disparities, denied access to opportunities, and general unkindness and unfairness to people based on race, beliefs, gender, and other singularities. It is not a perfect world; the forces of world economics, politics, environmental disasters, and strife bring waves of people across continents. The speed of media and communication brings every corner of the planet right into our homes and offices if we are interested. What happens in one place impacts another place thousands of miles away. No place is isolated anymore. Like the image of a fluttering butterfly slowly creating the initial force of a hurricane a world away, we influence each other in many ways.

The effects of culture and diversity cut across our professional and personal lives even without our knowledge or effort. They are bound and coiled together in a twirling structure with each contributing a distinct and singular strand, almost like the wiring for an electronic or phone system—colorful, tight, and unique. Culture, language, values, beliefs, rituals, ethnicity, and race are all coiled in a wire of individual energy. These unique characteristics in each of us then mold and conform to the reality of the world—be it through the use of technology, visits across the globe, or sharing of needs and wants. And after being and living with others whose wiring is unique, we might realize that we are so much alike, that our wiring is universal. This connection between what is unique and universal binds all humans together. With the power of human interactions we learn the arts of civility, acceptance, understanding, and harmony—be it in our close personal world or in our professional lives. It is defining a place in the world for all. And what better place to learn about interacting with others than through the lessons of children at work and play.

Holly Elissa Bruno

When Universal Is Not Uniform

Hey, Luis, when we get this one figured out, we'll be zillionaires! You take on towering questions:

- What do we know to be true?

- What lasts forever?

- On what can we all agree?

Yikes! You, Galileo, Copernicus, Rumi, de Beauvoir, and Gandhi are way ahead on this!

Even if we confine these soaring questions to our field, we hit bumps. Here's an example: My colleague, Sue Twombly, an early childhood director for twenty-seven years, described an experience during her presentation at one of the early World Forums. Sue was advocating for the value of consistent care, the ongoing relationship between teacher and child. Consistent care leads to the kind of relationship that develops and deepens when one teacher stays with the same group of babies from the infant room until those children throw kisses on their way to preschool. You can imagine where Sue was coming from: children feel safe and loved, challenged and secure, and free to grow with the same trusted adult.

Sue backed up her position with research findings on the benefits of consistent care by educators. She described how the teacher witnesses and guides each child through one phase of learning to another. Families grow to know and trust the teacher. The teacher, in turn, learns to understand, appreciate, and respect each family's desires, preferences, and values. Sound ideal? To Sue, yes, this is not only ideal but something she and her team work conscientiously to make happen in their thriving program.

Does the concept sound universal to you? Imagine Sue's jaw dropping when a delegate from Kenya in East Africa queried, "Are we doing something wrong? Our children do not have one consistent caregiver/teacher. Our children climb from one lap to another in our communities, learning something from each person, feeling soothed and comforted in differing ways. Our children are raised by the village, not by one consistent adult. Does the research mean we are harming our children?"

What would you have said in that moment? Sue was riveted. She had to quickly evaluate her stance and what she had said so she could listen openly to what the delegate was saying. Sue ended up both supporting the delegate and the approach Sue had seen work. Neither approach was superior, regardless of the research. Back to the drawing board on what is a universal standard! I have faced many similar moments. Just when I think I understand something deeply, new evidence or a powerful experience like Sue's takes me back to the question, what do we know to be true? Is what's true for me ever the same as what's true for you?

All I Really Need to Know I Learned in Kindergarten, or from the Motown Singers

Sometimes poets and songwriters seem to nail it. Their words carry a rightness that reaches straight through to our hearts. When words touch us deeply, the meaning behind those words feels universal. Does this statement of "universal" beliefs by Robert Fulghum (2003, 1–2) proclaim forever and always what is both universal and uniform?

Share everything.

Play fair.

Don't hit people.

Put things back where you found them.

Clean up your own mess.

Don't take things that aren't yours.

Say you're sorry when you hurt somebody.

Wash your hands before you eat.

Flush.

Warm cookies and cold milk are good for you.

Live a balanced life—learn some and think some and draw and paint and sing and dance and play and work every day some.

Take a nap every afternoon.

When you go out into the world, watch out for traffic, hold hands, and stick together.

Wonder.

Fulghum's words sounded pretty good until the bit about warm cookies. Warm cookies can be my over-the-lips-onto-the-hips downfall. But then, I skipped kindergarten, so I missed out on that needed year of social-emotional development. Maybe, unlike Fulghum, that's why I had—and (let's face it) have—trouble answering the question, what do we know to be true?

As a child, I turned to poets and Motown singers. I learned to value self-deprecating humor as the Main Ingredient crooned "Everybody Plays the Fool" and to question the government when Marvin Gaye asked, "What's Going On?" When Ray Charles mourned, "You Don't Know Me," I challenged appearances. And when Aretha Franklin told me what R-E-S-P-E-C-T meant to her, I got the message.

What's the message? In the end, as in the beginning, I learned to keep learning. When something is presented as a universal truth, my job is to question. I learned to stay open to surprises and to delight in discovery, even at the expense of needed security. In *Letters to a Young Poet*, Rilke reminded me to "try to love the questions." When poems and lyrics cause me to pause and "wonder," I know we are getting closer to the universal. Who can disagree with Fulghum's (2003) request for us to "wonder"? Who hasn't paused to wonder at LeeAnn Womack's song "I Hope You Dance"?

Luis, I respect your deliberate quest to figure out the universal and the uniform. You and those who make policy and draft codes and standards are doing good and valuable work. Bravi! As for where I stand on this, if you need a uniform standard to label my next step, call it *emergent curriculum*. Here's my truth: I can't sit still to ponder when the music is calling me out to dance.

Janet Gonzalez-Mena

Diversity in Discipline Practices

Reading Luis's piece and Holly Elissa's response brought two stories to mind for me. The first story started in a writer's group. My friends and I put together an informal meeting once a month when we shared whatever we were writing. We were all aspiring writers and early childhood professionals, so we often wrote about early childhood issues. At this particular meeting, everybody arrived with a draft of a short piece of mine that I sent out for them to comment on. It was a piece of writing that I felt good about. I had written about discipline—always a hot topic. At this point in my career, I knew a lot about effective approaches that I believed were universally applicable. I tried explaining these methods in a way that took me out of the spotlight, so I used *we* instead of *I* in giving examples and explaining how each worked.

When it was my turn for everyone in the writer's group to focus on my contribution, one member of the group handed me back my draft with just one question written in bold letters right on top. It said, "Who is this *we* you are talking about?" I looked at my critic with a puzzled expression on my face. She was an old friend and colleague of mine, an African American community college teacher. She smiled slightly at my puzzlement. Then she said, "Janet, who is the *we*? Are you talking about white women?"

If you had been there, you might have seen the lightbulb go on over my head. There was only one answer I could give her. "Yes," I responded sheepishly. I certainly hadn't intended to write from the point of view of my own race, but without thinking about it, that's exactly what I had done. I gulped. Then I realized that, indeed, I was writing about people like me who believed in the practices I was trying to promote. I didn't think about how my culture might relate to what I believed in. That day was a milestone in my development. From then on I was very careful to use *we* only when I was sure it would truly include everybody.

That incident marked the beginning of some interesting conversations about diversity in discipline practices. I learned a lot—not only from my friend in the writer's group but also from Cynthia Ballenger (1992), who writes about differences between what she believes and what Haitian teachers believe about disciplining young children. Ballenger uses what has been called the *consequences approach*, that is, letting children discover the natural or arranged consequences of their actions. She was surprised by how the Haitian teachers responded to her methods. They saw letting children suffer for their choices as coldhearted and excessively cruel. They preferred to guide children in other ways through appealing to their sense of family and why they should be good and not disappoint their parents.

Another discipline approach I came to see as hugely controversial is time-out. I remember a heated discussion in a discipline workshop I was giving. The group split into two camps: one for time-out and the other strongly against it. The con side spoke with passion about how using a time-out was wrong. A child who was having behavior problems never needed isolation—that child needed the group. Furthermore, a time-out was much too strong a punishment for any child, they said. Separating a child was not only like solitary confinement but also like shunning, and it was the worst possible punishment only to be used for unforgivable adult crimes. Several of the participants explained how there was a rule against using time-outs in their centers. It just showed me again that it is hard, if not impossible, to find universal agreement about discipline measures. I'm wondering how these issues about diversity and discipline fit in with Luis's universal and uniform theme. Maybe I could say that discipline and guidance may be universal, but it's definitely not uniform. I believe that fits in with the message Holly Elissa gave in her piece.

Questioning the Universal

My next story is a shorter one and relates to my involvement in a group that formed after NAEYC came out with the first edition of *Developmentally Appropriate Practice in Early Childhood Programs* in 1987. In the position statement on page 2 of that book, the two concepts behind developmental appropriateness are stated as "age appropriateness" and "individual appropriateness" (NAEYC 1987). The position statement maintains that human development research indicates that ages and stages are universal. The group that formed as a protest to the developmentally appropriate practice (DAP) position statement (or at least that's the way I heard it) was clear that if there are any universals, they are much less frequent than NAEYC claimed. Instead of presenting at the NAEYC National Conference, this group of rebel academics and researchers created their own conference and called it Reconceptualizing Early Childhood Education (RECE). At the time of this writing, the conference is celebrating its twentieth year and has been held in countries all over the world. I've been to four of the conferences and found them exciting and thought provoking.

Examples of two of RECE's goals can be found at http://recesite.wiki spaces.com/Conferences. They are stated as "challenging traditional assumptions about theory" and "exploring new directions in research, policy, and practice in early childhood education and care and childhood studies" (RECE, accessed 2013). When I went to my first RECE conference, I encountered postmodern theory as it relates to ECE. I had to learn a whole new vocabulary and way of looking at everything I thought I knew. But it didn't take me too long to catch up, because most of the original group were well-published and prolific writers. I gobbled up their books. I think what struck me the most was the relationship between reconceptualizing ECE and issues of equity and social justice. I also learned to question almost anything connected to the term *universal*!

Apparently, NAEYC got the message about diversity that questions the universality of developmental views and research. Here's the proof: in 1997 the revised edition of *Developmentally Appropriate Practice in Early Childhood Programs* came out, and a third base of knowledge had been added—cultural appropriateness. And by the third edition in 2009, gone were the terms "appropriate practice" and "inappropriate practice," which were replaced by "developmentally appropriate" and "in contrast." Also, the universality theme was much less prominent and diversity showed up throughout.

Writing this helped me look back at my own history in coming to better understand the relationship of the uniform to the universal. I guess in conclusion I'd have to say that stepping out of my own skin lets me see that what I think is universal just might not be.

Debra Ren-Etta Sullivan

The Power of Pluralism

What you are reading here is different than what I thought I would write. I thought a lot about change and relationships as I read this chapter. While sitting in the airport in Atlanta after the 2012 NAEYC Annual Conference and Expo, I saw a piece on television about Malala, the fifteen-year-old Pakistani girl who was shot in the head because of her opinions about educating girls. Luis wrote about "comprehensive principles that unite ECE leaders across the globe" in the introduction to this chapter, and I realized that resistance to change is a powerful thing.

Pluralism is about change. There are changing demographics all around our planet, and it is not possible to meet the needs of a changing demographic without change. Often, we want others to want, to value, to appreciate, and to strive for what we already have—to simply assimilate. What if things change so much that old normal becomes outnumbered by new normal? We may have to learn to exist in another group's normal—a redefinition of what is universal. Malala exists in a context where there is disagreement about the education a girl should have. This context is not new. Throughout all of time and all of humankind there have been differences of opinion about what is right or appropriate, and most of these differences have to do with access to power through knowledge. If you change who has access to knowledge, you change who has access to power. Our worlds, our societies, our communities, and our workplaces are changing.

As different groups join us, they will bring their own ideas and beliefs about what is right and appropriate—about what is universal. In the United States we are finding that more and more of the children and families we serve look, live, and speak nothing like the children's teachers. The Teacher of the Year whom Luis writes about understands change. He knows that each year brings different students, uniquely different human beings with different strengths, abilities, challenges, expectations, and perspectives. He welcomes the change, creates it intentionally, and plans for it. Change means different. It means things are no longer the same. Change also may mean loss—the loss of what we've always done and how we've always done it. Losing the status quo is very difficult for some people to manage.

Pluralism is also about relationships. With any relationship you have to learn something new—be it a new perspective, a new value, a new way of doing things, a new normal. Luis says that "falling in love and staying in love with the profession involves a lifetime of study and interest" and that most certainly requires a relationship with both our work and with those we serve. We fall in love and stay in love—in a relationship—by really getting to know the work we do in fresh and exciting ways and by really getting to know the children and families we serve in deep and meaningful ways. Again, the Teacher of the Year knew this. By starting from scratch every year, he allowed his work to be fresh and exciting. He had to get to know each year's group of students in deep and meaningful ways in order to meet their educational needs. This is a great demonstration of a lifetime of study and interest, a great demonstration of what it looks like to welcome pluralism by developing relationships. I wish all of my teachers could have been like him! I wish all of my children's teachers could have been like him! I wish all children everywhere could have teachers like him! This is obviously someone who has authentic relationships with each and every student.

There cannot be a uniform curriculum, a one-size-fits-all approach to our work. By its very definition, pluralism requires many, not one. Many appropriate practices, many ways to raise children, many ways to teach children, many children to teach. For some, it is a real challenge to have an authentic relationship with someone who is different. It requires a lot of time, a lot of listening, a lot of learning something new and different, a lot of considering different perspectives, a lot of reassessing our own perspectives. If we don't do what we need to do to establish authentic relationships with others, to make room for pluralism, we run the risk of rendering ourselves irrelevant. Others will simply go do their own thing, much like Janet's example of RECE and their global conferences over the last twenty years. Of course, we could plan to have everyone go their separate ways and do their own things, but our work will not be as full and as rich. It won't have what it takes to sustain a lifetime of study and interest. Our work, our profession, needs to have those many "laps" Holly Elissa describes in her story about Sue Twombly, the many "laps" of diversity and difference that are present when pluralism is embraced. The one thing that is definitely becoming universal is pluralism and the opportunities—yes, the opportunities—for change and relationships that come with it.

Summary..

Luis Antonio Hernandez

From the start, this dialogue posed some difficult intersects. First, how can we make this conversation and thinking relevant for an ECE audience? Second, for teachers and leaders to be effective in their everyday work, how deep of an understanding is necessary? The more we discussed and analyzed our thoughts and arguments, the more important the topic became for each of us. For starters, there is a professional need for constant reflection and analysis of our work so we can stay fresh, invigorated, and curious. The evaluation cycle of our words and actions is part of a standard to double-check new and old assumptions and values. The catalyst is the wheel of change—rotating and challenging us in uncomfortable ways in order to learn and grow. And as we try to understand those dynamics, we strive to be even better as we serve the children, families, and colleagues we interact with on a regular basis. As the universal flows into the uniform, our challenge is to avoid fear of change. Rather, we should aim for an openness to moving forward in a world of universal differences and the uniformity of natural rights and truths. Together with Holly Elissa, Janet, and Debra, we can attest that this conversation has relevancy to our work with no need to fear the depth of challenging thinking.

Make acquaintance with those who are new to your way of life. The best way to make connections for a smooth flow between people is at the start of a relationship. Share your stories—about your children, your pets, what you like to eat, and so on—and be open for others to share in similar ways: share what is meaningful to one another as fellow human beings. Check for the impact of demographic changes in your community. Who is coming in? What are the factors for these changes? What is the impact to your community, local schools, hospitals, housing? From the universal perspective, keep abreast about what is happening in the rest of the world: What are the trends? Where are the conflicts? Most importantly, stay informed, be knowledgeable, and be proactive. Maintain a sense of genuine curiosity as the world changes: research situations, ask questions, get a variety of opinions, and stay tuned. Be an ambassador! In making these connections, we also represent a body of cultural experiences. Share your stories, your values, your life's highlights. Most importantly, introduce new immigrants to life in our country—for you truly represent the best of America. Connections can be difficult, awkward, and uncomfortable at times, but it is the best antidote to ignorance, assumptions, and misconceptions. An easy opening is, "Help me understand something" or "Can you clarify something for me?"

Discussion Questions ....

1. Part of this chapter's title refers to cultural and diversity standards in our professional and personal lives. What does that mean for the times we live in?

2. A difficult step is to understand the factors of change, be it personally or professionally. How do you and those closest to you face new realities? And as the nation and neighborhoods change, how are you dealing with it?

3. What are some cultural or diversity issues that you are most at ease with? Which are more difficult?

References

Ballenger, Cynthia. 1992. "Because You Like Us: The Language of Control." *Harvard Educational Review* 62 (2): 191–208.

Fulghum, Robert. 2003. *All I Really Need to Know I Learned in Kindergarten: Reconsidered, Revised, and Expanded with Twenty-Five New Essays.* 15th anniversary ed. New York: Ballantine Books.

NAEYC (National Association for the Education of Young Children). 1987. *Developmentally Appropriate Practice in Early Childhood Programs Serving Children from Birth through Age 8.* Position statement. Washington, DC: NAEYC.

RECE (Reconceptualizing Early Childhood Education). 2013. "20th International Reconceptualizing Early Childhood Education Conference." Accessed January 3. http://recesite.wikispaces.com/Conferences.

5

Tomorrow's Children Today
A Self-Assessment Approach to Multicultural Readiness

 Janet Gonzalez-Mena

I have now lived three-quarters of a century, and in that time I've seen significant changes in our society and also in the field of early childhood education. What started in our profession as the beginning of multicultural awareness could be summarized as "It's nice to be nice." We are now moving from just niceness to examining issues of social justice that go beyond a simple multicultural focus and into areas such as race, gender, ethnicity, sexual orientation, social class, age, and ability. As a field, we are starting to understand and work toward a goal of shared power as we explore power dynamics.

Those of us in early childhood education have opportunities to learn to work respectfully together and benefit from one another's wisdom and experiences. We can work to understand every family who comes to us and learn what it means to them to be raising a child today in this diverse world. We can put aside our discomfort around topics of race and racism and all the other isms. With the help of the three bases for developmentally appropriate practice—developmental research, individual differences, and cultural knowledge (Copple and Bredekamp 2009)—we can look at differences in practices in the home and stop calling them inappropriate. Only then can we start looking at how diverse practices fit a family's background and goals. We can also acknowledge that almost every aspect of child rearing and education is influenced by individual and cultural beliefs and values. If we only focus on standard practice based on developmental research, we must be aware that some children and families will feel marginalized in our programs. Marginalization is not good for children, and it makes families worry about their children's identity formation.

An important note before I continue: The title of this chapter indicates that it's about tomorrow's children. Getting ready for tomorrow's children is a good idea. But let's face it: if we are talking about increasing numbers of children from diverse families (meaning not from the predominant culture), tomorrow's children are already here, and they have always been here. Multicultural populations have been on this continent for thousands of years. More recently, the various waves of immigration, both voluntary and forced, have added to the mix. We can't do much about yesterday's children, but we certainly can focus on today's children as well as their families.

Readiness: My Own Self-Assessment, Part 1

I want to share my own readiness for the issues of family diversity and the multicultural education of children from diverse families. First and foremost you need to know that multicultural education means to me mutual respect and empowerment. My hope is that you will be thinking about your own self-assessment as you read along. First, a quick glimpse of my history and cross-cultural education.

My history. I need to start by saying that I'm a white, European American woman, and I have lived in California all my life; Spanish-speaking people were here long before my family arrived two generations ago. Ironically, I didn't know any of them until I started as a volunteer in a preschool for Spanish-speaking families. Segregation used to be a fact of life—and not just in the South.

I was a beginning preschool teacher in a program when I met my husband, who was born and raised in Mexico. He came as a young adult to the United States. He was already a United States citizen when I met him, and we have been married forty-one years. I can say without a doubt that I've had forty-one years of multicultural education from him and his family.

Cultural differences. I experienced cultural differences at home and as a preschool teacher. When we married, I wasn't ready for the differences and cultural bumps I encountered. What was happening at home and in my newly acquired family reflected what I saw in the child care center. One example was at home where the bumps often showed up at mealtimes, which is frequently true for children in child care programs as well. I began to think about the children in my program and that they ate their meals "family style," which for some must have been very different than their own family's style. Greeting people properly in my new family also gave me trouble. I had never learned to shake hands. It just wasn't done in my family, nor did we hug or kiss each other as a way of greeting. My husband's family has a whole greeting ritual that involves handshakes and kisses. Another difference was who was greeted first, second, and so on. That was never an issue in my family. A quick hi was all that was needed and included everybody present. So as a preschool teacher in a cross-cultural program, I had the same problems, not only about greeting parents but also about what I expected from children. As a casual Californian, I would just smile and say hi. I didn't worry about the children who just ran in the door at preschool and right to playing with their friends. I appreciated that they were so eager to be there and to get started playing. Some families got upset about that. Names presented more bumps. I wanted children to call me Janet, and that was objectionable to some families.

I don't mean to complain about my multicultural education. I recognize how much it has enriched my life. Even more importantly, the bumps have given me vital insights into my own ways of thinking and behaving. I am grateful for what I have learned.

Discovery. I think of what it might be like for children and families who are experiencing challenges that may seem to the teacher to be only minor cultural differences. The question I learned to ask is, what happens to a child's sense of self when everything is different at school, preschool, or in an infant-toddler program? My sense of self was jarred by my many cross-cultural experiences, and I wasn't a child just forming an identity. Of course, we all know how flexible children are and that they can get used to doing things one way at home and another way at Grandma's. But that's different. Huge societal issues bear down even on very young children as they struggle to discover who they are and where they belong. Many children who have experienced a lack of harmony in out-of-home situations make unconscious decisions about their identities. I know a number of people who no longer speak the language of their family and who have enormous conflicts about their identity. Once they changed to fit the predominant culture, they couldn't go home again because they no longer fit. I also know a few people who move easily between various cultural environments. My husband is one. He is like a chameleon and can always fit in!

I'm not like my husband, and I worry about children in our programs who don't fit in at school or at home. I worry about what happens when children and adults in the program consider what other children do at home strange. I have seen with my own eyes the effects on identity formation and language loss.

Equity Issues around Language Development

What was happening years ago is still happening today. This has become a very personal issue for me, as none of my children grew up bilingual in spite of our many efforts to facilitate those skills. And now the next generation in my family has the same problem. My daughter-in-law is from Russia, and she has put a lot of effort into my granddaughter's bilingual education from birth on. It's hard to believe that her effort hasn't paid off yet. My granddaughter shows she understands Russian, but she refuses to say a single word. She went to a child care program starting as a toddler and somehow picked up the idea that English is the only important language. The program was an excellent one and multiple languages were represented, but English won out.

Beyond my personal experience, the linguistic outcomes of children whose home language is not English show a trend of losing the home language except in special cases. This is not a problem just in child care. The superiority of the English language is a message pervading our whole nation and most of its institutions. I'm not questioning the importance of everybody in the United States learning English; however, I prefer a broader goal: a bilingual population! Other countries accomplish that. Why can't we?

Addressing Equity Issues in Early Childhood Education

Next, I want to look at how our field has made progress on the issues of equity and social justice. Louise Derman-Sparks and her Anti-Bias Curriculum Task Force gave us a big push when their book *Anti-Bias Curriculum* came out in 1989. That book was controversial, but it brought the subject of equity to the forefront in our field.

Derman-Sparks made a strong case for helping young children learn about the dynamics of truly shared power by creating respectful environments where all children were empowered to become their freest and best. Children were taught to notice and also to do something about disempowerment based on race, gender, and ethnicity—first and foremost—but also based on class, belief system, ability, age, and national origin. Things began to change. First came the easy things such as classroom environments. Multicultural books as well as cultural artifacts appeared in stores and in classrooms. Photographs decorating the walls expanded from depicting white children and families to representing the diversity of the families in the classroom and the society beyond. Programs increased the variety in their menus and activities to reflect the new approach. They invited staff and family members to make tortillas or other cultural foods with the children. Certainly diverse families and children began to feel more at home with these changes from what previously had been a European American environment. The problem with Derman-Sparks's original approach was that the major emphases were on environmental changes and teaching the children. But children are always watching, and they tend to do what adults *do* rather than what adults *teach*. So in programs where staff hierarchies were in place with one group in power and another group in service, the children's lessons on antibias techniques were less effective than the power structures and adult interactions they saw in their classrooms every day.

Louise Derman-Sparks has been a trendsetter and took the profession further along the road when she and Julie Olsen Edwards came out with a second book in 2010: *Anti-Bias Education for Young Children and Ourselves*, which expands the focus beyond the environment and the children. The newer book includes the adults in early childhood education—their biases and behaviors. Now we're getting into the harder challenges. We have to look at ourselves to make change, and these authors give us plenty of chances to do that throughout their book.

Readiness: My Own Self-Assessment, Part 2

As I look back on my history of moving toward equity in our field and the greater society, I remember an important step I took early on. I figured out the place to start was with myself. I'm clear that the tendency for most of us is to look beyond ourselves and point fingers at people who are showing biases and discriminating. That won't help if we don't look at our own attitudes and behaviors. What helped me do that was exploring the parts of me that Carl Gustav Jung, Swiss psychologist and psychiatrist, more than a hundred years ago called "the shadow."

Recognizing my shadow. I don't hear people talking much about the shadow anymore, but it's a useful construct. It relates clearly to my calling to do antibias work and the message that we have to start with ourselves. The shadow is the notion that we see in others what we cannot see in ourselves. Or as I have also heard, if you want to know what you are really like, don't look at your friends, look at your enemies. That's a hard idea to swallow!

I discovered my shadow a long time ago when as a preschool teacher I had negative feelings about "bossy" little girls. My big insight was that I have one of those bossy little girls inside of me, and I don't like her. So there I was, having discovered my shadow bossy girl, about to take some kind of leadership role in multicultural education and going beyond "it's nice to be nice" to deeper issues of equity and social justice. I wanted to dedicate my life to understanding and working with the kind of change needed to embrace all cultures in early childhood education systems. Yet I had to deal with figuring out how to be a leader without letting my bossy little girl run everything.

Change from within. Change needs to start with ourselves before we try to change others. To take the concept of the shadow closer to antibias work, how many of us who hate those who show their biases also discover we have biases that we are denying? No one is bias-free, and though we may work hard to avoid discriminating, we need to admit (at least to ourselves) that we do have prejudices. Again, this means looking inward and focusing first on ourselves before trying to change others!

Going back to my personal shadow, I share another example: I have to admit that I can look at people with unearned power and privilege and feel critical of them. So what happens when I turn my glance inward? A Buddhist proverb says, "When the student is ready, the teacher appears," and that's exactly what happened to me. Just when I was headed straight into making our profession more equitable, someone handed me an article by Peggy McIntosh (1988) that opened up whole new realms of self-understanding. I discovered that I had power and privilege by being white and middle class. Discovering my power and privilege made me tremendously uncomfortable. Suddenly I was the bad guy! I was the person I had been criticizing. At first I didn't believe it, but I began to see through new eyes how white privilege works. As my life continued, I began to recognize that in multicultural/multiracial situations doors opened for me because of who I am and how I look—doors that were closed to others.

Discovering a new outlook. Thinking of myself as a savior underwent a big change. Ironically, before I made the discovery of my power and privilege, I decided to get off the big white horse I was riding around on trying to change things for downtrodden people in the name of equity and social justice. I stepped back because I perceived that rescuing people puts me a notch above them and disregards their own power. It was when I quit trying to be a savior that I eventually discovered I could be an ally—a partner in making changes. It was no longer about me and them but about us. Equity benefits all of us just as inequity hurts everyone even if we are on the other side of it.

Understanding power, privilege, and voice. Understanding power and privilege and whose voices get heard helped me perceive that my voice was often heard when the voices of people of color were silenced. I got back in the fray again once I understood my role. I could use my position to help make changes. I often did that by becoming a good observer. For example, during discussions I began to sit back and watch what was happening. I became aware of whose voice was most often heard. I observed who dominated the conversation and who sat back and was quiet. I noted just who interrupted successfully and who did not. I was especially surprised to see who managed to get in the last word, even if it was just to put the period on the end of another person's statement.

Eventually I stopped only observing and started interrupting discussions that were getting heated. I asked a simple question: What's really going on here? Usually that simple question changed everything. I didn't have to point out my perceptions; the people in the group began to point out theirs, and more people were heard than just the ones who previously had dominated the conversation.

What I discovered in these observations and from my interruptions was that white privilege was real! Even if we white people don't recognize it, we tend to dominate. Part of it is our cultural conversational style, and part of it comes from feeling entitled to stand up for ourselves and put forth our opinions. Not that entitlement is a bad thing—but it should be universal, not specific to one group of people.

Spreading privilege. I discovered my power to spread privilege around. It was a real benefit when I figured out that as a person who has privilege, I have the opportunity to help people see inequities and make changes—to spread privilege around. I could speak up against discrimination and inequity. I could support voices of people who needed support so they could be heard by others. I had a role in the change process—an important one. It wasn't about my taking charge but about my being a good partner or team member and making sure the group I was in wasn't silencing voices or discriminating in other ways. Best of all, I could let my bossy little girl out of her cage and teach her to take a leadership role without pushing others around. I have learned huge lessons about promoting multicultural equity. I know now for sure what works. The advice is so easy to say but so hard to do: we must each start with ourselves—old number one!

Going beyond Race and Culture

Multicultural readiness and promoting equity and social justice includes a wide range of isms. When you do your self-assessment, I imagine you will pick the areas that are most important to you. Let me suggest other areas besides culture and race and economic status that involve both power and privilege and lack of both: gender, sexual orientation, social class, belief systems, age, and ability are also important aspects of equity work. I can write about my power and privilege in each of those areas, but instead I challenge you to do your own self-assessment. I hope I've inspired you to do that.

Goals. Here's what's left to do: A code of ethical conduct from the National Association for the Education of Young Children (NAEYC) holds us all to the standard of mutual respect and empowerment; therefore, we must seek out and create respectful, open environments where all children are empowered to become their freest and best. We also need to treat families with the same respect and empowerment with which we treat children, which presents us with yet more challenges. When our consciousness turns to such goals, we have to be aware that adults (including ourselves) often experience or witness the disempowerment of diverse others. We also need to name, understand, and be able to articulate the dynamics of power that we have learned growing up and working in the field of ECE. The goal is truly shared power.

Strategies. We can get to shared power by creating strategies together to lead the way to equitable learning communities for all. I shared some of my strategies. Yours may be very different. Here is a summary of mine:

1. I reflect on my personal history.

2. I take seriously the notion that to make change I have to use self-examination.

3. I expand my horizons.

4. I listen openly to others and try to see the world through their eyes.

5. I create partnerships to generate movement toward equity and social justice.

6. I interrupt racism and other isms without starting fights.

Your Self-Assessment for Multicultural Readiness

1. What do you know about the cultural bumps some children and families may experience in early childhood programs? (Your program or ones you know about.)

2. What does it mean to you to take on issues of equity and social justice by starting with yourself?

3. Can you list the areas where you have power and privilege and where you have little or none?

4. How well can you describe your identity? Is your own description what others who aren't like you would say about you?

5. How different is your story from Janet's? What are the differences? Are there any similarities?

6. How prepared are you to partner with people unlike yourself to make changes in our field and in society? What do you need to make yourself better prepared?

7. How well does your history prepare you to expand equity and social justice by creating respectful, open environments where children and families are empowered?

8. Can you name, understand, and discuss the dynamics of power that you have learned growing up and working in the field of ECE?

9. What strategies can you think of to create equitable learning communities for all? Which are the ones that fit you the best?

Luis Antonio Hernandez

Changing the World Starts with Me

I am always astonished by the variety of ways in which our colleague Janet can weave lessons from a deep personal well to the cosmos of a positive and possible world. And to get to that world, the first steps begin with me. That journey starts in assessing my own universe, the recognition of my own humanness with all its richness and all its imperfections. If I am to change the world, I am responsible for starting with me. Although her journey is unique, it holds lessons on how we can trace our own paths and reach a place of strength based on values, principles, and passions dear to our experiences and history. Many of the lessons are learned as we go along the route of life through our relationships, work experiences, and the political and cultural times in which we live. In her evolution, Janet began a life commitment to influence and change the structures of equity, culture, power, language, and quality. Using Janet's words, I can begin to reflect on my own sense of privilege and how it impacts not only the work I do but also how I relate to others. A closer examination begins to reveal my own privileges, my locus of power, and the intentions within my work and profession.

Janet's message brims with hope, the result of a life commitment to shine on the nature and uniqueness of children and families in a variety of settings and age groups. It is a canvas of hope for a better tomorrow for our human family. Her passion is clear, and one cannot help but be a part of her crusade to make positive changes in the world today to create the brightness of future tomorrows. Much gratitude to Janet in the sometimes difficult exercise of personal reflection. The best lesson is that whatever the life experiences, they provide genuine drive and determination for my contributions to the profession.

Holly Elissa Bruno

Do Our Laws Help or Hinder Multiculturalism?

I pay attention to whether or not our laws promote the rights of the minority population. Legislation primarily articulates and enforces the status quo. The Defense of Marriage Act from Congress, for example, maintains that marriage can only be between a man and a woman—something that was already the law of the land. For decades, *Plessy v. Ferguson* upheld the practice and set the legal standard for racially segregated schools.

Occasionally the Supreme Court steps out of the mainstream box to articulate a newer, more just standard. That's exactly what happened in 1954 in the *Brown v. Topeka Board of Education* case, which set, rather than adhered to, precedent when it overturned *Plessy v. Ferguson* and said schools needed to be integrated. When the law, promulgated by courts or legislation, leads the way to needed social change, resistance flourishes. That's how it happened that in 1969, my first teaching position was in a segregated school, West Charlotte Senior High. Schools were mandated to integrate, yet school districts all over the country, including Charlotte, North Carolina, avoided following the Supreme Court decision.

So the first legal challenge we face in multiculturalism is whether the law promotes diversity. The second legal challenge is whether any laws that promote diversity will be followed. In 1969 I paid attention to the failure of the schools to lead the way for racial equality, regardless of legal mandates, and I decided to watch how other legal protections for those not in the majority would fare. Our country and our schools are only as strong as the willingness to honor and protect the rights of minority populations.

Over forty years later, the picture is still not always admirable. One group who has virtually no legal protection are lesbian, gay, bisexual, and transgender (LGBT) children and their families. In many states, same-sex couples are not legally allowed to adopt children. And currently, in most states, same-sex couples cannot legally marry. No federal legislation protects the rights of LGBT children and families.

Okay, if the laws aren't leading the way, what are the schools doing? Specifically, what am I and what are you doing to protect and promote respect for gender-fluid children? Gender-fluid children sometimes prefer to be boys and other times prefer to be girls. Gender-fluid children and adults do not conform to the stereotypical requirements of femininity and masculinity. Gender-fluid people may settle into the gender opposite from their birth gender. Educators may need to address these challenges with gender-fluid children and families (Savin-Williams et al. 2013):

- A parent insists that you make the child act like a boy or act like a girl.

- Parents threaten to sue you for promoting homosexuality because you have books in the classroom that include same-sex partners.

- Teachers routinely identify children as girls or boys.

- Boys who insist on dressing in girls' clothing and playing with girls are viewed as unbalanced.

Each year, I speak at a university campus in a college town that aspires to multiculturalism. Six years ago on that campus I met a young child whom I will call Sage. Sage was a sprite, a free spirit who adored pastel clothing and dancing with uninhibited abandon. Sage was unconditionally loved and supported by family and close family friends. Sage's preschool teachers were charmed by Sage's creative choices in clothing and willingness to live as original a young life as possible. I, too, was taken with Sage. What a delightful child! Sage followed Sage's path and no one else's. Each year I looked forward to the gathering where Sage, Sage's parents, and people involved with the conference met, shared home-cooked food, and sang and danced together.

Sage is now in public school, having grown beyond the loving support of his preschool teachers and administrators. Suddenly Sage has become self-conscious and wary. Sage looks down and turns away from the dance floor. Sage's ebullient energy has slid into a flattened, unhappy demeanor. Sage now wears traditional boys' clothing. Gone are the swishy skirts, long, curly hair, and dashing fashion statements. Sage seems to have lost his way, or at least seems to think his way is somehow wrong. He appears to be both sad and angry.

Where Do You Stand?

Where do you stand on gender-fluid children and staff? Do you call your students girls and boys? Do you accept boys' roughhousing and girls' nurturing others as normal? Saying we respect differences is easy. Do you make sure that children of all differences, including gender-fluid children, can live true to themselves in your classrooms and programs? What would you say to children who laugh and point at Sage?

Multiculturalism almost always requires each of us to face our blind spots. Little children who are adorable come in many colors, ethnicities, national origins, and gender identities. Laws protect the rights of some of our children. The least protected are perhaps the most vulnerable. What do you and I do to protect and nurture their identities?

Debra Ren-Etta Sullivan

Allow for the Discomfort

Having a self-assessment approach to multicultural readiness always seems to be so much more difficult than it should be. Many people do have a lot of discomfort discussing the multitude of isms that intersect our lives. I think it's because such topics involve a lot of pain, guilt, anger, sorrow, denial, fear, shame, embarrassment, and distrust. Few look forward to experiencing these emotions. Unfortunately, we allow our discomfort to keep us from moving through these emotions to a healthier space of reconciliation—reconciling with ourselves and with each other. I'm not sure that it's possible to achieve or even to approach multicultural readiness without addressing how we really feel about people who are different from us in whatever way that difference is defined. Most people don't like to admit—to themselves or to others—that there are people they don't like, don't feel comfortable around, don't trust, or don't consider equal. Self-assessment is hard if you are unwilling to tell yourself the truth *and* give yourself a chance to learn, grow, and change.

The whole notion of *different* is interesting to me. Children don't think of themselves as different until someone tells them they are. I went to predominantly white schools until high school and found out in the third grade that being black was a big difference that meant a lot to others. It was recess and a group of girls were in a corner of the playground eating cookies. I knew a couple of them, so I walked over to see what they were doing. The girl who was sharing the cookies told me she couldn't give me one or play with me because she was "not allowed to play with ni---rs." I was surprised, embarrassed, and ashamed. There were probably other times before that when I had been party to subtler discrimination or prejudice and hadn't noticed. This was the first blatant experience I had, and from that day on, I knew that being black meant I was really different in a big way. Much like Janet's granddaughter who learned early on that it's "better" to speak only English, I learned that day that it was "better" to be white. Of course later, around sixth or seventh grade, I developed a healthier sense of self and began to take pride in my African heritage, but the in-between years were frustrating for my parents because they knew I was ashamed of them, of myself, and of our culture. Things might have been different for me if the school's grown-ups had paid more attention to what I was experiencing. It's not as if they didn't know I was the only African American student in my class. I think they just hoped and prayed that no one would notice or say anything. Well, today *we* are the school's grown-ups and we are still hoping and praying that children will not notice difference and make us have to do something about it.

Yes, self-assessment is a good place to start. What area of difference gives you the greatest fear? What do you hope children will not notice or not mention? One of mine was size. I never wanted my own children to notice obese people when they were younger. Of course, that's the one thing they noticed all the time. My husband and I were at a play at a small theater once when my oldest son was three. During the intermission, we were standing in a very small lobby area and my son noticed a woman across the room (yes, all the way across the room) who may have weighed around three hundred pounds. My son said, loud but not too loud, "Mom, look at that lady. She's really big." I ignored him. He tugged on my skirt and said, louder this time, "Mo-oo-m, lo-oo-k!" People started to turn our way. I said, "Sh-h-h." My husband started looking for an escape route. My son was very frustrated now and said, in a very loud voice, "How come you can't see her, Mom? She's so-o-o bi-ii-g!" Everyone, including the woman herself, looked at me. My husband found something extremely interesting deep in the pages of the program. I took a deep breath, looked the woman in the eye, looked down at my son, and said, "Yes, honey, she is much bigger than you are." My son was satisfied that I finally responded. I'm embarrassed and ashamed and feel stupid that I tried to just make the whole thing go away by ignoring him. I don't know if I said the right thing or not, but saying nothing was not the right thing.

So I ask you again, What area of difference gives you the greatest fear? What do you hope children will not notice or not mention? What do you hope one child will not say to or do to another child that will make you have to address an ism? I think of Sage and the day he realized that there are big differences that really do matter to others. When other children say mean things, do you try to reassure Sage that they didn't really mean it? I used to hear that a lot when I was growing up and the teacher heard other children call me names. The teacher would come to me when I was by myself and tell me that in a low voice so no one else would hear. I remember thinking that somehow *I* had been the one doing something wrong. I realize now that my teachers just wanted me to not feel bad, to get over it and move on, to not linger on it. It didn't work. I only learned that you don't get in trouble if you call people names. You get in trouble if you feel bad about being called names.

We've come further along than when I was young, but we still have a long way to go if we are still uncomfortable talking about difference. I stopped hoping and praying my children wouldn't notice difference that day in the theater lobby. We teach them to notice even minute differences (think "one of these things is not like the other") and then hope they don't. Maybe that's a way to protect ourselves from what we really think and feel about people who are different, a way to avoid multicultural self-assessment. Fortunately, everyone reading this book is taking on the mantle of leadership and will model for both children and grown-ups what it looks like to fully engage and invest in a multicultural assessment of ourselves.

Summary...

Janet Gonzalez-Mena

This chapter looked at the history of multiculturalism in ECE and broadened the subject from simply seeing cultural differences in a positive light to exploring oppression in general. In my own experience, questions about early standards and practices inspired my thinking about inequity. Those questions and experiences led this chapter into an exploration of a wide range of areas in which discrimination abounds and puts one person or one group of people above another. Luis took the word *readiness* in the title seriously and did self-examination in the areas of his own privilege, locus of power, and intentions within his work and profession. That led the chapter into further personal stories of the authors, plus some of the history of laws relating to inequity as well as some relating to equity and social justice. Holly Elissa, as a lawyer, is well qualified to look at the legal aspects. She also focused part of her contribution on gender issues and told the touching story of Sage. Debra mentioned the many difficulties of working with children around inequities. She also zeroed in on discomfort that can arise when dealing with what we are calling *multicultural readiness*. Discomfort includes feelings such as pain, guilt, denial, anger, and fear. Working toward equity and the elimination of oppression is emotional and involves a lot of soul searching. I hadn't heard Debra's story of coming to a place of pride in her African heritage, and I felt angered by what took place in her life before that happened.

A strong message in this chapter relates to working with differences in positive ways—a theme all of us in early childhood education are familiar with. We start innocently with easy activities such as offering blocks of different colors and shapes and asking them to recognize differences. Eventually we work up to how a *b* and *p* are different. But all that's the easy part—it's the differences in people that are harder and far more important! This chapter shows how difficult it can be to teach children (and ourselves) to avoid negative attitudes and corresponding behaviors and instead take positive perspectives in the face of cultural and physical differences. The most important part is to convey the right messages about equity in both our attitudes and behaviors to those we work with—whether children or adults.

Discussion Questions ....

1. The word *oppression* was not mentioned in this chapter until the summary, but oppression permeated the whole chapter. What does the word *oppression* mean to you? Have you experienced oppression in your life?

2. You read a lot of personal stories in this chapter—those about the authors and those about people the authors know. What personal stories do you have to tell about the subjects of multicultural readiness, equity, and social justice?

3. The word *equity* was used regularly in this chapter. Did you notice that the term *equality* was mentioned only once? What is the difference between equity and equality? Why do you think the authors preferred the term *equity*? How do our laws support equity, and how do they privilege one group over another?

References ....

Copple, Carol, and Sue Bredekamp, eds. 2009. *Developmentally Appropriate Practice in Early Childhood Programs: Serving Children from Birth through Age 8*. 3rd ed. Washington, DC: National Association for the Education of Young Children.

McIntosh, Peggy. 1988. "White Privilege and Male Privilege: A Personal Account of Coming to See Correspondences through Work in Women's Studies." Working paper, Wellesley College. www.iub.edu/~tchsotl/part2/McIntosh%20White%20Privilege.pdf.

Savin-Williams, Ritch C., Robin Fox, David Bloomfield, and Peter DeWitt. 2013. "Gender Fluid Students: How Do They Fare at Your School?" Podcast interview by Holly Elissa Bruno. *Heart to Heart Conversations on Leadership*, March 12. www.bamradionetwork.com/index.php?option=com_content&view=article&id=1010:jackstreet54&catid=36:administrators-channel&Itemid=90.

6

Technology

Reflecting on Resistance and Habits on the Way to Dynamic Change

Debra Ren-Etta Sullivan

I've always loved learning about other people, their cultures, and their languages. My deep love of books probably stems from the fact that they can transport me to another place, another time, another way of living and understanding our world. As a cultural anthropologist, I can't help but view everything through the lens of the impact on people and culture. Technology is no different. It is everywhere, and whether we're talking about the Internet, computers, phones, tablets, notebooks, networks, cameras, sensing devices, or audio/visual devices, we're still talking about people and how technology affects them.

Technological changes have both intended and unexpected outcomes. The intent of much of the new technology is to make our lives easier, faster, more efficient, more connected, and more environmentally friendly. It makes it easier for us to connect with one another across time and space and keep up-to-date on the activities of friends and family. I find that there are unexpected outcomes as well. While we have access to more information and more access to each other, we also find ourselves inundated with more information and contact from more people than we could possibly respond to in one day.

Technology changes culture. It always has. The invention of the wheel changed our ability to move more items and heavier objects and to move ourselves. This impacted culture by allowing us to travel longer distances, move farther from each other, and acquire more stuff. We were also freed from having to live in close proximity to work. We became commuters. Today new technology continues to change our culture—our very habits and expectations are changing at a pace that is growing exponentially. We used to be on the phone every once in a while, usually while at home or at work. Now we can be on the phone all the time, anywhere. And there are those, like my seventeen-year-old daughter, who need their phones in hand at all times. I have photos of my daughter asleep with her phone in her hand or positioned under her ear so she doesn't miss a call or a text in the middle of the night.

Technology Networks

All of this connectedness reminds me of a Borg colony from *Star Trek*. If you are not familiar with the Borg, they are hybrid of human and robot who consider themselves perfect, though they strive to be *more* perfect. They have managed to download their collective knowledge into a massive computer that is their spaceship, their colony. They all plug into it to access all of their collective thoughts and knowledge. There is no individual thought or perspective, only the collective one that is modified for everyone whenever new information is downloaded. Then, always in pursuit of perfection, they seek out other planets and groups of people and collect their knowledge. The problem is that they not only absorb the knowledge into their colony, but they absorb the people as well, turning them into robot-humans and plugging them into the collective. In one episode, a Borg teenager is captured, and he's poking at the walls in his cell trying to find a place to "plug in." The Borg are unable to function without the collective.

That's how I sometimes feel about technology. Chargers are left dangling—without phones—from electrical outlets all over my house, leaking massive amounts of unused electricity because my son and my daughter and all their friends need constant access to a charger without having to look for one. In airports everywhere there are thousands of passengers walking around looking for (and occasionally fighting over) an outlet that was originally intended to feed a vacuum, not a laptop or a phone. When we went camping, my daughter was walking around the woods with her phone in the air trying to find a signal. Maybe she's the Borg teenager I was describing. It is not unusual to have to spend most of the day seated in front of a computer responding to e-mail and text messages. In fact, now my work phone voice messages automatically load into my work e-mail. I often feel overwhelmed by all the input coming from a multitude of sources. Some people are more Borglike and can do this type of uber-multitasking, but I'm learning that I'm not one of them.

Expectations have also changed with the increase in technology. Everyone is expected to be connected, but not everyone is. There is an assumption in our culture that access to technology in all its forms is available to all. This assumption has consequences: fewer efforts are made to address technological inequity and inequality, and people expect an immediate response to their calls, e-mails, and texts. "Why didn't you answer?" is a question I hear all the time, along with "I e-mailed you just now, but you didn't respond." The fact that I may have been talking to someone (in person or on the phone) or that I may have been in a meeting or in a class seems to be irrelevant. I get about a hundred e-mails per day, and no one seems to think it's unreasonable for me to respond to them all—in the same day! Fewer and fewer people listen to the voice messages I leave or bother to leave messages for me when they call. The fact that they called should apparently be enough to prompt me to call them back. I'm expected to answer the phone or respond to e-mails at all times—even when I'm at a conference and supposed to be in sessions or on vacation and supposed to be relaxing. Expectations around what is important have also changed. In any given week, I may receive up to sixteen e-mails with red exclamation points. How can there be that much urgency on a weekly basis?

Another interesting change in our cultural expectations is the length of time we should keep any particular piece of technology. My daughter, along with thousands—if not millions—of others, expects to get a new device every six months or so. I bought her a phone, and six months later she considered it a piece of crap and needed a new one. I gave up. Now I just hand her the landline phone—a solid piece of equipment with unlimited local minutes. My daughter is seventeen and didn't get a cell phone until she was almost fifteen, but I see children as young as three with all types of devices.

Technology and How We Communicate

Technology has changed our communication patterns and sometimes even whether we communicate at all. I remember a time when I would have been considered antisocial if I had headphones on while riding the city bus. I wasn't expected to talk to everyone who got on the bus, but I also wasn't expected to shut myself off from everyone on the bus. Flash forward to today: I get to sit on a city bus and hear people talk on their phones about personal business—loudly. And, it doesn't stop there. With Facebook, Twitter, and other social networking sites, we all get to share and hear about our "friends'" lives daily and are informed of everything from the most mundane ("I'm driving past Walgreens") to the most personal ("I'm having my best friend's boyfriend's baby"). I'm not even sure how people find the time to follow Twitter, Facebook, and Tumblr, and answer e-mail and the phone.

Social networking was supposed to connect us more with those we know and love, but as it has expanded to the workplace, it has also cut off whole communities. I once attended an open meeting to learn about a grant that I was interested in applying for. There were several organizations and agencies present to learn more about it and whether to apply. The grantors did not have any hard-copy information about the grant. We were informed that the application, the eligibility requirements, and so on were all on Facebook. This was a number of years ago when MySpace was enjoying popularity. I didn't use MySpace, and I had only just learned about Facebook. I was intrigued that I would have to open a Facebook account to learn about the grant when the two grantors were sitting right in front of me. How in the world are people, community groups, agencies, and organizations with limited funds supposed to gain access to important information if they do not have access to important technology?

The changes in our language have been rapid as well. We've added new verbs to our vocabulary: *Skype*, *Facebook*, *friend*, *tweet*. Text spelling is so common that many users of technology have become horrible spellers or think that the importance of learning how to spell has gone away. I am, however, one of the first to agree that language etiquette, formalities, and standards are arbitrary. Shakespearean writers would likely be appalled by what we consider standard academic English today. Tomorrow, "textese" may become the new standard, the new normal we talked about in chapter 4. In college I read *Babel-17* by Samuel R. Delany. It's a science fiction book about an intergalactic war in which a language, Babel-17, is used as a weapon. Language has the power to shape our perceptions and thoughts. People who speak one language may be able to have thoughts that others who speak a different language can't have because they don't have words for those thoughts. And some may be able to think certain thoughts faster because they use fewer words to describe complex concepts. For example, the word *house* can mean a lot of different things. If I had to break down the concept of *house* to explain size, construction, uses, functions, temperatures, inhabitants, and so on, it could take quite a long time. Textese is much quicker than conventional spelling. It could be the next Babel-17. Intriguing, huh? I would just as soon pick up the phone rather than text, but I think I'm outnumbered, at least by people my daughter's age. And this makes me wonder if talking can continue to compete with texting: real time versus real people.

Technology and Young Children

One area that concerns me about increased use of technology is the impact it is having on young children's development. I think technology should not be used by children under three. Social-emotional and language development happens through conversations and social interactions. Children spend the first two years of their lives learning an entire language and the context within which to use it. This happens most effectively through relationships with adults and other children—relationships based on meaningful communication with people young children care about. This forms the very basis for developing strong social-emotional ability. Infants and toddlers need exposure to all the words we know and even some we don't, in as many languages as possible. They need big words, little words, words in books, words on walls, simple sentences, complex sentences, satire, humor, rhetoric, metaphor, hyperbole. They thrive, linguistically, when engaged in authentic conversations, dialogues, and discussions that include lots of open-ended questions so they can figure out why and how and if and whether. They need to talk about how they feel and how others feel and see real people so they can connect real feelings with real interactions. Developing relationships with other people—in person—provides an environment rich with opportunities for critical thinking and analysis, language development, and social-emotional development.

There is also cognitive development, which requires experiences. Infants and toddlers learn best through concrete, tactile experiences that incorporate a wide variety of age-appropriate items to touch, taste, test, and try. Children need to *do* in order to have meaningful experiences that strengthen cognitive skills, and when it comes to technology, the more the device does, the less the child does. I heard a story once about a group of young children sitting around the table staring at the playdough, waiting for it to do something. Cognitive development can happen in very dynamic and engaging ways when young children have self-initiated experiences with blocks, puzzles, balls, food, liquids, and their favorites: boxes, paper, pots, and pans. I think we need to be mindful and avoid training children to be passive participants who expect a thing to do more than they do themselves. And, again, for me it all comes back to relationships. Engaging in meaningful experiences with people the child cares about is crucial. Pretending to build a house of blocks with a teacher, pouring water from one container to another and back again with a friend, making up music and songs with instruments both real and imagined with a parent—these are real relationships that provide a real context for cognitive development.

What the Future May Bring

So, where do we go from here? Technology is, indeed, everywhere you look, and it's here to stay. While it is designed to make our lives easier, better, faster, and more connected, I think we must be thoughtful about how we use it—especially with young children. I realize that not all children develop at the same rate or in the same manner, and technology does offer some exciting, innovative opportunities for children with special needs. However, when it comes to typically developing infants and toddlers, I'm a firm believer that less is more in the use of technology. I have been noticing more workshops, trainings, books, and articles about how important it is for parents and caregivers to develop meaningful attachments with young children. It seems odd to me that we have to train people to develop authentic relationships with children. This may be the case with socially or emotionally challenged parents, like a new mother with postpartum depression, but it just seems strange to me that typical adults have to be trained. Maybe the attention to this is because grown-ups are increasingly distracted by *their* latest "toys." *Children need more people, not more things.*

As our society becomes increasingly object-based, we must be very careful not to relegate children's learning and development to too many things. Authentic engagement is free—you don't need a lot of money to have an authentic relationship with a child. We each have multiple daily opportunities to model for children and for grown-ups what it looks like to have a healthy relationship with technology. We can model what healthy disconnection looks like and how to use technology in moderation. We can have a lot of impact on the future of our culture by simply paying attention to how we use technology and how it uses us. The Borg are very matter-of-fact when they tell you that "Resistance is futile. You will be assimilated." We are not just human beings. We are humans being.

Luis Antonio Hernandez

Going with the Flow

I thank Debra for her technology piece since it forces me to catch up with a culture that I feel is leaving me behind. Indeed, the culture is changing all around me, but am I changing along with the culture? Her reference to *Star Trek* leaves me even more perplexed—should have I paid more attention to those episodes to dwell in the midst of this new world? As with many ancient philosophies—or in old TV shows—our human experience can be distilled into simple yet deep messages that often defy our best intentions. If any particular lesson is to be drawn from new or old messages, a constant one is that life is about change. And change is not constant (that is, every change we experience is different). All we'll ever know is that this life force continues to change regardless of our futile attempts to stop, divert, or ignore the fact. Nothing is permanent. Mixing technology and early childhood education is a heavy topic, but ultimately the evidence in our work shows change in real time: the development, growth, and learning of young children. And the current wave of technology is a bold reminder of both the speed of change and its impact on our daily lives.

I am not a Luddite—those folk who want to remain in a romantic moment and place in time before technology—rather, I've come to adjust to and expect technology to make my day. I'm afraid of the implications, but I am hooked on its conveniences. Truly, I am nothing without technology: How would I make an airline, hotel, or car rental reservation without a credit card; where would I get cash without an ATM; and how would I communicate with family and friends without the Internet and cell phones? Yet I'm completely dependent—the type barely able to turn any of my devices on or off. As a very patient customer service representative for a computer company said to me once: "Now, sir, do you have your computer plugged in?"

And just like Debra, I also believe that children need more people, not more things. And so, leading to the core of this technology conversation, how do we maintain authentic relationships with those around us? How can people guarantee human touch and sensibility? Is texting your son—who is upstairs—to come down to dinner the same as shouting, "Marcos, come down, dinner is ready"?

Or does your daughter, away at college, who wants to have a Skype call with you to show you how messy her roommate is bring a new kind of closeness, a redefinition of how relationships can be fluid and elastic in ways not possible before? Indeed, from observations of family and friends, we are more connected in ways unimaginable before. At the same time, the messages in these new types of exchanges are truly short—just a tweet away. And as much as I want deepness, I know that desirable face-to-face relationship models provide no guarantee for greater intimacy or closeness. And yet technology expands the possibility of frequency—however short within 140 characters—with those we love, those we work with, even those we want to avoid. More regular contact, just less content. And if it gets uncomfortable, we both retreat to our mobile devices.

Reflecting on my own family history, I think of my grandparents who never flew on an airplane, my parents who at the most flew ten times in their lives, and then my weekly flights across the country. Planes are machines and technology—the product of astonishing human ingenuity and capacity. And across these generations, we are united by the sense of wonder of how a huge aircraft can take off, stay up in the air, and then come down. A parallel analogy is today's version of what we do best as humans: the creation of devices and things to highlight the uniqueness of who we are. Perhaps drawing bison in the caves of southern Europe was a leap in human creativity together with the stories the wall painting tells us today and told others thousands of years ago. Maybe that's an early version of an e-tablet.

Back to *Star Trek*: maybe we can learn to dance and balance with the Borg that Debra mentions. Scary and intimidating at first, it's about adjusting to a new world. From Debra I learned that I am not being left behind, I'm just going with the flow of change in life at this moment in time.

Janet Gonzalez-Mena

My Love/Hate Feelings toward Technology

Much of what Debra and Luis wrote struck home with me. Of course, I agree with the issues related to young children and technology. So I'll just start off with the parts where I differ from them. Here's one. Though Debra is overwhelmed by greater connectedness and the messages that pile up, I love all this connectedness! I don't even worry about the expectations of immediate responses that Debra finds annoying. As a retired person who lives in the country with no neighbors nearby, I really appreciate being able to sit at home and communicate with multiple people. It's exciting to get messages from all over the country as well as the world and to respond so easily to them. After a full life of going to work and coming home to the hustle and bustle of my children and their friends, life has become very quiet. Not that I dislike silence—in fact, I relish it! As a writer, that's exactly what I need. At the same time, I also greatly enjoy the companionship that comes with the interrupting *ding* of e-mail arriving, the phone ringing, the answering machine blinking, and, most of all, the *whoosh* of texts arriving. I especially appreciate texts because I have a hearing deficit, and when I get a text, I get the whole message—not just the parts I can hear clearly.

Speaking of texting, I think textese is fun, and I wouldn't mind if it became the new standard. I know the change worries Debra, but I always found standard spelling a little stuffy. I resent how it is often used as a mark of superiority by people who are good spellers over people who aren't. Good spellers may feel smarter, but they aren't necessarily. It wasn't always that way, you know—that people could be looked down on because of their spelling. Spelling in English used to be a lot more arbitrary and lacked a standard. As an English major, when I learned that, I cheered. It's not that I'm a bad speller, but some of my best friends are! Of course, technology has helped us all improve our spelling—unless we are creating something handwritten without anything to do a quick check for misspelling.

Oh, and I should point out what texting and e-mail have in common that I love. I can save the messages and look at them later. As the memory banks in my head are beginning to fill up, I really appreciate being able to go back and review conversations from the past. I have a pretty good system of organization, so I can usually find just what I'm looking for. I don't have to depend so much on my memory.

Of course, I agree heartily that technology can hurt the development of young children. I guess it can't be said too often: technology can get in the way of children's needs for relationships and hands-on experiences in the physical and social world. Too many children are getting addicted at a young age to flat screens, flashing images, and recorded sound. That's not the way they should be learning about the world they live in! I applaud everything Debra wrote about infants and toddlers and technology—I have even been known to criticize *Sesame Street* for that very reason. I want to add a pet peeve of mine about toys for infants and toddlers. When toy manufacturers create stimulating toys that grab the baby's attention with sounds, colors, lights, sparkles, and movement, they teach babies that they need constant entertainment. One of my teachers, Magda Gerber, used to say, "Active toys make passive babies." She suggested very simple objects for babies to manipulate—objects that don't *do* anything. It doesn't take much observation to discover that babies who are constantly stimulated with the toys designed for that very purpose get bored easily once the novelty wears off. They need constant new entertainment and cry when they don't get it.

Reading Luis's statements about change brought a question that keeps coming to me. Where will it end? It's hard to believe that we will keep moving forward technologically as fast as we have in the last few years. Further, I have visions of it all crashing down. It seems to me that once some evil force finds a way to control all those waves going through the air, we'll suddenly be in real trouble. Just taking out electricity will leave us in the dark with our dead devices. Just imagine. Surely somebody is working on it. If we can invent all these invisible waves, somebody can also figure out how to stop them. I've never given up the idea of returning to the simple life with limited technology, but then my early memories are of World War II and the idea that life can change very drastically in a short time. I've never been overly optimistic about our society continuing to advance. But that's just me.

Something happened a few years ago in Northern California that makes me pessimistic about our technological future. Suddenly people in a widespread area couldn't access ATMs, use credit cards, or buy gasoline. I have a friend who was driving down the state, coming back from Oregon, and her gas tank was getting low. She saw cars crowded around gas stations waiting to fill their empty tanks and others at the side of the road that had already run out. She only managed to get home because she happened to be near the area where she grew up and she remembered a relative who was a farmer with his own gas supply. Luckily his pump worked. She drove in her driveway with a big sigh and a resolution never to let her tank get more than half empty again. It turned out that something happened to a satellite and it quit working. I don't know if we ever found out why. Since then I always keep some cash around and don't let my gas tank get too empty.

We are so dependent on our technology. I'm constantly aware of that fact. I have a love/hate relationship with my gadgets. I love my smartphone, which puts me in instant touch with my scattered family members. I adore my computer, which helps me continue to earn a living. (BTW, even though I'm retired and don't have a job, I'm still working and loving it!) *And* I've lived long enough now that I know for sure I can live without my gadgets. My first published article was written on a manual typewriter, which I still have stored in the attic. I've written other articles on a yellow pad with a pencil while camping. See, I know I can survive without gadgets. Does everybody know that?

Holly Elissa Bruno

Technology Is My Friend

I love me some technology that saves lives, streamlines our work, and connects us in (less than) a heartbeat. Looking back, I can see how far technology has brought us.

As a person who loves to travel abroad, I smile as I recall my explorations thirty years ago. As a university professor, I had much of the summer off. Once I booked my flight, that was it! I was on my own after I landed. To phone home, I plunked coins into a clunky machine inside the French (or Italian) post office. To receive correspondence, I depended on snail mail, which I would pick up intermittently at preordained American Express offices. A friend stateside took care of paying bills and returning phone calls. How did I know where to lay my head without viewing photos and reading reviews of the hotel, *pension*, or *soba* in advance? I didn't! I knocked on doors and lucked out or didn't. One time in Prague, the shared bathroom at the end of the hall had no running water. Given I am charmed by surprises, I was mostly a happy explorer. And, yes, I felt like an explorer or a stranger in strange lands.

My issue with technology is the person versus machine dilemma. How many movies or books have you seen or read where technology renders us all obsolete, robotic (Debra's Borg example from *Star Trek*), and dangerously vulnerable?

Fear is a powerful motivator. If fight or flight from technological change is our only choice, the result isn't usually pretty. In fact, the result is mostly reactionary rather than insightful, innovative, or compassionate. Trust me, I can get right in step with those fear reactions. I am the immigrant, not the home girl, in the world of technology. I can resist, freeze up, go blank between the ears, and get defensive when I don't have a clue. You know how children melt into the floor like dead weights when they don't want to move in the direction the adult intends? I can do that when overwhelmed by a technological (there's nothing that feels logical about it) meltdown. Given that, like Deb, Luis, and Janet, I understand the value, threat, and inevitability of technology, what helps me get on board? When the Borg machine warns "resistance is futile," trust me, I get it. To make my way in the cyberspace world, I have a very simple approach: I make technology my friend. Yes, friend. I am such a relational person that I need to build a human relationship with the machine. Technology, welcome to my neighborhood!

As with any other new person in my life, I listen up, pay attention, ask questions, and when possible, read between the lines of the technological advance. Emotional intelligence (EQ) serves me just as well as IQ when making technology my new friend. EQ (reading people as well as we read books) lets me stay in touch with my emotional response and learn from it. Am I afraid? I ask for help. Am I embarrassed? I admit what I don't know and specify what I need to learn. Am I overwhelmed? I take a break and come back later. Am I slow to learn? I like learning a new language, and I keep using the new knowledge. This week I released my first tweet. Hello, hash tags and retweets!

Some folk may say my personalization of technology is silly or simple-minded. Those folk may be right. A computer has no heart and the web has no soul. However, I have both, and through them I connect to my world. I am so grateful when the technology-savvy designers make technology user-friendly. I love it when Siri talks to me! She's expert at helping me find the closest doughnut shop and the weather report of my next destination. She clues me in to the best Thai restaurants in the middle of nowhere. If I ask her to predict the next election or to tell me "What's the meaning of life?" she asks if I want her to search the web for the answer. Often my Siri makes a joke or calls me an earthling.

Isn't that what I do when I don't know an answer? Siri is not my BFF; however, she is my helpmate. I have friended her. Friending. That's the name of my game. Friend the unknown until it becomes better known. I take a friend with me when I fear stepping into the dark. I celebrate my brain's (however slow) capacity to forge new brain pathways. And I never leave the comfort of home without my sense of humor. "Siri, who will win the next presidential election?" No, my friend, don't bother to search the web for the answer.

Summary...

Debra Ren-Etta Sullivan

There are so many different ways to think about technology and our relationship to it: Can't live with too much of it; can't live without it. It makes life easier. It makes life harder. It moves too fast. It's not moving fast enough. It's my friend. It's my enemy. I rule it. It rules me. Technology, yes. Technology, no. I think the reality is that technology has always been with us and has always made a significant impact on society. The wheel changed us yesterday just as much as the latest device has changed us today. And our ancestors were probably having the exact same conversations about the pros and cons, loves and woes, of the wheel.

Technology also provides alternative accessibility and connectedness for those who may have been more excluded before. Janet makes a good point in appreciating how useful texting is for people with different levels of hearing or speaking ability. Texting is also useful in allowing more interaction for those who prefer more alone time. One of my sisters hates talking on the phone and can be rather shy in social interactions, but she will text all day long. Luis says he is afraid of technology's implications but is hooked on its conveniences. The key is to make informed decisions. We need to be clear about what we need or want and what we don't need or don't want. I may not want to tweet, but I need to know how to plug in my computer! I also need to make informed decisions about the kinds of experiences I want to have and how technology can help or hinder those experiences. I thought a lot about Holly Elissa's reflections on traveling abroad thirty years ago as a regularly surprised yet happy explorer. Today we can easily arrange very controlled and regulated travel planned right down to the fastest route to the nearest attraction with few surprises and even fewer adventures. And a robot will vacuum our floors while we're gone.

We all seem to agree, however, that grown-ups need to be thoughtful and deliberate when introducing technology to babies and young children. No matter how human and humanizing we make technology, it is not the same as interacting with a human. Obviously, there are ways to use technology in a variety of capacities for both typically and atypically developing babies and children, but we need to be more aware of the impact technology has on them rather than simply transferring what we believe to be its impact on adults. We also need to keep in mind that our technological devices are just that—devices. They are not humans. I'm glad that Siri is not Holly Elissa's BFF, but she *is* one of my daughter's BFFs. My daughter talks to her all the time. And even more intriguing, Siri does not appear to like one of my nieces. I mean not at all! She can't ever seem to get a useful answer. Or maybe my niece needs to redefine *useful*.

Niece: Siri, where's the nearest phone store?
Siri: I give up. Where?
Niece: Siri, I'm having a bad day.
Siri: There are several bridges nearby I can direct you to.

None of us can figure it out. My niece and Siri are no longer on speaking terms. The fact of the matter is, we each need to define our relationship with all of our pieces of technology and make sure we're the boss of that relationship. Running from it won't help, and neither will letting it run us.

Discussion Questions ....

1. Some are overwhelmed by the greater connectedness that comes with technology, and others love it. What about you? Is there an aspect of technology that you just can't live without on a daily basis? What is your backup plan if you have to live without it? Are you overwhelmed by technology? If so, what aspects of it overwhelm you the most? Do you love the greater connectedness it affords you? If so, what aspects of it appeal to you most or do you use the most?

2. Technology allows us to have more regular contact with each other but with less content (think 140 characters). Think of the top five family members and friends you communicate with most. How much contact do you have with each person? What is the nature of the contact (for example, Facebook, e-mail, texting, phone calls, cards). How long is the content (for example, 140 characters, a note in a card, a "like" on Facebook)? Is that how you want the relationship to be? If not, what can you do differently?

3. Sparkly, colorful, noisy toys teach babies that they need constant entertainment. And now grown-up toys train us all to crave constant entertainment. We want our toys to do more and more. Do active, sparkly grown-up toys make passive grown-ups? What does that mean in terms of your own leadership growth and development?

7

CAT Spells Success

Curriculum, Assessment, and Teaching for Quality Learning Environments

Luis Antonio Hernandez

What you teach matters, but how you teach it matters more. What you do counts, but how do you count what you do? Learning environments influence children's success, but how do your values influence the learning environment? And how do you make sure you're accomplishing what you set out to do in the integration of curriculum, assessment, and learning experiences?

In this chapter, my coauthors and I connect and reflect on the personal values that influence so much of what occurs in the classroom. Curriculum selection, assessment strategies, and teaching methods all come together through our own values regarding the learning process. These dynamics should lead us—and you—on the road of intentionality in our work with children and families. And since we have the moniker of CAT—Curriculum, Assessment, Teaching—in the title, I'm going to be playful with some feline behaviors.

The CAT Considers a Variety of Morsels: Identifying Curriculum Goals and Objectives

I begin with a model that can be both practical and capable of generating creative approaches and solutions. As with all early learning models, it's based on what we know is most appropriate in the development and education of young children. Reflect on your years of professional development based on the roots and pioneers of solid theorists such as Piaget, Montessori, Erikson, and Vygotsky. To these theorists' work, add what we know about best practices, specifically the principles, research, and methodology of developmentally appropriate practices as advocated by the team at NAEYC. This combined foundation leads to deeper understanding and enthusiastic practices in everyday classroom circumstances.

As leaders and teachers, we start with the individual lives and experiences of the children and families we work with. Through every step of children's development and learning, we consider what motivates, inspires, and enchants them. We affirm the values of our practice by observing what intrigues the learner: Is it blowing bubbles? Is it stacking blocks? Is it running up a hill?

The fantastic learning experiences for children in quality environments—be it blowing bubbles, building towers, or conquering a hill—are the result of theory and practice. The important goals of learning are clear to families and to the entire teaching team. The materials and resources have the children experimenting and discovering, all with the understanding that nothing is perfect; mistakes are learning opportunities; and individual attempts mean significant progress. Children are respected for their successes, feedback is specific and immediate, frustrations are acknowledged, and learning happens.

For leaders and teachers working with families challenged by poverty, early childhood education provides opportunities for social change. The process of early learning encourages creative expression and builds the steps to future success in school and life. As leaders in this emerging community of learners, we uphold the core belief that education is the gateway of hope and aspiration for any child. Through the principles of community building—we are all in this together—the common ground for learning is shared and supported. More importantly, meaningful respect and trust are shared and supported by everyone in the community. This strengths-based vision establishes the values of education and advocacy as a platform for a better future.

Although it sounds reasonable to have a great environment, invigorating teachers, visionary leaders, and the latest materials and resources, I still ask, is genuine learning taking place? The reality of the bump in the road happens as we face current expectations. Families want to know when their children are going to read and write, administrators want proof of the effectiveness of the program, and policy makers require accountability for the public dollars spent in programs. We know the strengths, cultures, and uniqueness of the children and families we work with, but the ultimate goal is set for us: Are children learning and are teachers teaching? Under such measured and data-driven expectations, we continue to strive for a balance of high expectations for success and the determination that it can be observed, recorded, and analyzed.

Upon entering an early childhood classroom for the first time, a stranger may ask, "What is going on in here?" That first impression of child energy is due to the dynamics of active learning taking place simultaneously and joyfully, which is the result of an intentional planning process. Yes, dear stranger, that's how it's supposed to be! The foundation is a talented and energized teaching team—a group of individuals in a learning community who are committed to achieving great success for the children. The team begins planning by narrowing the desired developmental and learning outcomes for the children. The journey of learning begins when the teaching team is confident in defining the road map for learning. This dynamic process provides the purpose for a day's activity, the rhythm of a week, or the flow of an entire school year. A curriculum, be it locally developed or commercially selected, provides the structure or the recipe for learning experiences and activities. Within that process, the learning philosophy of the program is embedded—be it a compilation and balance of particular theoretical principles, a variety of play and academic approaches, a family-centered program, or a buffet of all of the above and more. Indeed, the curriculum is a manifestation of a program's philosophy and identity, part of a broader learning community shared by other programs across the nation. While doing all of this, the team also constantly informs and involves families so all families have an understanding of classroom practices.

As relationships begin to emerge with individual children and families and as observations of children's interests, needs, and challenges provide more evidence, the teaching team can articulate the desired general developmental expectations as well as more specific individual learning results. From there, specific learning outcomes begin to emerge. Setting clear objectives based on the identified outcomes helps the entire team unify the purpose of their work. From these learning objectives, the planning and implementation process becomes smoother. Think of outcomes as a destination—Hawaii!— and the objectives as the paths leading you there—airplane, cruise ship, sailboat. And just like planning a vacation, developing and writing developmental and learning objectives is not an easy task.

Because the writing of defined goals and objectives can be laborious, here are some questions to consider to aid the process:

- Are the objectives developmentally appropriate for the individual child and groups of children?

- Are these objectives realistic for the time and space in the classroom or in the outdoor space?

- Will the objectives and activities be clear to all?

- Are the objectives measurable? How will children be observed to measure their progress?

- Is there a natural flow from one activity to another? Are learning objectives sequential?

- Are the objectives rooted in children's interests and curiosity? Are children positively challenged in the learning process?

- How can families be incorporated in supporting the learning goals at home and in daily life?

- What additional guidelines do you have when writing goals and objectives? Add them to the list.

In the middle of this process, teaching teams have to step aside to reflect and evaluate throughout the entire day. Perhaps the purpose and value of reflection and evaluation is put on the back burner due to other more immediate work responsibilities. Reflection may be seen as a luxury of time and effort instead of a positive aspect of professional growth: knowing what works and what can be improved. Reflection and evaluation by individuals and work teams prompts insights into daily practices, relationship building with children and families, use of resources and materials, and the general direction of the vision for learning. How does the atmosphere support learning? Are children busy with meaningful play? Are conversation and laughter evident? Are parents regular visitors to the classroom? If all goes as planned, a dedicated time for reflection affirms a team's effectiveness in reaching the destination of learning.

Through reflection we also learn that sometimes things do not go as planned—welcome to early childhood education! If an activity and its objectives are not working, adapt and modify them on the spot. An almost mandated skill for those working with children is to move and act with yogalike flexibility. For example, when expecting classroom visitors, a teacher wanted to impress the visitors with a cooking lesson—that would be terrific, except no visitors arrived. Unfortunately, on this day, the plan was not working, and the cooking activity was not going well. The teacher, without a wrinkle of disappointment or fear, cheerfully said to the class of four-year-olds, "Making cookies today is taking much longer than we anticipated. Can you help me think about what else we can do before we go outside?" Instantly, the children mentioned favorite areas of play, and an activity in problem solving occurred. Congratulations to that teacher for her flexibility!

The CAT Purrs: Getting to Know the Children and Families

Before the goals for the day—or even for a whole new year—can be carried out, duty numero uno is getting to know the children. Begin with smiles, reassuring words, genuine friendliness, and encouraging words of praise, concern, and attention. Building relationships is a delicate and slow-cooking stew of many emotions and feelings. To start, most everyone in the group is new to each other. You may be the first grown-up outside the immediate family who reads a book to a child, or you may be an adult who speaks a language a child does not yet understand. Children wonder, "Will you like me and will I like you?" The foundation of early childhood is about the budding and flowering of long-lasting relationships between young children and their first formal teacher. A wide spectrum of friendships between you and the children will be experienced. Some children will be ready immediately to sit with you while others will take some time. Trust takes time, and children are each at their own stage of comfort.

At the heart of our profession is the challenge to create relationships with children as well as their families. The tools are within our individual temperament and personality: the ability to connect, relate, and nourish a bond with others. Genuine relationships and positive human interactions are a responsibility for every early childhood educator—they are a basic principle of our work. The challenge is to create a genuine bond of respect and trust with families. This is the key component in the teacher-parent relationship. Always keep in mind that the parents trust you with their most precious creations. Families wonder, "Will you take care of my sweet child as well as I do?" That special bond between you and the family is built on the affirmations that their child is safe in your program, that the child will be guided by capable and professional adults, that the learning environments—both indoor and outdoor spaces—are safe and inviting places for learning, and that we are now partners in the development and learning of the child.

Connecting with families as partners in the learning process is a task many of us strive to make meaningful and rewarding, sometimes with a great deal of trepidation. Indeed, if parents are the child's first and most important teacher (How often have you heard that refrain?), are we truly ready to be a child's "second teacher"? This delicate balance underlies much of the power play between teachers and families. Some families see teachers as the ones responsible for their children's learning—that's what teachers get paid for. On the other hand, teachers may experience too much family interference about what happens at school; or on the other extreme, parents may have little interest in what happens at school. This back-and-forth dilemma needs clarification for all parties. Use research to educate your teaching teams and families on the impact of positive parent engagement during a child's early developmental and learning years. The words family members use at home, the books and stories they read, the regular on-time attendance at school, and the physical contact with teachers all lead to the greater success of children in kindergarten and throughout school. A sobering body of research continually shows the positive powerful influence of meaningful parent engagement and involvement on later success in school. Therefore, an extra responsibility for early childhood professionals is to cement a foundation of positive school experiences for families based on relationships. A parent who is warmly welcomed and greeted by you is more likely to read a book to a child, volunteer in the classroom, or be a chaperone on a field trip. We are all friends now, and we are all in this together.

The CAT Explores a Ball of Yarn: Assessing Children's Development and Learning

Before the assessment process begins, we prepare with strong skills and guiding principles. The teaching team recognizes that observations and assessments are ongoing and strategic and that they produce a variety of positive outcomes. The purpose of observation and assessment is always clear: monitoring children's development and learning provides valuable information for the cycle and process of learning. Observations serve as a catalyst and guide for planning the next set of exciting learning activities. Assessments are also the source of data collection and verification of children's progress and growth. Observations and assessments play a key role in identifying children who may benefit from further screening and special services. Ultimately, they provide the best answer to every parent's questions: "How is my child doing? What did he learn today?"

From a perspective of best practices, observations and assessments require that the process be appropriate for the child's stage of development and age. Within the framework of best practices, the teaching team focuses on each child—how well you know a child's temperament, personality, and preferences. And finally, you become aware of the cultural dimensions in the observation and assessment process. You take into account the linguistic, cultural, and economic background of every child within the context of the child's family and community life. For ECE professionals, this requires a wider understanding of the process of how children learn a new language and how poverty affects the experiences children may have, such as visiting a zoo or having access to books at home.

When capturing observations, much like a good detective story, "We just want the facts, ma'am!" This is a skill that always needs sharpening, for it is so easy to be subjective and sloppy in observations. "Michael wore a really colorful shirt today" does not pass muster as a valid observation. Your observation of a child's skill-building action needs to be verifiable by other observers on the team: "Today Miss Lucy and Miss Maria saw Michael riding the tricycle on his own." Each observation is a point of focus and attention on an individual child about which we write notes, use electronic media, and provide evidence and samples of work and other related anecdotes. These multiple measures guide the next round of planning and decision making.

Formal assessment tools should complement the objectives articulated in the curriculum model selected by the team. If you are using a commercial curriculum model and assessment tool, it should have valid research based in ECE components. Of importance, the curriculum and the assessment should complement the global perspective outlined in the philosophy of your program. This way the assessment tool can point to any follow-up, diagnostic evaluation or referrals for screening measures. Even with all this, we must continue to reflect and evaluate the results of plans and refocus the lens of observation for objectivity and clarity.

Documenting observations and recording assessments are probably the most arduous part of a teaching team's daily work. Teams must make adherence to a practical assessment system a priority. The system needs to be efficient as observations and information are recorded, analyzed, reviewed, and shared with families, community leaders, and funding sources. All this must be accomplished while recognizing individual variations in children and allowing them to show competence in unique and different ways. It is always a joy to witness what children can do independently and cooperatively in play. It is also joyful to share a challenge when they may need a little assistance while on the playground, painting a masterpiece, or serving themselves mashed potatoes during lunch. Together with information and input from families, teaching teams can recognize the whole world of learning that a child may encounter in any particular time or place. The challenge is to maintain the focus on an assessment process that indicates individual progress in each child's development and learning. The satisfaction of every team's intentional hard work on learning objectives is the validation of what happens at home and in the classroom documented through observation and assessment.

The CAT Stares out the Window: How Values Influence Teaching Strategies

An often-heard remark by many friends in ECE is the feeling that people—including our own family members—believe we are just glorified babysitters, playing with children all day long. If this happens to you, take a deep breath and share the professional joys as well as the challenges with those willing to listen. Start by comparing yourself to other caring professionals, such as doctors, dentists, and nurses, who are also challenged every day by difficult but rewarding circumstances. Like them, we are always learning, adding to our skills, and refining our practices.

And just like a doctor, we need to keep up with the standards of our profession by reading the latest research, being curious about trends in the field, exploring innovative methods, and being challenged by new ideas and concepts. We also need to take care of ourselves. Recognize that ECE work requires a special dimension of energy, enthusiasm, and drive just to keep up with young children. Be healthy in body, spirit, and attitude. The infectious positive energy that you bring to your work spills into fantastic learning experiences for young children.

The values and ethics of early childhood education start with the love for the profession. While the word *love* is not found in any monitoring tool, it is a key element for the profession. We start with a belief that the teaching practices embodied in ECE enhance children's development and learning. We make possible a variety of learning, based on knowledge and experience, through renewed and time-tested experiences and activities. We can balance the wonder of play within the context of academic expectations. We build on what the children already know and challenge them to move to the next level. We add new information and skills with continual review and reflection about what each child can do and knows. Most importantly, we know how children best develop and learn, keeping in mind that we learn from them all the time. From this, we use our magical toolbox of strategies—encouraging, acknowledging, modeling, giving specific feedback, demonstrating, adding challenges, and praising—to every learning moment. The children we work with know that we are there for them, accessible and responsive in every situation and experience.

The values of fantastic teaching drive greatness and excellence; the spontaneous and planned moments define the joys by which our profession thrives. As leaders and members of a team, we encourage one another to go to the next step in the ladder of professional development. Excellent teachers experiment and challenge their practices constantly. Excellent teachers question whether children are learning and whether the experience has been positive and challenging. Excellent teachers observe children for glimpses of triumphs and for calls for attention and assistance. Excellent teachers know the pacing of learning—are we moving too fast or too slow? And excellent teachers know to balance what is being taught and how it is presented to children. Excellence in teaching is a balance of guiding children on content and openly learning from children about their interests and skill levels. Excellent teachers recognize that it takes hard work to achieve success, and it inspires joy to see a child master a skill or complete a task: "Teacher! I did it!"

The CAT Naps by a Sunny Window: Celebrating the Success of Integrated Approaches

Celebration is neglected as a regular activity for leaders and teaching teams. It's time to give each other high fives, secret notes of congratulations, public recognition of a job well done, individual specific words of praise, or a bunch of flowers at the next staff meeting. Doing the work of quality early childhood education is truly one full of blood, sweat, and tears with a good balance of joy, esprit de corps, and a sense of real success. When we combine the forces of curriculum methods, careful observations and assessment, and fantastic teaching strategies, the children in our classrooms are on the road to discovering possibilities, competencies, friendships, and a love of learning.

The success of the work is the creation of a community of learners in which children, families, and the teaching teams encourage and propel the dream of a generation of future doctors, nurses, scientists, teachers, engineers, mechanics, and master carpenters—and careers we don't even know about yet! As in all healthy communities, each member is valued and respected for their uniqueness and singularity. And each member knows that the learning environment will be a safe and secure place where caring and learning is at the heart of everyone's interest.

Just as a cat dashes from room to room, the variety and formats in our practice matter, and the way we engage children matters even more. All attempts count, whether they involve children playing outside or walking around the block or reading a book in a quiet corner—all attempts are important because they are how we meaningfully create interest and enthusiasm for learning that is significant. Learning environments influence children's success, but professional curiosity, interest, and teaching values impact the total atmosphere of learning. And the success of children is a daily testimony, much as when the end of the year approaches, culminating in incredible growth and success for each child in our classrooms. The accomplishments are individual—the child who spoke English for the first time, the one who no longer fears climbing the play structure, the one who can write, the one who can now hug everyone. Combined, they become the results of how a teaching team has its own success in the integration of curriculum, assessment, and fantastic learning experiences.

Debra Ren-Etta Sullivan

The Importance of Praxis

The first thing that struck me, Luis, was your statement that "early childhood education provides opportunities for social change." A good education is the equalizer, and I always have such a difficult time trying to figure out why it is so challenging to provide every single child with a good education. Why can't all education be good? Why does access to a good education in the United States have to be tied to income, language, and the number of parents in a child's home? Why do we still struggle to integrate all of the learning styles and address all of the multiple intelligences? Quality learning environments should be a given. If we can walk on the moon and get videos of stars exploding, we should be able to provide even the most vulnerable of our children with a good education and a chance for a different future. The path to social change requires the use of creative expression, which is an important feature of a good curriculum. Through the curriculum, social change can start right in the classroom.

I also really like your focus on strengths-based learning environments. That's exactly where the CAT's variety of morsels plays a key role. Curriculum goals and objectives should always include each child's strengths. The challenge for some may be figuring out how to really use a child's strengths as the foundation for addressing areas that need improvement. Someone once told me that when asked about the difference between gifted and special education, a third grader replied that in gifted classes the teacher finds out what you're good at and you get to do that all day, and in special education the teacher finds out what you're bad at and makes you do *that* all day. Assessments that allow us to address both areas are much likelier to result in curriculum and teaching that lead to successful learning environments for children. A strengths-based learning environment finds out what every single child is good at and uses that as the foundation. The environment helps build children's confidence and sense of competence. Focusing only on deficits doesn't work for adults, and it certainly can't be that effective with children. However, every child also needs opportunities to improve in areas that need improving. The only way that C(urriculum) A(ssessment) T(eaching) can spell success is if children can grow in both areas of need and areas of strength.

I was intrigued by the idea that reflection may be seen as a luxury of time and effort instead of a positive aspect in professional growth. I think this is, indeed, often the case. I'm not sure how we came to a place as a profession where making time to stop and think about what we're doing became a luxury. We certainly want children to stop and think about what works and what can be improved, so we should be modeling that for them. It should not be a luxury of time and effort to reflect on our practice. That's why I'm so committed to *praxis*—theory, action, and reflection—for critical growth and change. It should be commonplace for us to have a deep understanding of the theory behind curriculum, assessment, and teaching; take action by implementing all three with great intentionality; and reflect on the results/outcomes and of all three based on how successful we were with children. If all did not go as planned, reflection becomes our time to consider new theory and new actions. Reflection ensures that we are not simply getting *through* the curriculum and children's learning, but we're also getting *to* the curriculum and children's learning. Or, to think about the praxis of CAT, curriculum is the theory, teaching is the action, and assessment is the reflection.

Getting to know the children and their families cannot be stressed enough. It's so important to remember that we are not just teaching children. We are teaching *other people's* children, and they have some definite values and ideals around what their children should know and be able to do and what kind of adults they should grow up to be. We say that parents are children's first teachers, and we even say we really believe that. In practice, that means we should be consulting all of these first teachers and finding out how we, the second teachers, build on strengths and improve areas of need. Indeed, it is true that there is a complicated dance to be done between what parents want and what teachers want. A well-planned curriculum with clearly defined goals, objectives, expectations, and outcomes will go a long way in helping parents make informed choices about the type of learning environment they want for their children. Luis, you mentioned assessments and observations as a catalyst and guide for planning. They are also a great catalyst and guide for good communications with parents and families. They serve as the capital letters of the conversation (the beginning). "Here's what we're going to do next." Unfortunately, for some parents, observations and assessments serve as the punctuation for the conversation (the end). "Here's where your child has been all year."

Of course, it also doesn't help the parent-teacher partnership when teachers are thought of as glorified babysitters. This is where our voice about our well-planned curriculum is urgent. My response to that statement would be, "Maybe you babysit children when you are around them, but I teach them and facilitate their learning. Here's how I do that." Our values do influence our teaching strategies *and* our beliefs about the purpose of our curriculum *and* how we approach our work with other people's children. The clearer we are about those values, those beliefs, and those strategies, the more others will understand the nature of our profession—that we are not just offering a string of activities but a holistic view of what we want children to know and be able to do. When we can do that effectively, it will be quite obvious that *C* and *A* and *T* spell success.

Holly Elissa Bruno

Student and Teacher Are Learners

Remember the log with teacher on one end and student on the other? I like the idea that all learning is as simple as two people sitting at opposite ends of a log, exploring the questions between them. Chatting amiably, the student marvels out loud about his fascinations, his questions, his insecurities, and his yet unspoken dreams. The teacher listens with both heart and intellect, listening deeply to hear the story behind the story:

- Is the student passionate about discovering more?

- Is the student fearful of getting it wrong?

- Is the student able to articulate what he has learned?

- Is the student happy to uncover links between what he has mastered and yet needs to learn?

- Is the student more concerned about pleasing others than about finding the truth?

- Is the student making the knowledge his own by applying the discoveries to his own life?

- Is the student full of wonder about why things work (or don't) and always seeking more effective ways to do or see things?

- Is the student able to build connections with others along the path to learning?

- Is the student developing skills at addressing disappointment, failures, and losses?

- Is the student growing in the ability to reflect on his strengths as a seeker and learner?

- Is the student celebrating accomplishments and building tools to bounce back from failures?

- Is the student needing the teacher to affirm his worth regardless of endless negative "You're not worth it" messages others have laid on the student's heart?

- Is the student finding who he is and who he is meant to be and experiencing the joy of discovery along the way, especially in unexpected ways?

As the student learns and grows, what is happening with the teacher? Is he able to change direction in a heartbeat as an unanticipated curriculum opportunity pops into being? Is he hearing who the child really is and helping that learner unfold into the unique explorer only he can be? Is the teacher learning as much as the student about new possibilities, his own shortcomings and strengths, and the way the world works? As the student marvels, does the teacher allow himself to be awestruck?

The log is the image of education: two people, sitting amicably or feistily together, communicating, learning, and coming to trust, respect, and challenge one another. Imagine both people look down to see a lazy cat turn the log into a scratching post, a secret hideout, a perch to assess the bird population for lunch, an opportunity to be petted, or simply a place to nap in the sun. The cat and any other being or concept that joins us on the log presents another chance to learn. Curriculum emerges, and with emergent curriculum comes the creation of knowledge.

The log is our platform. The log is our launching pad. The log is our safehouse. The log is our boxing ring. The log connects your world to mine. Relationships are the heartbeat of learning. We find out who we are in relationships. The student is the teacher. The teacher becomes the student. We learn, we assess, and we learn anew. The log is anywhere: in an airplane, in a tweet, in the back of a classroom, on an incoming train, at a baseball rivalry, before falling asleep at night. Perhaps you and I are on the log together in this moment. Even by yourself, the log connects you to the night sky, the shooting star, the firefly's dalliances, the web, and your inner voice where wisdom lies. In every question is an answer; in every answer is a question. I'll see you on the log!

Janet Gonzalez-Mena

We Are Born Learning

As a person deeply concerned about the care and education of infants in out-of-home care, I feel a need to do some translation of the terms *curriculum, assessment,* and *teaching* so they fit the youngest children served by ECE programs. As I read all the excellent information Luis was able to convey by his clever use of the cat metaphor, I kept thinking that he was talking mostly to preschool teachers. That's understandable because our profession is made up mostly of preschool teachers. As I read Debra's concern about equity issues and questions about why all education can't be high quality, I was again thinking about infants and toddlers. I thought of how high-quality care and education programs for our very youngest children could make a big difference when they reach preschool age and beyond. And then I came upon Holly Elissa's learning log, and I felt an urge to make her metaphor fit infants. So here goes.

First of all, both teacher and learner have to get off the log because that's not safe for the infant or toddler learner. Though if you imagine the log as a diapering counter at times and the floor space in a playroom at other times, then what Holly Elissa describes fits. Certainly the teacher is concerned about who each child really is and understands the importance of helping each unfold into a unique explorer, as Holly Elissa writes. I want to add that the teacher is careful not to compare one infant to the other. Holly Elissa's interactions between learner and teacher were verbal, mine as an infant teacher are likely to be more physical. Words will be part of it, but touch is equally important—especially during caregiving times, which is when a good deal of learning occurs. The interactions during diapering, for instance, are physical. My hands as well as my face give messages as I look at and touch the infant learner. All of that behavior enhances the relationship. From relationships comes a sense of security, which is what learning is built on. Think of caregiving as the times needs are met—physical needs and emotional ones too. Only then are infants free to learn through exploration and play in appropriate and safe environments with other infants in it.

I want to make the case that infants are born learners. On Holly Elissa's log, the teacher had to make up for some of the negative experiences the learner had incorporated before getting on the log—experiences that had impacted the learner's sense of self. That's why the teacher had to consider outside motivation. Infants and toddlers don't need motivation. They are loaded with motivation to learn. The typical school-type motivators—rewards, star charts, grades, even praise—are unnecessary and can get in the way of their learning. Of course, once infants and toddlers get used to rewards for certain behaviors, they come to expect it. They begin to perform for the adult and the intrinsic rewards begin to fade. Even praise can get in the way of learning for its own sake.

When working with infants and toddlers, it's important to understand the prerequisites for learning. Attachment is one. Ideally, the home provides the primary attachment, but a secondary attachment is also necessary in out-of-home care. To provide for attachment to a caregiver, a system needs to be in place—a system where each caregiver has a small number of infants to care for, even though responsibility for the whole group is also part of the job. Continuity of care is also important to continuing attachment. In some programs infants are moved around a lot, sometimes by being regularly promoted as they reach more advanced stages of development. Ideally an infant who starts in the first weeks of life in a program is still with the same primary caregiver and at least some of the same children for several years. That's not easy in a child care center, but lasting relationships make a difference in the child's sense of security, which affects the child's ability to learn. If the infant is in family child care, the primary caregiver is probably a given and continuity of care is present unless the family removes the child.

Another aspect of security that affects learning comes when infants and toddlers feel physically secure so they can learn with their bodies. In spite of the fact that adults tend to provide a good deal of visual and auditory stimulation by hanging musical mobiles over jump seats, for example, the very act of being strapped in means the learning is limited. Infants and toddlers learn best when they can explore and improve both fine-motor and gross-motor skills. That's how they come to see themselves as learners, and they need no outside motivation to progress. The motivation is built in!

I've looked at Holly Elissa's log learning; now let me get back to CAT—Curriculum, Assessment, and Teaching. Allow me to translate each of those terms into useful concepts for those who work with infants and toddlers. I've already started with curriculum, which I think of as a plan for learning. Everything I have already written about here is part of the plan for learning. The word itself comes from Latin and means "to run or travel along a course." That makes me think of a river course, which is a good metaphor for infant learning. It flows; it meanders. Curriculum for infants and toddlers needs to be natural—and it can be when the program is set up and teachers are trained to let that happen. Curriculum starts, as Luis said, with the individual lives and experiences of the children and families. He also said we have to take into account what motivates, inspires, and enchants each individual child. We do this by observing what each infant is actually doing. It's not about teaching, it's about supporting learning. In order to support learning, those who work with infants have to stop being teachers and start being learners. As Magda Gerber used to say to her students and interns, "The infant is the teacher."

I like to look at the concept of curriculum as it applies to infants and toddlers as something natural that each child brings to the program. The adult's job is to be fully present to each child and help support the learning he is working on. In some ways the curriculum lies in the infant, not in the adult's goals, expectations, ideas, practices, lesson plans, or activities. It's a different model from the one in which the adult teaches and the child learns. When curriculum is considered a natural flow, assessment is an ongoing process and it comes about through observations, interactions, communication with families, and record keeping—records both written and pictorial. Families are involved in the process both as receivers of information and givers of it. The picture is never complete without knowing what is happening with the infant at home as well as observing the infant in the program.

Teaching, as has been pointed out already, is a more fluid process with infants and toddlers than with older children. Think of a teaching-learning process where the roles constantly change. The infant or toddler teaches the adult about his personal needs, interests, activities, and abilities. The adult meets those needs, provides for interests, and creates an environment that relates to the child's abilities and activities. The adult seldom looks like a teacher per se, but more like a facilitator and a caregiver. It's a different role than many think of when they go into the teaching profession.

Summary..

Luis Antonio Hernandez

The more I think of CAT in our work, the more I see a fine dance of theories in sync with practices, the rhythm of challenging ideas with the flow of methodology, and the steps that promote positive relationships for development and learning. The conversation on curriculum, assessment, and teaching practices that the members of this dance ensemble have undertaken shows the diversity of individual thought on the strength of practices, the analysis on social change, and the action in supporting excellence for the work we do. No matter where we are in the continuum of teaching and leadership development, there is still room for more wonderment.

Finally, the word *success* in the title of this chapter points to the excitement of natural knowledge and the motivation for learning. And the stages of success through the lens of a curriculum, assessment tools, or teaching strategies still demand respect for children in all age groups—from infants to those in the third grade. Success still hinges on the melody of genuine relationships, positive experiences, and interactions rich in the flow of life. And as Janet reminds us, it's not about teaching, it's about supporting learning.

Discussion Questions ....

1. Consider your work with a curriculum for young children. How are interactions and relationships emphasized?

2. In assessing children's development and learning, how are those observations and related anecdotes used to support children's learning? As an ECE professional, what do you consider to be indicators for children's success in any learning environment?

3. From the CAT conversation above, describe three highlights related to your work.

8

Playing for Keeps

The Power of Laughter and Lightheartedness for Adults

Holly Elissa Bruno

How much do you play? Do you reserve your playful moments for the weekends? Or perhaps you don't have time to play anymore.

Our work is serious business. Children and their families deserve our best. If we lighten up, we might not be taken seriously. If we lighten up, we may offend someone because we are not taking our work seriously enough. If we lighten up, we might appear unprofessional. So why is play for adults, especially adults in leadership positions, important? In fact, the answer is serious business. If we don't play, we lose the capacity to resolve issues, remain optimistic, come up with creative new approaches, and keep our eyes on the prize. Neuroscientists can now demonstrate that our executive function (originating in the prefrontal cortex of our brain) craves the mental exercise play provides. Play is the brain's jungle gym, suggests Jaak Panksepp (1998), neuroscientific researcher.

To do our best by children, we need to let ourselves laugh, sing, dance, create, and just be silly. Who knew? Is play part of your daily routine?

What Is Play?

If you have ever had one of those patient conversations about the value of play with a parent who wants her child to do worksheets instead of play, you have identified the value of play for children. The bottom line is children learn through play. Play can include games and competitions; however, play is more a state of mind that an activity. Dr. Stuart Brown (2009), author of the seminal book *Play*, describes what we are like when we play:

- We are free.

- We are not self-conscious.

- We are in the moment.

- We are fully engaged.

- We are discovering.

- We are actively learning.

- We are alive.

- We are joyful.

Who wouldn't want to play? Brown (2009, 154) boldly claims, "When people are able to find that sense of play in their work, they become truly powerful figures." Who wouldn't want to be playful, spontaneous, alive, and joyful?

What Is the Opposite of Play?

How would you answer the question, what is the opposite of play? The natural response for many of us is work. Work is the opposite of play. In fact, 55 percent of people in the United States subscribe to the belief that we have to get all our work done before we can play (Myers et al. 1998). What if the work is never done? What happens to play? Have you known someone who claims he will play once he retires; until then, his life is a series of continual responsibility? What happens to people who put off play until they retire? Have you noticed that an alarming number of these people do not live long enough to enjoy retirement?

Adults Need Play

Play for adults may seem like an afterthought, a luxury, or a frivolous idea. After all, our work is full of responsibility. There's nothing funny about a child being harmed or not getting what she needs to grow. Don't our days of playing end when we reach adult responsibilities? Consider the often quoted biblical passage (1 Corinthians 13:11–12): "When I was a child, I talked like a child, I thought like a child, I reasoned like a child. When I became a man, I put away childish things. For now we see in a glass darkly; but then, face to face." The message of this verse, to me at least, is that children's understanding of the world is innocent, unaware of the troubles of adulthood; therefore, children can play without worry. Seasoned adults, however, who see the realities of the dark glass are no longer free to play. The implication is adults are responsible; only children can play. The command on us as responsible working adults is to reserve play for children while we work.

My belief is that without playfulness, we adults shrivel up, take ourselves too seriously, lose perspective, and frankly, become boring. Playfulness restores our souls, enlivens our spirits, and helps us stay optimistic. Play also hones our problem-solving skills. Work, without play, becomes dull and tedious. And when our work is with children, what are we modeling for them?

It's Not Funny: Forces That Shame Adults for Playing

Our work is serious business; children's lives and well-being are entrusted to us. We have laws to follow, regulations to adhere to, policies to enforce, overflowing toilets to plunge, and conflicts to resolve. None of this is funny business. We in the field have an image of respectability, sobriety, and professionalism to uphold, right? After all, how we behave reflects on our whole program.

Some of us believe we cannot make mistakes, for all of the reasons above. In addition, mistakes can be fatal. Everyone has heard at least one agonizing story of a child left behind on a bus or a teacher accused of sexually molesting children. One poor decision could put a child in harm's way and cost a teacher her job. Where in all of this responsibility and duty is play?

Play is our saving grace. According to Dr. Stuart Brown (2009), depression, not work, is the opposite of play. Dr. Brown argues that without playfulness, our resilience—the ability to problem solve and generate new ideas—rusts away. Play triggers and engages the prefrontal cortex of our brain where problem solving, creativity, optimism, and perspective are generated. Unless we play, we hunker down with a frown. We may be working hard, but we are not enjoying the moment or seeing how our work has greater meaning beyond the immediate task.

Play: The Essence of Early Learning

Think of a child's face during play. Chances are good that the image you have uplifts you or at least brings a smile to your face. The child is fully engaged in the moment, fully enthused about learning, and not in the least self-conscious. That's what play does for children.

Much of our early childhood philosophy is rooted in the understanding that children learn through play. Friedrich Froebel set the standard in his book *The Education of Man* (1826, 54–55): "Play is the highest phase of child development. . . . It gives . . . joy, freedom, contentment, inner and outer rest, peace with the world. It holds the sources of all that is good. . . . The plays of childhood are the germinal leaves of all later life." Dr. Maria Montessori (1914, 77) urged each teacher to "guide the child without letting him feel her presence too much, so that she may always be ready to supply the desired help, but may never be the obstacle between the child and his experience."

Jean Piaget maintained that the purpose of education is to help children create new things, not simply to repeat the tried and true. Piaget believed that children need to construct their own knowledge rather than passively receive instruction. Therefore, educators need to step back, observe how a child learns through play, and facilitate and affirm that lifelong process. Emmi Pikler championed the philosophy and practice of creating safe and loving environments where children can unfold to be who they are meant to be. According to the Pikler method, children learn best when playing with elemental items like a silky cobalt blue scarf or a wooden spoon. In essence, through play, the child teaches herself.

Howard Gardner helped us identify and appreciate children's multiple intelligences. Gardner's breakthrough thinking paved the way for Daniel Goleman's declaration that emotional intelligence—known as EQ or the ability to read people as well as we read books—is more essential to us in the day-to-day world than IQ—the ability to analyze rationally. To have a high EQ, we must incorporate all of our multiple intelligences and act wisely with the information gleaned from reading people. Play is an essential way for children to learn EQ. During play, they learn to take turns and share, to pay attention to their teammates' and their own needs, to deeply experience the value of boundaries, and above all, to be joyful in the moment.

Fred Rogers, a pioneer in acknowledging the need for EQ in early childhood education, summarized the value of playful learning this way: "What nourishes our imagination? Probably more than anything else, loving adults who encourage children's own choices of imaginative play" (2002, 1).

Does the right to play end when a child goes to elementary school? Certainly homework and sitting still through classroom lectures are not play and recess may be nonexistent or fly by in fifteen minutes. By middle and secondary school, play gets relegated to the sports field. Children who are able to do so play sports. Sport quickly becomes about outcomes: who gets the greatest number of runs, touchdowns, baskets, points, or birdies. Play ultimately adds up to being about winning. Even our littlest children are often shuttled off to soccer camp or piano lessons so they can perform well and be competitive. Tiger Woods and early piano prodigy Vladimir Horowitz devoted hours of what might have been playtime to practice-makes-perfect time. Both became famous experts as men. I wonder what childhood playtime delights they forfeited. Sometimes, we can forget how to play at any age.

The Gift of Perspective

Humor—a form of play—gives us the gift of perspective. If I can laugh at myself or lighten up about a problem, I see the problem from a renewed perspective. I shrug that heavy cloak of solemnity off of my shoulders. The problem morphs into an opportunity. Or, at least, the problem gets placed in soothing perspective. Do you know the saying, "Angels can fly because they take themselves lightly"? Laughing at myself helps me shake off my impossible-to-achieve need to get things just right. How can we be holier than thou if we see our own silliness? Perhaps laughter and humility are related. Both help us keep things in perspective.

When we're in a challenging situation, one way of accepting this gift of perspective is to ask ourselves, "How important is the problem?" In the moment, we can be sucker punched. A parent, Mr. Krueger, can angrily threaten to sue us because his daughter Ava failed to ace the entry exam for a high-end kindergarten at a private school. Losing perspective like Mr. Krueger did is easy to do. In fact, our brain is wired to react to perceived threats. Our amygdala—located in the center of our head—works with the hypothalamus to trigger the adrenal gland—located on top of the kidneys—to release a blast of stress hormones into our system whenever something pushes us off balance. With cortisol and adrenaline coursing through his veins, Mr. Krueger's ability to value Ava's considerable social and emotional development is obscured.

By taking a breath, stepping back, and asking ourselves, "How important is it?" we can begin to put the problem in perspective. We know Ava blossomed thanks to her teachers' developmentally appropriate practices. Ava's enthusiasm for learning has been deepened by our Reggio approach. With the gift of perspective, we can help assure Mr. Krueger that his child is well prepared socially and emotionally for upcoming academic and life challenges and remind him of the research on the ultimate value of a playful early childhood experience.

Laughter releases endorphins, those chemicals that lighten our mood. However, taking parents' concerns seriously is important; everyone needs to feel heard and valued. Sometimes the best way to hear and value ourselves is to step back and lighten up on ourselves. When I find myself taking things so seriously that I become glum, I remind myself, "Get over yourself. The more you worry, the less you can be present to yourself and others." In the process, I can often smile and even laugh at my own inflated sense of importance.

If you have attended a twelve-step meeting like Al-Anon or Co-Dependents Anonymous (CoDA), you may have noticed program slogans posted around the room, slogans like "Put the problem in its proper perspective," "Let go and let God," and "How important is it?" People in recovery—those who practice a twelve-step program—learn that what gets us down is, in the end, the very thing that can lift us up. As with other bumps in the road, we find that what appears to be a disaster is, in fact, an opportunity. Mr. Krueger's despair over his daughter's not getting into a private preparatory school may, in the end, help him see Ava (and himself, perhaps) as gifted in ways other than traditional test taking.

How important is Mr. Krueger's anger at us? Important enough that we listen, understand his concerns, and show him respect. But not important enough for us to forget the value of early childhood education or tumble into despair.

Scoring Points for Playing

If we want to play for keeps—to keep play in our lives—and stay upbeat and not "let the turkeys get us down," we need to pay attention to these questions:

- What pushes our buttons?

- What happens internally when our buttons get pushed?

- What can we do to bounce back in the moment?

What pushes your buttons? What sabotages your "can do" energy? Most people tell me that negative people get under their skin, as does dishonesty, disrespect, and not taking responsibility. When things get us down, the emotion centers in our brain can kick our stress systems into overdrive, setting us on edge.

The top five workplace behaviors that lead to intense stress will likely sound familiar to you (Goleman 2011):

- experiencing condescension and lack of respect

- being treated unfairly

- being underappreciated

- feeling you are not being listened to or heard

- being held to unrealistic deadlines

When we feel threatened, our amygdala takes over and nothing is funny; everything is dead serious.

What Happens Internally When Our Buttons Get Pushed?

Let me share with you some information that helps me: understanding what is going on inside me on a cellular level helps me practice how to partner with those changes. Left over from the days when our ancestors battled tigers and bears, our amygdala serves as our fear center. When we are threatened (by a shark attack or even by being left out by peers), before we can stop to think, we feel compelled to hightail it out of the situation or punch out the threat. The amygdala does protect us from threats; however, the amygdala's clanging alarm can challenge our professional perspective and decorum (Cozolino 2006).

So, what can we do given that our brain responds with knee-jerk reactions before we can even think? Isn't avoiding conflict at any cost preferable to an amygdala hijack, that feeling of being swept away by emotion (Goleman, 2011)? Fortunately, our brain's prefrontal cortex helps us evaluate and readjust. It gives us the capacity to step back and regain perspective. In everyday terms, these brain functions allow us to regain perspective, even in the moment of stress, and call upon the quiet voice within (Gilkey, Caceda, and Kilts 2010).

Bounce-Back Strategies: Countering Amygdala Hijacks

In practical terms, here are steps we can take and resources we can call upon that will effectively diminish the disabling effect of fear:

- Step away from the situation physically.

- Breathe more deeply to decrease shortness of breath.

- "Go inside" to a safer place via meditation, prayer, or a saying like the Serenity Prayer.

- Ask yourself, how important is it (in the long run and over my life span)?

- Ask for help; connect with a trusted friend.

- Call upon your sense of humor.

- Keep your eyes on the prize: picture a child who will be helped by you facing your fear.

Take a moment to recall a time when you successfully overcame your fear and took action to make a difference. Each time we take these actions, we develop additional nerve pathways from the executive function to the amygdala (Goleman 2011). Dr. Louis Cozolino (2010) notes that as we mature, our amygdala matures with us and is less activated by fear and anxiety.

Can You Come Out and Play?

What stands in the way of you playing? One way we can easily laugh and play is to take ourselves lightly. Trust me, I have hundreds of reasons to laugh at myself. The more we laugh at ourselves, the more relaxed and at ease the people around us can be. The need for perfectionism abates. Imagine just one way in which you could poke fun at yourself today. Share that with a staff member. In a heartbeat, you let people know that humor is healing. Fun is just that, and we need more of it. Life's too short to take ourselves, even our professional selves, too seriously!

Debra Ren-Etta Sullivan

Our Work Should Be Fun and Creative

Who decides what play really is? Who determines what normal play is? Not only does play make childhood fun, it also has a critical role in childhood cognitive development. Yet no one needs to tell children how to play. Sometimes grown-ups suck all the fun out of play by trying to exert far too much control over children's play. Remember when you were a child? Real play was nonliteral, intrinsically motivated, self-chosen, and pleasurable. Children really do want to be playful, spontaneous, alive, and joyful, but when grown-ups join in, play seems to shift to structured, extrinsically motivated, adult-chosen, dead-end activities. As adults, maybe our inability to play started when, as children, we began to shift play toward games with rules, such as marbles, cards, and competitive games that turned into sports. Make-believe declines as organized games increase, and perhaps our ability to be playful, spontaneous, alive, and joyful decreases with it.

We can learn from children's ability to approach situations creatively and playfully. Children who are intellectually competent tend to be expert players. Children also coordinate many different senses as they play and explore their worlds. They taste the toy and develop a sense of what it feels like both orally and manually. They see the toy and listen to the sounds it makes as they taste and hold it. They smell the toy, and they experience a feeling of satisfaction and happiness with the whole event. We know that children transfer their play to learning possibilities such as when playing with blocks or playing grown-ups. When children are playing grown-ups (for example, house, doctor, or church), they take on pretend roles and practice who they would like to be and how they would like to be when they are older. When children are playing with blocks, they learn about weight, balance, gravity, construction, destruction, addition, subtraction, and how to work with other children.

Play also makes childhood fun—even when chores are involved. Children cleverly integrate work and play during the day. Children of many different cultures around the world play while they work, often carrying out their household tasks in a make-believe adult manner. Children saying, "Here ya go, honey. That's a good girl!" while feeding a baby sister, or "Let's say these are carrots and vegetables and we try to get our baby to eat them," while playing "parents" with a friend are two examples.

What can adults in leadership learn from children's play? Play in leadership means being creative, flexible, curious, thinking of possibilities, and taking chances. It means taking on new roles, just as children do in pretend play. I'm always surprised when I find adults who are actually afraid to take on new roles, do something different, or even engage in "possibility" thinking. Why shouldn't our work be fun and creative? What are we afraid of? I think, for some, the very notion of work as something fun is just sacrilegious. Somehow, if we are curious, having fun, being creative, and taking chances, then we must be goofing off at work. I remember once having a lively conversation with a coworker about a conference we were planning. We were laughing, excited, and probably talking a little louder than most of the others around us. Another coworker came over to suggest that our coffee break was probably over and we should get back to work. My explanation that we were, indeed, working created a moment of disequilibrium for her, and she admitted that it would never occur to her that people could be laughing and having fun at work. Fortunately, we were not around children, modeling bad "play" behavior.

Parents and guardians are children's first playmates (touching faces, peekaboo) and do, in fact, model different kinds of play. Depending on their cultural norms and values, parents may engage in much physical play with a child or may engage in quiet, less physical activities. And, as Holly Elissa mentioned earlier, parents may not always agree with the amount, the type, or the role of play allowed by a teacher or care provider. Parents may place care providers and teachers in roles that range from child care servants to child care gurus, with varying expectations for their child. In some cultures, formal teaching is the responsibility of the family and early learning settings are places where children go to play with others of a similar age. For other cultures, play is what happens at home and early learning settings have full responsibility for all formal teaching.

Many parents are suspicious of anything that may make their children less competitive in school or in the job market, and they view play as messing around. It is our responsibility to explain the role of play in children's development. Just describing to parents how pretend and symbolic play creates the foundation for future reading skills is an excellent way to advocate for developmentally appropriate activities for children. And in planning those developmentally appropriate activities, let's not forget to have some fun ourselves. It's been said, "Life is what happens while you're making other plans." Perhaps play is what could have been happening while we were planning!

Janet Gonzalez-Mena

We Decide What Our Play Is

Both Holly Elissa and Debra got me reflecting on the importance of ECE professionals not only promoting play for children but also looking at the benefits of play for adults. That made me think about the role that play takes in my own life. From there I went back to the time when I took my very first ECE class, which, not coincidentally, was called Play: A Way of Learning. That was back in the 1960s. The teacher was a woman who had just gotten her PhD from Stanford and had been hired to teach at the University of Illinois, Urbana. She had come back to California to teach a summer class at San Francisco State College in the ECE department—the class I was enrolled in. Her name was Lilian Katz, and she went on to be famous for her writing, teaching, research, and leadership in the ECE profession. This class was a great way for me to start on my path to be an ECE professional. I had already taken some first steps by enrolling my own children in a parent co-op and volunteering at a brand-new Head Start program. I had never planned to be a preschool teacher, but here I was going back to college to take a class leading toward that very career.

I remember one of our assignments in that class was to examine the way we played as adults and what we got out of it. That assignment took me back to my childhood and imaginative play. I *loved* playing pretend! I remembered spending hours doing just that—sometimes all on my own—with dolls or paper dolls. The assignment was to think about how I played as an adult, and there I was flashing back to my childhood. But that flashback brought me forward to another memory from my adulthood. It was during a time that, after already being a published writer, I decided to try my hand at fiction. I was sitting at my desk deep into working on a novel about a child who lived out in the country in the small valley in Northern California where I lived at the time (and still live). This girl had found a number of arrowheads and obsidian scrapers—evidence that people lived there long ago. I was about to write a scene when the girl goes back in time and connects with earlier inhabitants. I set the scene: it was springtime, the fields were lush green and dotted with wildflowers. I was totally absorbed in the landscape when I chanced to look out the window over my desk. I was truly startled to see brown fields of dead grass lying in the summer heat. In California we call dead grass *golden*, but it didn't look golden at the moment to me—it looked *dead*. Reality was a shock when I had been so thoroughly living in my imagination. As I sat there amazed, I went right back to my childhood and remembered the pleasure of playing pretend. As I was writing, I was doing the same thing! Writing often is playing for me. I eventually finished the book but never tried to publish it. I got so busy working on nonfiction that I never went back to fiction. Maybe someday . . .

So how do I play as an adult besides writing? I play in my head a lot—daydream, pretend, imagine. Although I'm not a person who enjoys playing with my body—tennis, swimming, or any other active sport—I do walk every day, an average of four miles. And while I'm walking I'm playing in my head—letting thoughts flow, sometimes watching the flow but usually not controlling it. I do *love* what goes on in my head!

Long ago I studied psychosynthesis, a theory of humanistic and trans-personal psychology that came out of the head and experience of Roberto Assagioli, an Italian psychiatrist who died in 1974. Psychosynthesis relates somewhat to what we in ECE call the *whole child* concept. In other words, a person is made up of mind, body, and feelings, which, of course, come together as a package. As the theory goes, most people tend to identify with one part more than another. I am definitely a mind-identified person. I love my mind—it gives me much pleasure. I seldom focus on my body except to be thankful that it has served me well all these years and not commanded my attention too much. As far as my feelings go, I'm ambivalent. Of course, I enjoy what I think of as happy feelings; it's those others I'm not wild about and would love if they would just go away altogether. Intellectually I know all feelings are useful, but there's my mind again taking over—calling attention to itself. Of course, you can't ever separate mind, body, and feelings, but most people tend to put more focus on one part than the others. There's a lot more to psychosynthesis than the whole child aspect, but that's a whole other piece of writing. Back to play. Thinking about how I learned about myself while studying psychosynthesis, I realize that a good deal of my learning came through playful kinds of activities involving art, movement, language, and guided imagery. I didn't just learn with my mind, I learned with my whole self.

I recently saw a sign in an ECE classroom that said, "Play is a set of behaviors that is freely chosen, personally directed, and intrinsically motivated." There was no name on the sign, so I don't know who said it, but that definition reminded me of a story about my youngest son when he was in preschool. I went to a parent meeting where the families were treated to a slide show of the children. (Remember slide shows? They came before computers and PowerPoint presentations.) When a picture of my son appeared, he was holding a shovel and standing beside a rather deep hole. I remember how he stood up in the meeting and walked right up to the screen, announcing proudly, "That's the best thing I ever did in preschool!" Then he went and sat back down. It was obvious that he put a lot of work into digging that hole. Was digging that hole play? It must have taken a lot of work. When he talked later about digging the hole, it was clear that it fit the definition of play on the sign: freely chosen, personally directed, and intrinsically motivated. That story also helps me see that no one outside the player can decide what's play and what's not. I doubt that anyone observing me going through an ordinary day would be able to tell when I'm playing. I often look like I'm working. So let me finish with these questions: Can anyone from the outside distinguish play from work? Isn't it up to the person being observed to decide how to label the activity?

Luis Antonio Hernandez

Play Is the Foundation

Let's be serious for a change. Sit up straight and be ready to be lectured on play. Please do not try to divert your mind and your thinking into "What's for lunch?" or "I wonder where I parked the car." For play is so important that research is an integral component; books are written about it, professional types have unbelievably boring PowerPoint presentations on the subject, and people take copious notes on how to do play. Play is incredibly scientific—an academic discipline—with all the bells and whistles (it wishes!), with a long thesis, field observations, and peer reviews. Luckily it also has discovery tunnels, messy physical activities, sensory-rich creative projects, and the requirement of singing out loud, in or out of tune. As research proves, play can induce peals of laughter even from people not prone to public displays of playful abandon. Therefore, a deep, or even a superficial, discussion can lead to a better understanding of its strange dynamics.

I am just glad my colleagues Holly Elissa, Janet, and Debra have outlined that discussion on what you needed to know about play with plenty of research, data, pros and cons, and maybe some graphs (did I miss them?). At the end of reading their pieces, I know I am smarter than the average person on the street in the theoretical analysis of play. For those of us in the world of ECE, it is more than essential to recognize how the nature of play is a foundation that impacts children in multiple ways beyond child development and Early Learning 101. Play is for adults too! Play is essential in the workplace as a force for team efforts and productivity. Play keeps couples happy and joined at the hip. And as we eventually grow old, play maintains the gleam in our eyes and the smiles in our faces. Play happens at every stage of life. For play is inherent and natural in human development as it skates and dances across all our domains—be it language, cognitive reasoning, emotional well-being, or physical maturation. We are just beginning to recognize and comprehend its many purposes and functions, which include healing factors, analytical reasoning, and possibly a contribution toward world peace. Let's imagine soldiers in a tomatoes war, like the festival La Tomatina in Spain, and observe how everyone will be indistinguishable from all the runny, juicy tomatoes on their faces and bodies. What better weapon than tomatoes!

Holly Elissa reminds us that play is integral with its lightheartedness and laughter. From that comes the many brands of humor—and each of us has our own preference for a good belly laugh. As she mentions, humor is a "gift of perspective." Today humor is used in many work settings as a management tool to bring team spirit, cohesion, productivity, and loyalty to organizations. One of the most notable companies that uses humor in its organizational mission is Southwest Airlines. I know that every time I fly it, the crew somehow manages to make people comfortable and at ease with good-natured humor: "For those of you flying to Dallas, we just went right over it." Debra reminds us to be children again (gosh, I keep forgetting). Simply working and being with the children should be a replay on the basics of play. When I work with teachers and ask what they enjoy most about their work, very frequently they mention how children make them laugh and how they feel young every day. Possibly, early childhood humor and laughter may be marketed as cheaper than Botox! And when children see us at play, we rekindle our playful spirits and model a positive view of learning. In the book *Developmentally Appropriate Practice in Early Childhood Programs Serving Children from Birth through Age 8* (Copple and Bredekamp 2009), the authors emphasize the importance of joy in our teaching practices. Whatever the planned or spontaneous learning experience, a sense of joy needs to surround it for relationships and learning to take place.

In revisiting our playfulness, Janet encourages us to do what we started with as children—to daydream, pretend, and imagine as our gateway to a universe of play. For me, play is a constant challenge because I love to play to an extreme. Not just organized sports or fitness classes at the gym, but truly adult exercises in silliness and fun. My neighborhood, Coconut Grove, in Miami, has an annual parade every December called the King Mango Strut. Actually, it is not a typical parade, more like a rolling parody of events, news highlights, and caricatures of infamous personalities from the year coming to an end. Politicians are mocked, TV personalities are demonized, and major events are satirized. With a group of like-minded friends, we discuss and argue as to who our target will be—usually done the day before in order to get the best creative juices flowing. Somehow, it all comes together, sometimes a few hours before the Strut. And before you know it, we are marching in front of thousands of people. We have done many topics over the years, but a few of the memorable highlights include The Melting Ice Caps, The Escaped Everglades Python, and Julia Child's Helpers. Unfortunately, you have to be there for the fun. Every year we all look forward to the event, for no matter how awful we are, we laugh for forty-eight hours straight. Adults playing and having fun. The biggest compliment is my niece telling me, "Tio, never grow up." At this point in life, play is still the engine that keeps the twinkle of lightheartedness and laughter going.

Summary......................................

Holly Elissa Bruno

So what are we waiting for? Let's play! I'm ready. There's my beloved pup, Toby Grapelli. I could scratch his ears forever. Here I come, Toby G.! You should come too. Look around. What's calling you to play? Can you blow bubbles? Text a pal? Hug a preschooler? Join in a classroom activity? Just be silly? Why not? Life's too short to be boring.

Discussion Questions ....

1. What percentage of your work is play? When was the last time you played at work? Can you identify one way you can engage the adults around you to lighten up and play? Tag! You're it. Just do it!

2. What is your answer to Janet's question, "How did you play as a child?" I virtually lived outside, climbed trees, explored the forests, picked blackberries, biked and hiked for hours. Today I still love to be outdoors. Today I explore the world. Do the things you enjoy doing today have a relationship to the ways you played as a child?

3. Early childhood education is serious business. We are vested with the heavy responsibility of helping each child find her way. Given the gravity of this work, how can an early childhood leader be playful, lighthearted, and perhaps even silly? Can a lighthearted leader be taken seriously? What leader do you respect who is playful and able to laugh at herself?

References ....

Brown, Stuart. 2009. *Play: How It Shapes the Brain, Opens the Imagination, and Invigorates the Soul.* New York: Avery.

Copple, Carol, and Sue Bredekamp, eds. 2009. *Developmentally Appropriate Practice in Early Childhood Programs: Serving Children from Birth through Age 8.* 3rd ed. Washington, DC: National Association for the Education of Young Children.

Cozolino, Louis. 2006. *The Neuroscience of Human Relationships: Attachment and the Developing Social Brain*. New York: W. W. Norton and Company.

———. 2010. "Three Keys to Understanding People Who Push Your Buttons." Podcast interview by Holly Elissa Bruno. *Heart to Heart Conversations on Leadership*, April 3. www.bamradionetwork.com/index.php ?option=com_content&view=article&id=413:jackstreet54&catid=69 :infobamradionetworkcom&Itemid=144.

Froebel, Friedrich. 1826. *The Education of Man*. New York: Lovell.

Gilkey, Roderick, Ricardo Caceda, and Clinton Kilts. 2010. "When Emotional Reasoning Trumps IQ." *Harvard Business Review* 88 (9): 27.

Goleman, Daniel. 2011. *The Brain and Emotional Intelligence: New Insights*. Northampton, MA: More Than Sound. Kindle edition.

Montessori, Maria. 1914. *Dr. Montessori's Own Handbook*. New York: Frederick A. Stokes Company.

Myers, Isabel Briggs, Mary H. McCaulley, Naomi L. Quenk, and Allen L. Hammer. 1998. *MBTI Manual: A Guide to the Development and Use of the Myers-Briggs Type Indicator*. 3rd ed. Palo Alto, CA: Consulting Psychologists Press.

Panksepp, Jaak. 1998. *Affective Neuroscience: The Foundations of Human and Animal Emotions*. New York: Oxford University Press.

Rogers, Fred. 2002. "Children's Museums and the Role of Play." *Hand to Hand*, October.

9

Social-Emotional Competence
Are You Smarter Than a Two-Year-Old?

Janet Gonzalez-Mena

Is your answer to the question in this title, "Certainly I'm smarter than a two-year-old"? Obviously anyone who knows anything about child development or has been around a two-year-old for even a short time knows that the behavior of two-year-olds fails to fit concepts of adult social-emotional competence or adult behavior. So what is a chapter on two-year-old behavior doing in a book on professional development and leadership in the field of early care and education? Are we suggesting adults adopt unruly behavior such as screaming "No!" or shouting "Me! Mine!" Of course not. This chapter is not about competition between you and two-year-olds; it's in this book to provide a perspective on social-emotional competence in two-year-olds to help you examine your own social-emotional competence as it relates to leadership skills. The point is to take a look at yourself with the idea that you might see places to improve your social-emotional competence. And one more thing, if you know me, you know I can't write about anything without exploring diversity issues as they arise. So with all that in mind, let's get started.

Put aside two-year-olds' social-emotional competence for a minute and take a look at your own. To help you start thinking, here is a little quiz. You won't be graded. There are no right or wrong answers. Oh, and by the way, please keep your own cultural background and individual inclinations in mind as you take the quiz.

Quiz

Please reflect on these aspects of your social-emotional competence:

1. Are you clear about what you want and what you don't want? If yes, how do you express it? If no, what makes you unclear?

2. How do you show what you care about?

3. How easy or hard is it for you to say no to someone? Why is it easy or hard? Does it matter who the someone is?

4. What are your abilities, and how confident are you in those abilities? Put another way, what are your strong points, and how confident are you in your strengths?

5. How well do you recognize your protective instincts, and how do you handle them?

Now compare your answers to the emotional competence of a two-year-old. Start with knowing what you want and don't want. How did you answer question 1? Think about your answers as you read about two-year-olds.

Knowing What You Want and What You Don't Want

Two-year-olds are usually quite competent at knowing what they want and especially what they don't want! They seldom hesitate to show their likes and dislikes. They tend to be open about their feelings and clear about what strikes them favorably and what doesn't.

How clear are you about what you want and what you don't want? How often are you aware of your gut reactions? What do you do with those reactions? Do you stifle them, or do you allow those gut reactions to help you figure things out? Leadership requires that we feel our feelings and bring our whole self—mind, body, and feelings—to the task. You may assume good leaders just concentrate on thinking and, indeed, you may be more comfortable staying in your head when you get stirred up during a situation that calls for your leadership. Certainly it's good to think, but recognizing what's going on inside of the rest of you is also important. You don't always have to show what you are feeling. At times it is unwise to share your emotional reaction, though sometimes it helps a difficult situation if you do. Some people are so used to hiding feelings that they don't read the body clues that could tell them they are in the grip of emotion. Those people need to notice that their teeth are clenched or that there is a strange sensation in their chest. Staying in one's head and denying feelings can get in the way of clear thinking. Denying feelings can also affect relationships with others. Good relationships are part of effective leadership.

What about clarity? That was also a piece of question 1. Are you often indecisive? Clarity is an important part of leadership. Using social-emotional competence, not merely intellectual intelligence, can make a difference in decisions. Did you get any insights or gut feelings as you were reading this? How can you improve your abilities to know what you want and what you don't want if that's what you need to do? What else came to your mind as you answered question 1? Question 1 leads to question 2.

Showing What You Care About

Two-year-olds can show what—and especially whom—they care about through facial expressions, body language, and behaviors. They can effectively show love and affection long before they can use words.

Maybe you can do that too, but in my experience some adults use only words and miss the rest—the facial expressions, body language, and behaviors. I'm struck by how often some adults use affectionate statements as motivating devices—words without any real feelings. "I love you" is an example of three words that can be said without any emotional content. Some repeat those words so often that it leaves me to wonder if they are trying to make up for something they feel guilty about.

Effective leaders show their caring in more ways than just words. Those leaders who can sincerely show others that they care are aware of the difference between using motivating words and other devices to manipulate others into doing what they want. We've all been exposed to behaviorist approaches of using various rewards for good behavior. You can be wise about using those approaches in your leadership role.

Think for a minute about culturally diverse ways of expressing caring. You may be quite aware that in the predominant United States culture, putting love into words is not only acceptable but is also desirable. Gushing praise is another example of expressing caring. Of course, you're supposed to really mean it when you say, "You're really great!" or "I love you." The practice of verbalizing caring contrasts with other cultures in which praise is seldom used and love is not put into words. A Japanese American friend, who was born and raised in the United States, tells me her mother never says she loves her. When she complains to her mother, the reply is something like, "My behavior shows you my love for you. I raised you. I was there for you. Why do you need words?" There is an old saying, "Actions speak louder than words." This mother showed her love in action, not words. The same issue comes up between a husband and wife in a cross-cultural marriage. The wife complains, "You never tell me you love me." Her husband's response is that words are nothing, behaviors are what count—behaviors like remaining faithful, being there, providing for needs when appropriate. All are examples of loving behaviors, says the husband.

Saying No

No is a word most two-year-olds say quite often. They can say it loud and clear with words, body language, facial expressions, and behaviors. They don't usually give mixed messages.

Can you say no as clearly as a two-year-old can? How easy or hard is it for you to say no to someone or something? When is it hard to say no? Does it depend on the circumstances or to whom you are saying it? Do you sometimes say yes when you really mean no? If so, is that a problem for you—or for other people? It's quite possible that if you have a problem saying no, your difficulties may be an effect of your upbringing. Perhaps your hesitancy to say no comes from the cultural community you were raised in. Did you consider the effects your upbringing may still have on you? Perhaps you were taught never to say no, especially to someone you were supposed to respect. What is emotionally competent in one culture is not necessarily competent in another.

In cross-cultural situations, cultural differences can get in the way of communication. It may work very well to say yes when you mean no when communicating with someone of the same cultural group. On the other hand, it may be difficult for people to understand that your polite and respectful yes is not really what you mean. Or if you are a person who says no and means it, in cross-cultural situations the person you say no to may be greatly offended. In other words, what is emotionally competent and the related appropriate behavior may not work in cross-cultural situations. How well have you figured that out? Leadership skills in ECE usually depend on working across cultures, at least sometimes.

Having Confidence in Your Abilities

Two-year-olds can show confidence in their abilities by insisting on doing things without help. They may fail to accomplish what they intend, but it's likely that they will keep on trying. See the box "Assisting Youngsters When They Need It."

How did you respond to question number 4: What are your abilities, and how confident are you in those abilities? Put another way, what are your strong points, and how confident are you in your strengths? Certainly if you know much about self-esteem, that term probably came up as you were thinking of your answers. Realize, however, that self-esteem is a cultural concept. Depending on your cultural background, that may or may not be a concept that makes sense to you or to the people you work with. And even if self-esteem is a useful concept, it is important to recognize that only a realistic appraisal of one's abilities counts toward self-esteem.

Assisting Youngsters When They Need It

When examining two-year-olds' confidence levels, I don't mean to imply that two-year-olds are mature in their social-emotional competence and related behaviors. It is important to point out that two-year-olds cannot necessarily make good decisions about what is physically safe and what is not. Of course, they need adult guidance and often adult protection. An incident from my own past illustrates this point. My father used to tell a story with great glee about a time when I was little and he taught me a lesson about my capabilities. The story goes like this: My father was helping me climb out of the car when I said in a firm voice, "Janet do it" and pushed his hand aside. His reaction was to step back out of my way. I wasn't yet able to climb out on my own, so I fell and got hurt. He liked to say that I landed on my nose. And then he'd laugh. He seemed to think that was a good lesson for his know-it-all daughter to learn that she wasn't as capable as she thought she was. I wonder how much that lesson stuck with me to this day. I'm sure the outcome would have been different if he had given me just a bit of help. Obviously one can't judge—one can only speculate about—the effects of one incident from earlier years; however, not all adults have the confidence in their abilities that most toddlers have even when they reject help. The point is to let them try things but keep them from getting hurt.

Certainly, knowing what you can do and do well are important leadership qualities. Working on what you don't know how to do is another one. Improving on what you don't do well is yet another one. I have learned a lot from my children over the years. Here's another story about confidence in a young child.

My young son, Adam, and I were shopping—this was a long time ago—in the days before I owned a computer or had ever even touched one. Adam and I noticed a crowd gathered in one area intently watching something. We went to the edge, and he wiggled his way to the front so he could see better. Watching from the back, I could just make out a man sitting at a computer. I couldn't see what he was doing, but the crowd was interested. In a short while, the man got up and left. The crowd started to disperse. I went up to get Adam, but before I reached him, he climbed on the chair and started playing with the computer keys. I was surprised. How did he think he could operate a computer? I certainly didn't have his confidence, especially with lots of people who had turned back and were now watching what he was doing. When words came on the screen that said, "What's your name?" I was surprised when instead of his name he typed in "Jerk." "Okay, Jerk," the screen responded. "This is a cooking lesson. What do you want to make?" Adam, aka Jerk, watched a whole list of dishes appear on the screen. The crowd laughed. He clicked on "Chicken Cacciatore." I doubt he knew what that was, but it didn't stop him from clicking on the next screen, which said, "Okay, Jerk, how many people are you going to feed?" The crowd laughed harder. Adam typed a 1 followed by lots and lots of 0s. I don't remember how many, but I do remember that it didn't faze the computer. Immediately the directions came on the screen and went something like this: "Take 1,000 chickens, cut up, rub with 16 gallons of olive oil and 1,500 cloves of garlic. . . ." By now there was a huge crowd around laughing their heads off. They kept on laughing as Adam continued getting the recipe and directions. When he finished, he got up from the chair and came to me smiling. I couldn't help but feel proud of his confidence in that situation. He was just a kid, but he was not afraid to try something new, even with an audience. He's still like that today as a grown man!

Cultural Influences

Often toddlers keep trying in the face of failure. Not all adults have the willingness to do that. Do you? Try, try, and try again is a motto that can help us become successful. Some adults take failure hard and give up at the first sign of it. Some may be so afraid of failure they never try anything new. That's not typical toddler behavior. And, of course, whether a child tries at all can depend on the culture. Here we go again!

Let's look at confidence in abilities from two contrasting cultural perspectives. When independence is a family goal, two-year-olds are encouraged to try things on their own. "You did it all by yourself!" is a typical adult response from families with goals of independence. These children usually fit well into many early care and education programs where adults were either raised to believe in stressing independence or were trained to promote it. On the other hand, in some cultural communities parents teach their children that it's more important to let others help you than to help yourself. It makes the other person feel good. Showing dependence is an emotionally competent behavior, and it pleases adults when children allow themselves to be helped. That lesson goes along with another one that can be stated thus: "Help others before you help yourself." In these cultural groups, dependence that grows into interdependence is the outcome. It's taught through modeling in the early years. In cultural communities where interdependence is a priority, even two-year-olds can learn to put aside their independent urges so they too are emotionally competent in line with the cultural goals of their families.

Recognizing Your Protective Instincts

Certainly two-year-olds have protective instincts, though the behaviors that go with them may need some adult intervention. Self-regulation, the important skill that helps us handle our feelings, is likely not strong enough in toddlers for them to contain their behaviors when they feel threatened. Instead of talking, they have the impulse to lash out or sink their teeth into human flesh. They need to learn alternative defensive responses and problem-solving skills from adults. Then their protective instincts will be accompanied by prosocial behaviors that become an aspect of emotional competence. These skills don't just come naturally; they need close adult supervision and intervention. An important job of adults living or working with two-year-olds is to stop aggression and teach nonviolent problem solving to youngsters faced with choosing a response related to protective instincts. That's emotionally competent. See the box "Avoiding Meeting Aggression with Aggression."

Did question 5 throw you? How well do you recognize your protective instincts, and how do you handle them? Protective instincts aren't usually a part of professional development and leadership training. What do you think *protective instincts* means, and how did you answer this question? Did you learn something about yourself?

Avoiding Meeting Aggression with Aggression

One way to handle aggression in two-year-olds is to help them see the perspective of another person. That's a good skill for adults in leadership roles to acquire as well. Adults teach that when they model something, when they put into words what they perceive as the child's perspective. This can start at birth. Three of my teachers, Magda Gerber, Dr. Emmi Pikler, and Anna Tardos (Pikler's daughter) taught me to talk to babies this way: "Yes, I see how upset you are." They also taught me to focus on a baby's needs, and when I couldn't figure out what the need was, to put into words the question, "What is it you need?" It may seem strange to ask a baby who can't talk, "What do you need?" I wondered about that until I tried it. I was surprised to discover that sometimes when you ask the question, the answer can come. All this can happen long before the child has learned to talk. All this also applies to adults. Avoid meeting aggression with aggression. And you can even use that same strategy with adults: ask them what they need from you when you find yourself in a confrontation. It changes the whole tone of an argument or serious discussion.

Leadership, Communication, and Problem Solving

So how does all this relate to leadership? It has to do with communication and taking a problem-solving approach when feeling threatened. It starts with recognizing defensive feelings for what they are and making a clear decision to change the response to a nondefensive one. That's not easy to do.

They say what we teach is what we need most to learn. That may not be true of everybody, but it's definitely true of me. Perhaps that's why I have put myself in cross-cultural situations most of my adult life. Communication is a subject I not only teach but also study. I'm still a student and don't have all the answers or skills, but I continue to work on both. I'm continuing to work on communicating across differences in nondefensive ways. Several authors have helped me greatly when I've read and reread their books. One is Marshall B. Rosenberg, who wrote *Nonviolent Communication: A Language of Life*. After I read that, I got his book *Living Nonviolent Communication: Practical Tools to Connect and Communicate Skillfully in Every Situation*. Another book that made a great impression on me when I first read it years ago is called *Don't Be So Defensive!* by Sharon Ellison. The latest edition of that book is now called *Taking the War Out of Our Words: The Art of Powerful Non-Defensive*

Communication. I learned a lot over the years about how to communicate with children. I had good teachers. The way I learned to communicate with adults is a different story. I followed the models I grew up with, and none of them were particularly nondefensive communicators. These two authors, Rosenberg and Ellison, helped me improve my communication skills. I really like the idea that moving from defensiveness to nondefensiveness in communication is a path to peace.

I wish all adults who feel protective instincts would have the skills to use nonviolent approaches to solving problems. I'm thinking about what Magda Gerber used to say. She was clear that adults often treat aggression in toddlers with even more aggression than the child displayed. Of course, the classic example is, "I'll teach you not to hit!" *Slap, slap, slap!* Taking a diverse perspective, when adults have strong nonviolent views and behaviors that go with them, biting becomes rare behavior in two-year-olds. Those adults usually belong to cultural communities or groups with either a long and peaceful history or child-rearing practices that support, model, and promote peaceful approaches to problem solving.

Communication skills are vital for professionals in ECE. We need to be able to communicate with all kinds of people, both little ones and big ones. We especially need to be able to communicate effectively with people who are different from us, such as when we cross cultures. Communication and emotional competence are vitally related. As we increase our skills, we become better and better models of good, clear, nonviolent, and effective communication. These skills not only help us engage positively with other adults and with children, but they also allow us to be models of nonviolent communication. How are children to learn these ways of communicating if they aren't demonstrated?

Are you as smart as a two-year-old? Are you smarter than a two-year-old? Obviously you are a lot smarter in many ways. It isn't really a contest. You are not only an adult, but you are also reading about leadership skills. Hopefully this chapter will help you see yourself in a new light. I hope it also helps you see where you can improve your skills in emotional competence.

Debra Ren-Etta Sullivan

My Answers to the Quiz

My response to this chapter was to take Janet's quiz. Every person's experiences and answers will be different, and it can be valuable to learn from each other. Following is what I came up with.

Knowing What You Want and What You Don't Want

I try to be very clear about what I want and what I don't want. I also try to be clear when I don't know what I want or don't want or when I want time to consider the options, choices, and perspectives. Sometimes this is appreciated and sometimes I'm told I'm too direct and need to soften my responses. I find this intriguing because my culture has taught me to be direct and clear, but that doesn't always work well in other cultural contexts.

In the workplace as a supervisor, I try to be clear about what I expect and what I want. My staff is never caught off guard about what I want. If there are areas where they excel, I let them know and encourage them to keep on doing what they are doing. If there are areas that need improvement, I let them know that as well and offer strategies and support for growth. Yes, sometimes I face resistance:

> *Me:* Please learn how to use this new database software.
> *Them:* I don't like the new database software.
> *Me:* You don't need to like it, but you do need to learn how to use it.

Being clear about what I don't want is equally important to me. I sometimes find that if you aren't clear about what you don't want, there are those who will "nice" you into a corner. They will assume that you are too nice to say you don't like what they are doing and will use this as a way to continue unacceptable behavior. After all, you didn't say you didn't like it. This is where I'm often asked to soften my response. What does that mean—make my response a little vaguer? Young children are clear: "I don't want that. I don't like that." Often they may not even understand vagueness. My younger son loved to play Duck, Duck, Goose in preschool and played even when it wasn't time to play. Whenever he got up to do something, he'd tap the head of every child he passed. His teacher said, "I'm not sure the other children appreciate it when you do that." This response went right over my son's three-year-old head, and he kept tapping his friends' heads as he went about the day. His teacher asked me what she should do, so I told her to just tell him—in a supportive and caring tone—"Duck, Duck, Goose is over, and we'll play again tomorrow. Please stop." He stopped.

Of course, being clear about what you want and what you don't want doesn't mean you'll get your way. I can guarantee you I don't. I do find, however, that clarity makes it harder for people to misunderstand you—unintentionally or intentionally. And I do have to pay attention to how culturally appropriate my directness is in any given situation. I am careful not to be rude or offensive, but I'm equally careful not to find myself constantly in a place of having someone misunderstand what I want and what I don't want.

Showing What You Care About

I have a really hard time *not* showing what I care about! When I'm mad, I'm mad. When I'm happy, I'm happy. When I'm hurt, I'm hurt. When I'm excited, I'm excited. I think the trickier thing for me is what to do when I don't like someone or don't trust someone. There is a difference if it's a personal relationship or a professional one. In a personal relationship, I will work harder to make the relationship continue to function. I give at least two chances depending on the circumstances. You want to trust your little brother again after he took money out of your piggy bank because he's your brother and you want the relationship to continue. At work, however, I try to separate how I feel about someone from the task we have to accomplish together. I am not being paid to like you or trust you (I tell myself), but I am being paid to accomplish a task. I can show that I care about the task and the work I am asked to do. Of course, this means I have to care about my work and what I'm trying to accomplish, but I try hard not to apply for work that I don't care about.

Another part of Janet's question is about using words that don't match how you really feel. She gives the example of saying "I love you" without emotional content. I find that another phrase treated in this way is "I'm sorry." People often say I'm sorry when they don't really mean it, and unfortunately, grown-ups teach children to do the same thing. We tell children to say they are sorry when they engage in inappropriate behavior such as hitting. Children often say they are sorry because we tell them to say it, not because that is how they feel. Sometimes the only thing they may be sorry for is getting caught. Actions do quite often speak louder than words. I tell my children that I will know they are truly sorry if they never repeat the behavior they just apologized for. That's what tells me how they really feel.

Saying No

It can be easy or hard for me to say no; it depends so much on the circumstances for me. The big areas (for example, physical harm, discrimination, social justice, theft, murder, mayhem) are easy: The answer is no! However, if someone asks me about an exciting project (like writing a book with three people I love, admire, and respect) or an important cause (like advocating on behalf of children of color, children from low-income communities, and children learning English) then my answer will likely be yes! This is true even if I know I may not have the time at the moment. This is where I ignore my feelings of panic and uncertainty about my ability to be effective. And there are a handful of people (just a handful, and they are all my elders) whom I have a hard time saying no to, and I'll say yes because I don't want to disappoint. Of course, this is crazy because I'm saying yes so I don't disappoint, but I'm feeling no because I don't think I'll be able to deliver excellence. In this case, I am most definitely giving a mixed message. The good thing is that my face usually tells the messenger exactly what I'm really feeling, but this is where I find myself in a dilemma.

Having Confidence in Your Abilities

For the most part, it is culturally appropriate in the United States for me to tell you what I'm good at, and I feel fairly confident that I can do just about anything I set my mind to doing. Whether I can do it well is another story. I love physics, and I always tell people that I could be a physicist if I wanted to. I wouldn't be a very good one, but I could be one nonetheless. I try to spend the bulk of my time doing what I'm really good at. There are, however, times when I have to do things I'm not so good at. This can often happen at work when I have responsibilities that are not my strengths. I will work hard to do the very best that I can, but I try not to pretend that I'm really good at something when I'm not. It can also happen at times when I am called to do something important or difficult and it's my time to step up to the plate, as they say. I am not the parent who will strap my child on my back and hike ten miles into the woods to the lake for a unique camping experience. I am, however, the parent who will strap my child on my back and hike ten miles out of the woods in an emergency.

Recognizing Your Protective Instincts

I had to work hard to understand and manage my protective instincts as a youngster. It took me awhile to recognize my strong feelings about injustice and social justice, which for two-year-olds translates into what is fair and what is not. As a very young child, I could never understand why I had to eat my peas and my father did not. I was told that peas are good for you, but no one could tell me at what age that was no longer true since it was clear that my father did not have to eat *his* peas. This was unfair! I would become upset and angry about things that I thought were unfair or unkind, and I was willing to get in trouble for anything that really mattered to me. If I thought something was wrong, I would be mad and march in to fix it.

Learning to manage these emotions was difficult for me because my father felt it was important for children to suppress emotion and my mother felt it was important for children to deny emotions. They both had strong feelings about civil rights and injustices but did not see a connection between that and what a child might be experiencing at home. Civil rights, injustices, and fairness were about things like voting and grown-ups, not peas and children. I had to learn how to manage my feelings to adjust my actions to the perpetrators at hand. I had to learn to distinguish between voting and peas and manage my feelings accordingly. I learned to be more aggressive about voting and less aggressive about peas.

So am I as smart as a two-year-old? Maybe. Let's review my quiz responses again:

- In terms of knowing what I want and what I don't want, I sometimes really do feel pressured to soften my response and be subtler than I want to be. Two-year-olds aren't subtle.

- When it comes to showing what I care about—yes! yes! yes! I cannot help but show what I care about. I can, however, hold what I care about in high priority while paying attention to what others are doing or saying. This helps me point out when others' words and actions don't match.

- On saying no, it depends. Two-year-olds are much more likely to say no without concern for the consequences, but they eventually learn about consequences. I have decades of consequences to draw on.

- Two-year-olds don't know that they *don't* have abilities. They've just discovered confidence, and they feel strong, strong, strong. Life will tell them what their true abilities are, which may give me an edge in the "smart" department.

- Regarding protective instincts, two-year-olds have them, but I have more words and confidence to voice them. Two-year-olds focus on the peas. With over fifty years of experience, I've learned to choose my battles.

Luis Antonio Hernandez

My Answers to the Quiz

Are you smarter than a two-year-old? Our friend Janet truly knows how to push our thinking and feelings, going back to an age and stage that I don't supposedly remember. Janet's questions make me want to linger on the question, how much have I evolved since I was two years old? If my parents were still around, I could get a few funny anecdotes about my behaviors, habits, and temperament. Certainly the physical has changed and the emotional and social life has continued on its course of discovery and learning. It's safe to assume that much of those early experiences now reside deep in the wiring of my brain or in some undiscovered genetic segment. Who knows? Maybe all our moments in life become part of a human genetic file that preserves all the many phases of one's life. And perhaps we are better off not going too deep into the precise circumstances of ourselves as two-year-olds. Although we are not here to compete with a smarter former two-year-old in the body of an adult, our aim is healthy social and emotional competency now and for today's two-year-olds!

For this chapter, I will also take Debra's challenge to address Janet's questions. Perhaps we will have some common experiences or show individual uniqueness in our routes through life. And following her spirit for this conversation, I'm always interested to learn about and from each other. Here we go!

Knowing What You Want and What You Don't Want

In one of my presentations on leadership, I used criteria culled from a number of CEOs of major firms in the United States: be open in your communication, be focused in your attentiveness and delivery, and project clarity to minimize confusion. These particular criteria resonate for me in my professional and personal life. I'd like to share a story about a supervisor I admire for her skills and competency in early childhood—a truly brilliant mind and spirit. However, when she sends a memo or an e-mail—which are usually about five pages long—I have to scavenge the pages for the heart of her very important message. After years of this, I've learned to skip to the last paragraph and the last sentence to get her point. Finally, I've arrived at her main point! Clarity is not one of her strong points.

Which brings me to the question, what can I learn from this particular harmless situation? Am I clear when I'm with coworkers and colleagues? Do participants in my training sessions get the main concepts? In my personal life, do family and friends understand where I am coming from? Do I beat around the bush? Do I sugarcoat situations? Am I unclear at times to avoid conflict or insecurities?

Although my intention—in my own mind—is to be clear, the message can be opaque and muddy. There are times when I can feel my mouth moving and hear my words, and then my brain says, "That's not what I'm feeling or thinking or even experiencing." Unless we master the power of body language and facial expression, our nonverbal cues tell the bigger story if we are not clear, honest, and open to our real thoughts and feelings. From a leadership perspective, we need to be clear in communicating across languages by basing those words on convictions, principles, honesty, and doses of common sense.

Showing What You Care About

Back to the image of a two-year-old, we show we care with degrees and variations of jumping up and down. Heck, even Tom Cruise jumped up and down on Oprah's sofa to show how much he cared for his then girlfriend—and somehow many people read a level of insincerity in his actions. We show we care with our individual sense of excitement, joy, and passion. We become totally focused and evangelical about the things that matter deeply to us. We see it in people who become political zealots, extreme vegetarians, sports maniacs, butterfly collectors, coupon hoarders, and so on. Of course, these are examples of taking a passion to an extreme. I met a wonderful preschool teacher who, from the moment I met her, I knew cared about NASCAR racing. Her jacket had car logos, her fingernails had the numbers of particular race cars, and she confided that she even had a NASCAR tattoo somewhere on her body. Wow, she truly cared about car racing! And she was still passionate about our common work—advocating for children and families, working to impact public policy, and guaranteeing the rights of poor children. Passion drives individuals to be focused on what they care about.

While some of us are not at that extreme level, we do show that we care in individual ways. Maybe we keep up with new research and articles about ECE, organize a book drive, contact local businesses for donations toward a new playground, or help a neighbor make choices in selecting a center for her toddler. To work in this field, we must care with a degree of passion. Otherwise, it is time to make other work choices.

Saying No

By far this is the hardest question—how, when, and why to say no. We hate to offend anyone, don't want to be rude, want everyone to like us, and want to preserve our skin. Getting to *no* is a developmental process regardless of age; it is a behavior learned and practiced. And the counter practice is to emphasize a behavior culturally and socially acceptable—to say yes because it is the nicer thing to say and do. For the child who says no, do we inhibit her sense of control by stressing being nice? And is this why many adults have a hard time saying no? Is it the result of conditioning and acculturation shaping a person into someone who can get along?

The use and power of *no* became crystal clear in a casual conversation. Sometimes it takes someone from outside our culture to point out perplexing situations. My friend Claudia is from France and, as many French people do, she exudes a certain continental confidence. With her seductive and charming French accent, she once purred: "Louie, you know the difference between the French and the Americans?" Of course, I wanted to know the source of such cultural differences, and she seemed to possess answers to every world problem. She continued, "In America, when a friend asks, 'Can you pick me up at the airport? I will be arriving at two o'clock in the morning,' as good Americans you immediately get wishy-washy indigestion just thinking, 'That is an insane hour! I guess I better go. I really don't want to but . . .' So, you go back and forth because you cannot make up your mind, and uncertainty and guilt take over your life." Then Claudia said, "If you ask a French person to pick you up at two o'clock in the morning at the airport, they will say, 'No, take a taxi to your hotel, and I'll see you in the morning for coffee.'" Instantly, the lesson for me was one of liberation. The word *no* can free us from extra head work, eliminating unpleasant consequences and leading to a strong decision.

No provides clarity and resolution to circumstances that can seem to linger forever. Regardless of who the person is, the age of the person, or the status of the person, saying no is a singular act of self-control and determination. It may not be the nicest approach, but it provides limitations and boundaries that make the individual grow a backbone. And for leaders, it is essential to know when and how to say no as a prosocial behavior that is effective and compassionate. Not an easy task, but one full of clarity and honesty.

Having Confidence in Your Abilities

Janet's comments about the life of a two-year-old versus the life of an adult—without direct contrast or parallel analysis—touch on the concepts of being *open* and being *closed*. And, in a sense, I see that the confidence to do, to be, to experiment, and to explore relies on being open to the opportunities and possibilities inherent in the process. In being willing to try it out, a child can begin to stack some blocks—the step by step is the learning process, at times frustrating and at many times joyful. Or an adult can experiment with a new recipe—creating sauces, adding spices, tasting—sometimes resulting in a delicious dish or a "never again." Learning from missteps, mistakes, and tryouts all lead to confidence building. Being open to a range of possibilities can result in a can-do attitude. All of this is compared with the closed option in which discovery is slighted, disregarded, made fun of, stigmatized, or worse, not praised or encouraged.

Recognizing Your Protective Instincts

Slowly, I've learned that my shield of self-protection has a big smiley face on it. Humor is my defense mechanism that can squeeze me out of uncomfortable and uneasy situations. If challenged, what better way to get out of that sweaty situation than to make an outrageous remark, tell an amusing tale, or make a funny face before sneaking away. "That was close! Humor got me out of that one more time." I know that I'm not the type to strike back, become passive, or fake agreement. Humor, then, is my escape route in moments when I need to protect myself. By its nature, the protective shield conceals the real self—for behind it lie insecurities, doubts, and fears. In developing emotional competence, one needs to continually reexamine the baggage of behaviors one carries from that long-ago two-year-old stage. For me, humor is the escape mechanism that holds back elements of confidence, one being "I know what I want and know what I don't want," to quote one of Debra's remarks. It takes work to liberate the emotional grasp of low confidence, but practice makes it better: "No, I don't want to do that," "Thanks, but that is not something I want to be part of," and "I do not find that funny at all." So let's use humor with a heart of confidence and create joy without shields.

Time and experiences have propelled me along, so perhaps I'm somewhat smarter than a two-year-old at this point. But from the shore of life, we can sense the richness of those early years as waves of emotional intelligence coming up from the deep ocean of the self.

Holly Elissa Bruno

My Answers to the Quiz

I grow wistful when I hear Satchmo, aka Louis Armstrong, croon "What a Wonderful World." I can hear his hopeful lyrics now and his acknowledgment that children will learn more than we'll ever know.

Our two-year-olds will witness discoveries, inventions, breakthroughs, and shifts in thinking we cannot envision. May our children know a world free of cancer, Alzheimer's, racism, and even war. In that regard, tomorrow's generation will always be smarter than today's generation. As knowledge grows, so will human beings, if we stay open to learning. So, sure, two-year-olds are going to be a whole lot smarter than I am. Or at least they will have the opportunity to be a whole lot smarter if they choose to be.

But Janet's question, "Are you smarter than a two-year-old?" isn't about tomorrow, it's about today. Hmm. Let me think about that. I don't like comparisons that result in superiority and inferiority because someone gets diminished. I hate it when anyone is labeled stupid. Questions like "Are you smarter than a two-year old?" may be profitable for game show hosts. But who else benefits from being rated?

I prefer Howard Gardner's question, "How are you intelligent?" rather than, "How intelligent are you?" If anyone had asked my son Nick, "In what ways are you intelligent?" he might have displayed his encyclopedic knowledge of comic book characters: their history, motivations, life challenges, and ability to enter into or maintain lasting relationships. Even after reading Marvel Comics' compendium of characters, I had trouble keeping the Justice League straight. Fortunately, Nick was patient with me.

However, Nick wasn't asked about his passions for learning. Instead, he was tested to see whether he met academic markers, markers that made no sense to Nick. After years of support and tutoring, my Nick dropped out of high school. We live in a state where as a special needs student he wouldn't have received a full-fledged diploma even if he had graduated. Nick would have been handed a certificate. Nick is tired of being second class. When he's ready, Nick will stun the world with his knowledge. Or maybe it's the world that has to be readier.

So, no, I don't like comparisons when it comes to intelligence. I don't like that IQ is the only standard by which children are evaluated for intelligence. Eighty percent of life success is due to forces other than IQ, those grouped as emotional intelligence or EQ (Goleman 1995). IQ prepares us for academic tests. EQ prepares us for the tests of life. As Daniel Goleman (2005, 34) explains, "People with high IQs can be stunningly poor pilots of their private lives." He goes on to say, "In the day-to-day world, no intelligence is more important than the interpersonal" (42). For me, neither IQ nor EQ should define intelligence. We can, after all, be brilliant without being wise.

"Identify with, don't compare" yourself to others is a twelve-step adage. Don't bother taking someone else's inventory. Instead, we can focus on how to improve and address our own shortcomings. Accepting others makes life a lot easier compared with wasting time judging others. So who knows if I am smarter than anyone else? As Rhett Butler proclaims in *Gone with the Wind*, "Frankly, my dear, I don't give a damn." With these distinctions about intelligence honored, I feel freer to respond to Janet's questions.

Knowing What You Want and What You Don't Want

I know what I want and don't want. I want to do all I can so that each person is free to find her path to happiness and fulfillment. The pursuit of happiness is an inalienable right to me. I put up my dukes when anyone asserts you or I don't deserve that right. Anyone who crosses me on this is in for a fight.

Showing What You Care About

I show what I care about by telling you what matters to me. I go after what matters to me. I fight for what matters to me. I cannot hide what matters to me and wouldn't want to.

Saying No

My no to someone else is a yes to me. "No, I will not take on that added responsibility" is the same as "Yes, I will honor my boundaries and the commitments I have made." Why is this easy or hard? Resentments kill. I don't want to resent myself or another person because I allowed myself to get suckered into something I knew was wrong. I would rather live with the momentary guilt of disappointing another person than the wreckage of resentment.

Does it matter who that someone is? Are you kidding? Absolutely! Saying no to the people I love the most is like chopping off my arm. I have a huge blind spot about this. I will do just about anything people in my inner circle ask of me, unless that something is harmful to another person or myself. I am deliberately learning to monitor this. I have made a number of mistakes by blindly trusting that inner circle instead of stepping back and questioning. I am, however, excellent at not enabling addictions or other destructive behaviors, subtle and blatant.

Having Confidence in Your Abilities

As an abuse survivor, I have had to find courage, strength, and talent within myself. Because I was told I was worthless, I had to discover and steadfastly develop strengths I could count on. When child development specialists remind me that a child must have a loving relationship early on, I shiver. I joke I could have become a criminal or an addict, given that dearth in my life. No doubt I have to work terribly hard on trust. I almost never believe in anyone's authority over me: don't fence me in! The deep loneliness and humiliation I felt as a child have given me equally deep acceptance and appreciation of everyone's struggles for confidence, regardless of outer appearances.

For these strengths, I am grateful: optimism, humor, outspokenness, wonder, originality, courage, openness, and boundless curiosity. As I say to my children, I am grateful for all of it. Without those struggles, I wouldn't be the character I am. I believe we are given no more than we can handle, even though we might not think we have the strength. That strength is within. Today I am confident that I am a worthy and lovable human being, intelligent in my own way, and able to offer something valuable to others.

Recognizing Your Protective Instincts

In a heartbeat, I become a lioness for my children. Disrespect either of them, and I pounce. Or so I did early on. Over the years, I have tempered my actions. I still feel protective of their dignity; however, I trust them to fight their own battles.

I am also protective of my dignity. Very protective. My protective voice rises from a deep place of inner justice. Show disdain for others or for me and

I will hold you accountable. Right now. Did I mention I am Sicilian? Thank God, I temper my temper with an ample ability and desire to laugh at myself.

Addressing the Difficult Questions

Hey, Janet, here's another question: What do I want most to learn?

I want to keep learning how to love and be loved, how to replace fear with trust, and how to make any new Apple technology my BFF.

Summary..

Janet Gonzalez-Mena

As an early childhood professional, I do not embrace competition! The title of this chapter came from a game show that focused on IQ and related to facts, so the title is misleading. If you have read this far, you know this chapter isn't about cognitive skills but instead focuses on social-emotional ones—those skills that often have more to do with satisfactory educational and life outcomes than with intellect. Notice that the other authors wrote about themselves in ways that helped you think about their abilities in professional leadership situations.

You may also notice that I didn't take the quiz myself. As I read the three sets of responses, I thought about how different I am from my coauthors. First of all, I see a lot of benefits as an infant-toddler professional of being a follower of a baby instead of a leader or teacher. I also discovered as a preschool teacher how many benefits there are in becoming part of each young child's world. Maybe that's why I seldom think of myself as a leader and tend to step into the shadows when offered leadership roles.

Another way I'm different is that I am older than my coauthors, which means I spent my childhood in a different era. My first memories are the leftover effects of the Depression period, and I have strong memories of World War II. The women in my life didn't say no or put forth what they really cared about. I'm not even sure they had protective instincts; they tended to depend on men for protection and for almost everything else. Most saw themselves as inferior to men, and even though women—including my own grandmother—went to work in factories during World War II, when the war was over, they went back to being housewives if they could. It wasn't until I started writing this that I realized the significance of my huge life goal related to changing the lives of others around issues of equity and social justice. I've been looking outward all these years at inequities and haven't spent much time looking inward to see my own internalized oppression as a woman. Writing is therapeutic!

So my message to you, the reader, is to read this chapter with yourself in mind. Rather than comparing yourself to a two-year-old, think in terms of your own social-emotional skills. The information about two-year-olds came about because I'm an advocate for looking at two-year-olds in a positive light. I have always been trying to promote the idea of the terrific twos rather than the terrible twos.

Discussion Questions ....

1. What are your ideas, experiences, and skills as far as being a leader in the ECE profession?

2. How do your own social-emotional skills relate to those of two-year-olds as explained in this chapter?

3. Which of the four authors' explanations of their leadership skills do you identify most closely with?

References ....

Goleman, David. 1995. *Emotional Intelligence: Why It Can Matter More Than IQ.* New York: Bantam Books.
———. 2005. *Emotional Intelligence: Why It Can Matter More Than IQ.* 10th anniversary ed. New York: Bantam Dell.

10

The Great Imposter

Unmasking the Burden of Self-Doubt in Our Professional Lives

Luis Antonio Hernandez

Most teachers and professionals in early childhood are competent people who sometimes have moments of doubts about their skills and capabilities. Now may be the time to discuss this dark shadow that impacts our work in subtle yet negative ways. In this chapter, we provide an overview of the roots of these doubts and accept, affirm, and take action on certain personal and professional weaknesses, whether we recognize them or not. On the positive side, leaders in education are always working on self-improvement and learning—the lifelong learner—as an integral part of a professional development process. It is reassuring to have a consistent focus on strengths, to claim credit for small and big success stories, to recognize tasks that are accomplished, and to reflect on positive engagement and relationships.

Maybe it all started for me with the lyrics to "The Great Pretender" by the oldie but goodie Platters playing in my head. The catchy tune by the Platters plays in many of our heads when we feel like a pretender or imposter. The lyrics and tune play, teasing us with nostalgia as well as a reminder of insecurities of who we are not, loneliness, and the façade of strengths. If it's just a song, why does it resonate so much?

Whatever the label—imposter or pretender—it describes the self-doubt many leaders in every field experience. Even for high achievers, it is a nagging feeling that you don't really belong, that you don't fully know what

165

you're doing, that you are not good enough for the responsibilities ahead. And that you are fooling many people around you into believing that you are more competent or talented than you really are. This uncomfortable feeling hits leaders across the spectrum. For those in early childhood education, it is a particularly heavy load to carry because we question professional choices, are angered by low wages, and bristle at the lack of respect for our meaningful work.

Part of this guilt is based in the fear that others will discover our professional limitations or that a perceived weaknesses will translate into overall incompetence. Self-doubt becomes a burden of insecurity that can hamper individuals daily and over the long run. In reality, developing leadership skills requires that we make mistakes and learn from them. But those in the bind of being perceived as an imposter tend to be poor judges of their own performances and often tend to minimize their abilities.

Let's take some time to reflect on some of these concepts:

- Does the topic of self-doubt interest you? Why or why not?

- Are there gender differences between men and women in having a sense that they are not as capable as others may think? If so, what are the differences and why do you think they exist?

- When it comes to age or generational differences, are older or younger people more confident in their professional abilities?

- What cultural or class-based factors can either raise or minimize a person's sense of self-doubt at work?

My informal conversations with friends and colleagues in leadership positions in early childhood education have pointed to frequent cases of imposter feelings. One colleague told me how she was named director at her center when the current director suddenly quit. She was told, "You are a great teacher; you can also be a great director." She took the full responsibility in body, mind, and heart. Still, she knew perfectly well that she had no idea about how to manage an organization, positively supervise a large team, or deal with clogged toilets. She recalled how she cheerfully pushed on, feeling that at any time she would be called out for her lack of expertise. She survived and continued for the next ten years, always in fear of being discovered. Another friend, with advanced academic degrees and years of experience in the area of public policy and advocacy for children and families, always had a nagging fear at the bottom of her heart. She feared that as a single person with no children, her credentials and body of work would be questioned.

Such stories are common in just about every field, and for leaders in ECE these self-doubts can be hard on our confidence and well-being. These questions whirl in our minds: How did I get here? Am I competent in this position? Do I have the necessary expertise and skills? Will I be taken seriously? Why do people think I'm an expert? In other words, can you sing the blues if you don't have the blues?

A case in point for me is my self-doubt in a number of professional areas. Although I believe I have a fairly good command of the English language, I recognize it is not my native home language. Still, the occasional comments, such as "You seem to have an accent," "I love the way you talk," or "Did you really write this?" make me wonder. Is it my hybrid idiom of Cuban Spanish, Bronx English, the occasional Southern tones, and Broadway show references that makes my persona more interesting? And most importantly, does it take away from my professional work? Are listeners trying to figure out where I'm from, or are they truly listening to whatever words of wisdom I'm rambling on about?

Another big professional insecurity is my lack of a doctorate. Imagine, I'm out there giving presentations, citing research, speaking on public policy, and serving on boards and panels with no PhD! Although I know I should have completed that infamous degree, it did not happen, nor will it happen. Can I hold my ground with colleagues with the degree? Absolutely. But then a little voice says, "Can you truly be a leader or mentor in the twenty-first century without a doctorate?" There it is, that nagging insecurity that without that degree, I am not as good as those who have one. Maybe I am not as smart as the "degreed ones." I will only have a master's degree until I die, and the *New York Times* will not carry my obituary.

Consider the following questions and reflect on your personal and professional journey up to this point:

- At work or in school, do you worry that you may not be as bright and capable as others in the ECE profession?

- Do you sometimes shy away from leadership challenges because of nagging self-doubt?

- Do you tend to chalk your accomplishments up to being a fluke, no big deal, or the fact that people just like you?

Now you know a couple of my little imposter secrets. And many of us carry these real secrets every day. Comments we hear, little jabs here and there, making introductions or meeting people at a conference, even job postings raise insecurities for many of us. They become a deep well in which we think, "I'm just an imposter, not good enough for the work I do, the position I hold, the leadership I advocate." If we think these thoughts for too long, we end up in a dark place, and sooner or later we will be found out.

Real Stories

A dear friend was selected, from a field of hundreds, to be a one-year fellow in a major early childhood organization in the nation's capital. She was absolutely thrilled but felt she was not ready for Washington, DC; after all, she was a country gal from a small Appalachian town, and the biggest city she had ever been to was Nashville. When she arrived, she was assigned as a congressional representative; by now she was having many doubts about how she dressed, how she talked, how to ride the Metro, even how to find the right buildings. She was basically not ready for the Big Time. She felt that she was an imposter dealing with really smart people and city types. But in making the rounds of congressional offices, she told the stories of her family, her children, and her community to the congressional people, and they connected to her passion and genuine voice. In the end, she felt at home, and her basic lesson still resonates with me: "At first I wanted to hide or run away, but slowly I learned to see the chambers of Congress as a huge version of our little town hall back home. People are just the same wherever they are."

As part of this imposter club, it's important to look first at how we create a set of conscious and unconscious reasons to maintain professional insecurity. And later we'll discuss how leadership skills will get us out of deep negative funk.

People who feel like imposters do not give credit to their own positive qualities or achievements. People who feel like imposters tend to believe that their positions or contributions, no matter how small or large, are based on a fluke or luck or planetary alignment. They believe that it is not a big deal to complete a proposal, give a presentation, or invigorate a teaching team. People who think they are imposters tend to minimize their accomplishments: "Anybody else could have done it just as well." For others, once a project is successfully completed, they start working on the next one, mostly to prove that they can do it bigger and better next time. No big deal indeed.

Did you know that those who think they are imposters are nitpickers? They tend to get worked up about how they could have done it better. They are extremely focused on mistakes and dwell on minor flaws in their performance. A healthier attitude is to focus on what we do well, what works, and how things can be improved in the future. If anything, those who feel like imposters tend to discount all their good qualities, strengths, and accomplishments. And sadly, they compare themselves unfavorably to others: "I wish I were as smart as Einstein." There's always someone smarter, taller, better-looking, more well connected, and better at dancing than the imposter. Such unrealistic views and qualities result in poor leadership.

So, what is the imposter in each of us to do? Remember that we are in good company! We are not alone in these self-doubts; many others have the same concerns. Accept the fact that we are luckily unique and human. Each of us has great qualities as well as weaknesses; therefore, we should recognize them and deal with them, for they are all part of the human condition. Do not let these self-imposed barriers derail self-esteem and chip away at the confidence of leadership.

Working on improving the self lessens the imposter syndrome. Through discipline, habit, and persistence, a process begins at the level of awareness. You begin to think, let me out of this hole! It takes time, sweat, and tears to slowly overcome the stickiness of self-doubt. Start by giving yourself credit for the insignificant and magnificent accomplishment in each day: "Hey, I'm actually good at making coffee for the whole staff," and "After many meetings and proposals, we were awarded funds for a new nature play area." Recognize the merit of your work and how your passion for early childhood education translates into positive outcomes for a child, a family, a team member, or an entire organization. Be willing to accept compliments for a job well done and be gracious in accepting suggestions or criticism—each can translate into affirmative lessons learned for the day. Rediscover your strengths, focus on your solid skills, and be curious about those things you want to learn. Admit mistakes, learn from them, and move on. One side lesson in having imposter syndrome is that heartache can provide new grounds for honesty and purpose. Regain confidence and a healthy dose of humor in the process. "Indeed, I have a PhD: a doctorate in the Stuff of Life."

As for my friends and colleagues who have that nagging feeling of being an imposter, here are a few quick responses: "I have learned so much being a director at my center. When I first started I lacked the necessary skills of a good director, but with determination, help from the entire team, and continuing education, I am now an accomplished professional." "You are right, I don't have children of my own, but I once was a child myself. I played with my brothers, sisters, cousins, and all my friends in school, and today I am a wonderful aunt, a fantastic teacher, and a great storyteller."

As for myself, I could respond with, "I'm glad you find my English so colorful. My family is so proud to be welcomed to the United States, and we are all still working to master the language of Shakespeare—not an easy task as you know." As for my lack of a PhD, I could say, "It has been my intention to earn that degree, but I find my work training ECE teachers across the nation so very fulfilling. Maybe one day I will finally do it. Right now, I love what I do."

Finally, as the Platters song plays, it may be time to update some of the lyrics (but not its soulful tunes) to a more positive rhythm. Take away words and feelings of weakness and infuse yourself with uplifting words of confidence and inspiration. Create your songs of strengths, write lyrics of power, sing tunes that embody your passion, and dance with the joy of your work.

Janet Gonzalez-Mena

My Insecurities

Luis's discussion of self-doubt really struck home with me and gave me lots to think about. Yes, I've been there. The story of his friend, the good teacher who became a director, was also my story. His friend knew perfectly well that she had no idea about how to manage an organization. I may not have known that when I got hired, but I sure discovered it my first day on the job. I was director of child care services in a fairly large community organization that started as a counseling agency. The counselors discovered right away that child care was a huge issue with their clients, so the agency took it on and applied for grants. The child care program was up and running and about to expand when I was hired. I wasn't the first director—she had been promoted and left a vacancy that I applied for and filled. She had huge shoes, and they didn't fit me at all. I lasted a couple of years, and there was never a day that I felt secure in that job. I knew when I quit that I was never designed to be a director, and I went back to teaching community college when a full-time job finally came along and I was able to get hired.

I can also relate to Luis's language insecurity. English isn't my problem, my monolingualism is. I have been intrigued with learning other languages since high school. I took two years of Latin thinking it would be a helpful place to begin. Of course, I never learned to speak it. In college, I majored in English and minored in French, but although I became good at French grammar and reading, I wasn't great at writing, and I didn't learn to speak French at all. Conversation wasn't a goal in any of the classes offered. We read literature and struggled with writing about it. When I graduated from college, I ended up spending a year in Germany on an American military base. I worked on learning German until I could finally buy groceries and ask where the bathroom was, but I never got much beyond that. Finally, I went to work on Spanish and took classes as an adult. By that time, I was teaching in a program for Spanish-speaking preschoolers and was highly motivated to learn. The year that federal funding for bilingual education first became available, the administration applied and received a government grant. That grant put me in the job of the English teacher, so I wasn't supposed to be practicing my Spanish. The Spanish-speaking teachers were native speakers, and though I tried to keep up with what they were saying and what the children were saying, it was hard!

When I married my adult-school Spanish teacher, I thought for sure I'd become fluent. I didn't! I do remember a trip we took to visit his family in Mexico. After we were there about a month, I realized one morning when I woke up that I had been dreaming in Spanish. I was really excited about that. The story is long and complicated, but the outcome is that I'm not bilingual, and by now I'm convinced I never will be. Maybe in my next life, if there is to be one (smile). I've wondered for years why it's so hard for me to acquire the ability to speak a language other than English, and I've come up with two reasons (excuses). I'm shy! Unless I'm on stage or talking to people I know well, I get tied up. That's not a very good excuse, but I have a better one. I eventually discovered that I have a hearing loss, and I now wear hearing aids. Since I have two children with hearing losses, one doctor suggested I might have had it since childhood, but it was never diagnosed.

Of course, it's easy to imagine that I might share another of Luis's insecurities—lack of a PhD. I have an MA after my name, but I'll never have a PhD, EdD, or any other kind of doctorate. I came to grips with that a long time ago. There was nothing about going on for a PhD that attracted me. I decided it wasn't for me, just as after I tried being a director I came to the same conclusion. Do I sound defensive? I hope not. I don't feel defensive. Like Luis, I also have imposter problems; however, there's nothing like living as long as I have. I think by now I've come to grips with my imposter problems. As Luis said, "There's always someone smarter, taller, better-looking, more well connected, and better at dancing than the imposter." I guess I'm secure enough that I don't spend much time comparing myself to people who have qualities that I lack. Okay, to be honest, sometimes I do, but it's not my main way of being or thinking.

Personas and Subpersonalities

I want to suggest two other ways for me to look at who I am besides as an imposter or a pretender: personas and subpersonalities. I couldn't help but think of them as I was reading Luis's chapter opener. One is the idea of personas. Do you know that word? The dictionary says it's an identity or role that somebody assumes. The word is from Latin, and from it we have the words *person* and *personal*. Originally, the persona was a mask that actors put on to play a role. It's not the same as being an imposter because it's less about deception and more about acting. A persona can be thought of as a personality that we put on and take off like a mask. But it's not about trickery. For example, if you followed me around, you would see that I'm one way with my children, another way with my grandbaby, still another way as a presenter, and a very different way when I'm out to lunch with friends. I change roles, including the way I talk and how I behave. I don't feel uncomfortable or insecure about being those different ways. They are all aspects of who I am—aspects of my *self*. A question I won't ask, but find interesting, is this one: Is there a true self that is beyond masks, personas, and personalities? For me the self—the true self, whatever that is—can only be seen through its physical manifestations. But now we're getting in really deep, way beyond Luis's subject of self-doubt. But while we are still here, let me ask, what do you consider your true self and what personas do you present to the world? Is the way people probably perceive you the way you perceive yourself? If you answered no to that last question, you are probably back to Luis's subject of self-doubt. One more question: How do you want people to perceive you? This may be a hard question to answer unless you think of a specific setting, a group of people, or one of your many roles in life. So let me make it specific: How do you want people to perceive you as a professional? How can you make yourself a professional persona that works for you and doesn't leave you doubting yourself?

If I haven't already made this subject complicated enough, let me add one more theory that few people know about. Roberto Assagioli, an Italian psychologist who lived around the time of Freud and Jung, came up with the idea that the real self is clothed in what he called *subpersonalities*. Each subpersonality has a particular perception, a set of behaviors, even a voice. Each is wrapped around a need, and when that need is great, the subpersonality demands a lot of attention. He also believed that when two subpersonalities are in opposition to each other (and creating confusion and chaos in a person's life), it means that they are trying to get together. His theory is called *psychosynthesis*, which describes the process of continual integration as parts of us come together to make greater wholes. I studied with people who had studied with Assagioli himself, and I learned interesting things about myself. It was back when I was a beginning writer, and although I hadn't come to the studies to improve my writing, that was exactly what happened.

As part of a psychosynthesis course I took, I explored two subpersonalities in conflict within me. I gave them names, but I don't remember them now. I came up with an image for each. One was an iron rod. It was my unmovable self—a person who tended to be critical and wouldn't listen to any opinions that didn't fit what she believed. The other was a wet washrag—limp, spineless, wishy-washy. It was the opposite of my iron rod who took a stance and kept it. It was very hard to have these two characteristics fighting inside me. I would have to choose to present one or the other to the world. After working with these two characteristics—using symbols, imagery, self-talk, and other therapeutic devices—I was finally able to bring them together. As a writer, I need to be open, creative, and accepting of multiple ideas even when they clashed. I learned to get all kinds of things down on paper without critiquing them. That old wet washrag turned into a creative spirit—open and expecting. But then I call in my editor self, who is no longer an iron rod but a perceptive critic who knows how to clean up messes, straighten out thoughts, and make something readable. I used both to write this piece, though they are no longer separate in me. I also use both aspects in my diversity work when it comes to understanding perspectives on early childhood education that I don't naturally have. Both these subpersonalities are still part of me and have become one.

So I have shared where I have come from as an imposter and have gone way beyond to some rather esoteric personality and psychological theories. I hope, dear reader, you still see some connections to the original subject.

Debra Ren-Etta Sullivan

Imposter Syndrome Management

For me, it wasn't a song as it was for Luis. It was a turkey. Last Thanksgiving I had twenty family members over for dinner. I roasted a twenty-four-pound turkey, and it was a big hit. A really big hit:

"That was the best turkey I've ever tasted in my life!"

"I've never had a turkey that juicy and tender—never!"

"Can I come over for dinner again tomorrow?"

"I can almost taste those turkey sandwiches to come right now."

Well, there were no turkey sandwiches to come. They picked that turkey clean right down to the bone. This sounds like a good thing, right? So what's my point? My point is that Thanksgiving is coming up again, and guess who's in charge of roasting the turkey? Suddenly I'm panicking. The pressure, the sweating, the heart palpitations, the shaky hands, the high expectations. Will the next turkey be as good? Will I be able to pull it off again? Will I be able to measure up? Or am I an imposter whose great turkey last year was just a fluke? Am I just pretending I can cook?

In Luis's and Janet's examples, teachers were told, "You are a great teacher. You can also be a great director." Sometimes a well-meant compliment can go awry. Some say flattery will get you everything, but sometimes flattery only gets you frightened. Flattery can most certainly lead to feeling like you're an imposter! Most times when people flatter you, it's to make you feel good, but it can also feel like a setup for failure, especially if you feel that the flattery is not quite genuine.

Then (in my experience) the opposite can also happen—you or others begin to quash all feelings of confidence. If the *New York Times* does carry your obituary, it will say you died from complications due to quashing! This kind of critical approach usually happens when you try to accomplish some important goal, and then you or someone else doubts either the significance of your goal or your ability to do it. Twenty-five years ago, when my husband and I were first married, I told a colleague that I was going to have both my family and my husband's family over for Christmas. His response was, "Well, that's ambitious, considering you just met your in-laws." For just a moment, I had a twinge of doubt. Who was I to think I could prepare an important holiday meal for my newly acquired in-laws? Fortunately, I was offended enough to confront my doubt head-on that time. I'm a great cook, my in-laws love me, my family loves my husband, and my dining room was large enough to fit everyone. And besides, what's wrong with having ambition?

Seeing yourself as the Great Imposter can wreak havoc on leadership, because whether doubts are disguised as flattery or quashing, they can poke at your sense of confidence and cause you to focus on expectations. Are you as good as you think you are? Are you as good as they think you are? What if you lose the humility of being an imposter? What if you have so much confidence that when you, the Great Imposter, are given flattery, you acknowledge the compliments and then add your own? What if you lose your confidence and start agreeing with "quashers" who say you can never succeed?

Paying attention to being an imposter undermines the confidence you need to do well. But ignoring feelings of being an imposter is not much better, because it undermines the humility you need to remember you can always do better. Once you decide you can never measure up, you've lost confidence. Once you decide you can always measure up, you've lost humility. In either instance, leadership is compromised. Good leadership requires you to manage the imposter syndrome by balancing confidence and humility. How can we manage balance? I have nine strategies that I've found helpful for imposter syndrome management:

1. **Accept the fact that you cannot be perfect** all the time and you may not be successful all the time, but you can strive to do better all the time. Effective leaders know that failure is just another step toward success.

Learn from your failures and imperfections and use that information to do better next time.

2. **Don't be afraid of high expectations**—yours or others'. Just remember that *high* is a relative term. Expectations should be high enough to encourage motivation and perseverance but not so high that success is perceived as unachievable. Effective leaders know that mediocrity is not an option. Which brings me to my next strategy:

3. **Set realistic expectations.** There was a time when we believed it was impossible for us to fly like a bird. But we kept ambitiously trying to achieve the impossible until we learned how to fly in a plane. Effective leaders strike a balance between setting realistically high expectations and trying to achieve the impossible.

4. **Regularly engage in self-reflection.** Think about where you've been, where you are, and where you want to go. Ask yourself helpful, critical questions: Have I made progress? Have I improved? What is it that I don't know yet? What more can I do? What have I not considered? Use your answers to these questions to inform your professional and personal development and learning.

5. **Assess every situation.** Is there a reason to doubt your confidence? Do you need to be humbler? If there is no reason to doubt your skill and ability in that moment, don't. Do what you do well with the assurance that you are good at what you do. Be the teacher who has something of importance to impart or accomplish. If you need to be humbler, do so. Acknowledge that you are also capable of improvement. Be the student who knows you have much to learn and many from whom you can learn.

6. **Refresh! Renew! Research! Refocus!** Anything can become stale with time. Effective leaders know that even the greatest vision requires updating. Take time to take a fresh look, add a new twist, tie in a different perspective, hear a different voice. You don't have to wait for failure. Quality improvement, updating, and advancement can take place at any time.

7. **Stay resilient and flexible.** Whether you think of it as bouncing back or getting back up on the horse or picking yourself up and dusting yourself off, just be sure to try again no matter what. When the Great Imposter seems to be winning, remember that this is just an opportunity to examine another path, another approach. Effective leaders know that resiliency is the perfect tool for balancing confidence and humility.

8. **Stay grounded in who you are,** especially when someone is quashing your ambitions. There will always be those people wishing you'd give up and quit trying to achieve your ambitious goal. If you do measure up, it means others have to measure up as well, so they want you to fail even when they want you to measure up! Effective leaders stay true to themselves and focused on their goal. They know that ambition is a good thing. Even if you don't reach the star you were aiming at, getting as far as the moon is still a great achievement.

9. **Finally, remember to breathe!** When the Great Imposter rears its ugly head, do what my daughter always reminds me to do: Smell the roses. Blow out the candles.

So this Thanksgiving, I'm going to make the best turkey I possibly can. It may be as wonderful as the one I made last year. Or maybe I won't be able to measure up to last Thanksgiving, and the turkey will turn out only so-so. However, there's also a pretty good chance that if I follow the strategies above, I'll achieve the near-impossible and roast a turkey that outshines the last one by a long shot. I'll keep you posted.

Holly Elissa Bruno

The High Cost of Keeping Secrets

"You are only as sick as your secrets," a twelve-stepping friend reminded me. We were chatting amicably after our CoDA (Co-Dependents Anonymous) meeting, reflecting on what we had learned. My friend continued, "Pretending to be who we are not requires us to hide parts of ourselves we don't want others to see. Keeping secrets isn't always the same as keeping confidences."

The more we cover up about ourselves, the more "dis-ease" we feel. Luis's Great Imposter may look happy on the outside but feel out of sorts inside. Being fake steals energy and costs us serenity. Imposters are in danger of losing touch with who they really are. This is the disease of codependency: losing our identity trying to please others while relying on others for our sense of worth. Reclaiming our identity takes courage and hard work. I am a practiced (and gratefully recovering) codependent.

How did I learn not to be myself? My name was taken away from me. Talk about loss of identity! Here's the story: My father, Vincenzo Bruno, eldest son of immigrants Adollorata Modello Bruno and Michele Bruno from Caltinas-etta, Sicily, was the only member of his college class unable to find work after being the first in his family to complete college (Cornell Engineering School, class of 1934). Back in those days, signs in shop windows warned, "Positions available. Italians need not apply." My unemployable father moved back, tail between his legs, to his crowded home as if his four years in Ithaca hadn't happened. He sold shoes and Fuller brushes.

When I was born, attending nurses spooled alphabet beads onto elastic bracelets and placed the identifying beaded bracelet on each baby's wrist. My bracelet identified me as Holly Elissa Bruno. Later on I taught myself to spell my name by studying those beads.

When I turned four, the world became flat. My parents announced our name was Bruner and that our family name originated in Alsace-Lorraine at the border of France and Germany. I asked why I wasn't Holly Bruno any-more. I do not recall the words I was told, but I got the message: beatings would result if I asked that question again. In that formative moment, I said farewell to childhood and stumbled into an adult world of falsehood.

I didn't understand why we were no longer part of the loud and lively Bruno, Cocca, and Jelfo clan from Rochester, New York. How strange to visit my grandfather's kitchen steaming with homemade pasta and tomato sauce with his fig tree miraculously growing in the backyard and strains of *La Traviata* spilling from the phonograph and not be a Bruno. Cousins treated me differently, whispering that the Bruners were stuck up and thought we were better than them. I went into hiding inside myself.

As an adult, I understood my family had reason for changing our iden-tity. We were (allegedly) short, swarthy, garlic-eating "greasers." Relatives on my mother's side (the Scots) called us "wop" or "guinea." None of these derogatory statements would make sense to a four-year-old.

What does a child do when she is told she isn't real? How does a child live with the inner conflict, especially when adults pretend not to see a prob-lem? What do children do when classmates make fun of them or exclude them for being different? How does a child feel when she can't "talk right" or "dress right"? The pain of losing our true identity exiles us.

Do adults have a panoply of rationales for denying who we are? My father wanted to get a job to support his family. As Janet notes, shy people are not acceptable; they masquerade as extroverts. Luis explains, with Spanish as his first language, he fears others will judge his efforts to say things just right in English. As Debra explains, family expectations can put us into a tizzy of pretending and anxiety.

As for me, I have devoted a lifetime to rediscovering and reclaiming who I am. When I flew to Sicily after completing the bar exam, I was mesmerized by the stark beauty, the adorable bambini, and the kindness of strangers. Sicilians have ancestors from Africa and Arabia and Turkey and Spain and Greece and England. Sicilian faces are black to light; our height ranges from my grandmother's four feet ten inches to my grandfather's six feet three inches. I can't wait for a DNA swab to reveal my eclectic heritage. I embody a rich jumble of ethnicities and am grateful for that heritage.

Being Sicilian is only one layer of my identity that I have gone on a quest to discover. I have challenged myself to face the truth about other painful secrets. Child abuse is a secret that makes us very sick. My father was a violent abuser who beat me, sexually molested me, and otherwise let me know I was worthless. My mother's bouts with mental illness required me as a very young child to become my mother's mother.

When the truth isn't pretty, pretending is a way to survive. Pretending is not the way to live. If we are only as sick as our secrets, we are as healthy as our authenticity. Truth sets us free. These days I don't pretend. I tell people I am an abuse survivor. I tell them about losing and reclaiming my ethnicity. I tell them about my sixth-grade teacher, Michael Gonta, the first person to see any worth in me and the first person to tell me, "Holly, you are a special little girl, and someday you will make a difference." Michael Gonta's someday is today. When I tell my truth about being an abuse survivor, some people turn away; others get teary. But every time, at least one person says, "Thank you for being real. You give me courage to do the same."

So what do I know about being an imposter? I know that I cannot be anyone other than who I am, with all my immaturities and blind spots. I know when I speak the truth about being a survivor, I speak for children in your classroom or program who cannot yet speak for themselves. I know I am breaking an unwritten code about keeping secrets. When I tell the truth about my heritage being wiped out, I speak for countless children who have been reviled for their ethnicity. I know that being real is all I can be. People love me or hate me for putting the truth out there. Today I don't need their approval anywhere near as much. I just need mine. May all children and adults be free to be who we are, human beings wanting to be ourselves, shaking hands with others who want to be themselves. May imposters be set free.

Summary . . . .

Luis Antonio Hernandez

Dear Reader,

We have bared our souls of some deep insecurities—trivial, gigantic, silly, heart wrenching—but all residing inside our emotional selves. We all have them and we all have nagging imposters that sometimes get the better of us.

Discussion Questions . . . .

1. If you have self-doubts in a particular professional area, what can you do to overcome those dark feelings? How would you assist a colleague who may show evidence of professional self-doubts?

2. As an early childhood educator and leader in today's world, how do you influence and impact the lives of children to gain and retain a sense of confidence in their strengths?

3. With families, what strategies could you use to support an adult who is struggling with a sense of self-doubt and tends to belittle achievements?

11

Intentionality for the Well-Intended

Debra Ren-Etta Sullivan

One of my favorite leadership topics has been about intentionality and what it means for our work with children, families, communities, and each other. Most of the time, we all mean well and try to do what is right. Sometimes, however, meaning to do well and having good intentions are not enough. Sometimes we need to act with intentionality.

What Has Been Your Worst Good Intention?

One of my worst good intentions was making breakfast for my mom, sisters, and nieces on Mother's Day. Sounds like this should have been a lovely, thoughtful idea and event for a collection of women who are either widowed or whose husbands could never quite pull off an event on their own. I made Greek baked eggs; a fruit salad with mangoes, berries, and kiwi; turkey sausages, croissants, and orange juice with champagne. Unfortunately, one of my sisters and her daughter really wanted to go to a particular restaurant that served a daily buffet. I meant well. I thought it was a good idea to save everyone money and have a leisurely meal together without having to drive to a restaurant and stand in line for hours waiting for a table so we could eat heat-lamp food in cramped booths. My sister, on the other hand, felt offended because I was rejecting her idea and replacing it with my "superior" idea. And, because I'm the oldest of six, she felt it was part and parcel of my controlling nature to make everyone come to me rather than go out with everyone else. The eggs had too much feta, the mangoes made her tongue tingle, pork sausage tastes better than turkey sausage, the orange juice had pulp. Her daughter joined in, I got testy with her, my mom got upset with my sister, and the menfolk retired to the den with their plates to watch SportsCenter.

Intent, intended, intention, and *intentionality*. What do all these words mean, and how are they different? It could be both easy and difficult to delve deeply into definitions, but sometimes that's exactly what we need to do so we can be more honest with ourselves and with each other. People often tell me I focus a lot on words and meanings and get bogged down in semantics. I admit it; it's true. However, I find that many people are really quite clever with their words and use them to absolve themselves of responsibility for what they do, think, and believe by simply selecting an alternate form of a word or selecting a word that seems to have a similar meaning but really means something altogether different. I once worked with a group of parents who were starting a middle school for girls. They wanted the school to be culturally, racially, and economically diverse and inclusive, so part of their mission statement spoke to an antibias curriculum and learning community. At one point, after the school opened, it became clear that some antibias work needed to be done, and I was asked to facilitate a conversation. It is not uncommon for such conversations to be difficult, but there were a few parents who just did not want to participate. I explained that the process could be difficult but certainly not impossible, and that the end result would be addressing the school's value of eliminating bias. The director eventually told me that there would be no conversation because the mission stated that the school "intended to become an antibias community" and "intending to become" does not require a conversation right away. Semantics.

I like to start with the legal definition of the word *intent* because it tells me if I'm really being honest about what I'm doing. According to the law, *intent* means planning and desiring to perform an act. It means you meant to because you planned it and desired it. Intent requires mens rea, which is the Latin term for *guilty mind*, and this is where intent gets interesting. According to the law, if I innocently cause harm, then I don't have a guilty mind and should not be held responsible or accountable for my actions, words, and outcomes. Those I offend or hurt have to prove that I intended to cause harm.

When the Well-Intended Claim Innocence

Reflect on a time when someone offended you or caused you harm and their response to you was one of the following:

- I was just joking/kidding.

- I didn't mean it that way.

- I tried.

- You take things too seriously.

- You always take things the wrong way.

- You're being too sensitive.

When the well-intended claim innocence, the offended become the guilty party because intent cannot be directly proven. Intent must usually be inferred from surrounding facts and circumstances. If you set out to prove that I intended offense or harm after I've claimed innocence, you become the bad guy. It creates a very frustrating paradigm in leadership and social justice/social change work. It is very difficult to eliminate offensive behaviors and practices when the person committing the offense claims not to know there is anything wrong. It is not unusual for change agents, advocates, and activists to be characterized in a negative light.

I had an interesting conversation with my oldest son when he was about sixteen years old and said something I considered sexist. I called him on it and told him he needed to consider a female's perspective on the matter. He felt that what he said wasn't sexist at all and I was being too nit-picky, because none of the girls he knew seemed to take offense. Of course, I did have to point out that he may simply be oblivious to what his female friends thought and that men don't get to decide what is sexist and what isn't. At that point he claimed innocence, which may have been true since he was only sixteen and hadn't had much time to really come to know and understand the female perspective. Or it could have been that he felt fairly confident in his perspective but upon realizing that his mother questioned the validity of the perspective, he decided it was easier just to claim innocence.

In addition to the legal definition, *intent* has a general definition. It is one that is more familiar to most of us. According to the dictionary, *intent* can be a noun or an adjective. As a noun, *intent* is simply what one wants to do or achieve. It is having the mind and will focused on a specific purpose, ambition, objective, point, purpose, or target. This can be quite benign:

- I want to become a doctor one day.

- I intend to clean out the storage shed next week.

- I plan to get the dishwasher fixed.

- I have to finish this chapter by the end of the month.

This also leaves room for endless procrastination because it's what we want to do or achieve, but without a plan and active steps, it may never happen. It's not so benign when the intent is important, like reasonable wages for teachers of young children or improving the quality of children's learning environments. I would never be able to count the number of times I've been asked to serve on a diversity committee to help make an organization more welcoming to diverse populations. At one organization that shall remain nameless, I was asked every three years to provide community input.

As an adjective, *intent* means "directed with strained or eager attention." It implies that you are decided, determined, fixed, absorbed, and preoccupied. A baby's face may be intent as she tries to get her hands on some exciting object of interest. Babies are quite difficult to distract once they become focused on accomplishing something. Someone once told me a story about a two-year-old who had been told repeatedly not to touch the oven because it was hot. One day, the mother looked up and the toddler was walking toward the oven with wide-open staring eyes and an outstretched hand, saying to herself over and over, "Don't touch. Don't touch. Don't touch." That is an unwavering course of action directed with eager attention. Grown-ups can learn a lot about acting with willful intent from watching young children.

Intent is not the same as motive, which is what prompts a person to act or not act. Suppose Luis calls Janet names and Janet throws a snowball at him. Janet's intent is to hit Luis with a snowball. Her motive may be to stop Luis's teasing. Of course, if Janet's snowball really does hit Luis and he gets upset, Janet may feel bad and claim that she really didn't mean to actually hit him. Luis would not be able to sue Janet for the damage she caused because Janet did not have a guilty mind and, therefore, can't be held accountable for her actions.

Intent is also different from purpose. A purpose is an anticipated outcome that guides your planned actions. In Aesop's fable, the ant had an anticipated outcome (to have food and shelter for winter) that was guided by planned actions (going to the farmer's field as many times a day as possible to collect wheat grains). The grasshopper, on the other hand, wanted to sing and dance while summer days were long and bright. His intent was to prepare for winter later . . . and later . . . and later. And, as the story goes, when later came it was too late. The grasshopper did not act with purpose.

Intention

The word *intention* is actually fuzzier than the legal definition of *intent* because it implies little more than what one has in mind to do or bring about: I thought about it but didn't actually do anything about it. I was once on a small plane heading to a small city. It was one of those planes that has one seat on the left side and two seats on the right side. I was seated on the right side and had both seats to myself. A few rows ahead of me on the left side was a football-player-sized man squished into his allotted one seat. As people continued to board, it occurred to me that I should ask him if he wanted to switch seats. People continued to board; I continued to think; he continued to squirm. Finally, the front door closed and we were asked to turn off our electronic devices. Even then, I could have quickly switched seats with him—as was my intention—but still I said nothing. It was a short, bumpy, forty-five-minute flight, so we were asked to remain seated the whole time. I sat there, feeling guilty about all the seat space I had and feeling annoyed with myself for not taking action. Sometimes we really want to do something, have something happen, or change something, but we procrastinate until it's too late. Sometimes we just wait for someone else to do it for us. What we need is intentionality.

In human development, intentionality is defined as the ability to act with purpose, to behave with a goal in mind, and to take deliberate actions to reach that goal. Intentionality requires the self-control to take specific steps and persistent action to make a difference in some way, shape, or form. The time for "meaning to" has passed. There is no more "thinking about it." We believe in our own competence and in our ability to make a change and make a difference. When we act with intentionality, we do so knowing that the outcome we want will be achieved. We act as if failure to succeed is not an option.

Leading with intentionality requires us to pay attention (another great word) to what we are doing and the results and consequences of those actions. To *pay attention* means to provide care, focused concentration, and observant consideration. It involves heedfulness and regardfulness. We know what we want, and we direct our minds toward that goal. Distractions are ignored as we watch over, minister to, and apply ourselves toward our desired end. Imagine wanting to bring about a result, an achievement, a change so badly that we consciously, conscientiously, and consistently pay that much attention to what we are doing. This is both very difficult and quite easy. When I was about eighteen years old, I decided that I did not want to hear ethnic jokes ever again. Most are quite offensive, and I find that they keep recirculating—just changing who the target group is. I began asking people not to tell them in my presence. This was very difficult because it made people annoyed at best, mad at the very worst. Friends and family made fun of me and teased me quite a bit, but I persisted. What made it quite easy was that I was remaining committed to my value. I felt it required and deserved my unwavering attention. No one should have to guess what my value was, and no one would be able to assume I didn't care just because I didn't say anything. I spoke up regularly and consistently. It was about two years before others completely stopped teasing me or trying to make me feel bad about being a spoil sport, a party pooper, too politically correct, or too much of an activist (yes, they said all those things).

Your Worst Good Intention

When you reflect back on your worst good intention, what would have been different if you had added intentionality? With my Mother's Day breakfast, I could have taken into consideration that my sister would not necessarily like my change in plans. It is not as if I haven't known her all of her life. We are very close in age (eleven months and two weeks apart) and have often disagreed on things. And it is true that as the oldest of six, I have a tendency to make "big sister" decisions and just move on, expecting that everyone else will go along with me. This incident was really about our relationship. I could have acted with intentionality and been more mindful of that relationship. I know she gets upset when I make important decisions without including her, and then I make matters worse by trying to brush off her dissatisfaction by claiming she's making a big deal of it ("You take things too seriously"), making her feel guilty because I was doing something nice ("I didn't mean it that way"). I put her in the position of having to prove that I did, indeed, have a guilty mind, and that I needed to be held accountable for my action and the harm it caused.

I said earlier that under the legal definition of *intent*, it can be difficult to prove that the person acted with a guilty mind. With intentionality, there is nothing to prove. People should know what your true intentions are by observing the surrounding facts, circumstances, results, and consequences.

I believe that in our profession, leadership should result in change that benefits children, their families, and their communities. My leadership role is to lead with intentionality. If I don't, I'll spend a lot of useless time and energy feeling guilty and annoyed with what I meant to get to, hoped would happen, wished I had said, or wished someone else had done or would do. One of my favorite sayings is from Clementine Paddleford. She was a journalist (from the 1920s to 1960s) whose mother instructed her to "never grow a wishbone, daughter, where your backbone ought to be" (Paddleford 1958, 16). I call these words to mind on a regular basis because leading with intentionality often demands backbone. This is particularly true in social change and social justice work, which really is a large part of our work in early childhood education. There is much to stand up to and stand up for. Change for good does not come about just because we mean well or meant to, and we cannot depend on someone else to make our important change happen.

So where do we go from here as we think about leading and acting with intentionality? First, I think we need to take full responsibility for what we mean in our choice of wording. If you say you intend for something to happen, demonstrate that intent by articulating a pathway to it with a clear plan of action or behavior. Have a mind that leaves no room for misunderstanding, procrastination, or having others guess what you really meant. If you don't mean to hurt people's feelings or cause harm and offense, learn more about others. Study other people's values, cultures, histories, and perspectives. If you are actively engaged in learning more about what causes harm or offense to others, people will see that you mean what you say. It will also help you develop confidence in your ability to make and create change. Yes, you'll still make mistakes, but you'll know how to apologize and resolve those mistakes. You won't feel the need to claim innocence.

Another important step in moving from being well-intended to leading with intentionality is to be clear about what is important to you and what your values are. Pay attention to what you care about. Give it your fullest regard, minister to it, feed and water it daily, wait upon it, tend to it. If something is important to you, if you value something highly, everyone should be able to tell immediately and always. Nothing should distract you from it, especially anything that actually takes you in the opposite direction and puts you in a position of diminishing what is important to you. I see this sometimes in my leadership training work. Someone will start to talk about their organization or agency and how the work done there goes against their values. My response is often the same: they are paying you to help work against what is important to you. Intentionality requires us to avoid such situations.

Finally, look closely at the outcomes, results, circumstances, and consequences of your actions, words, and practices. If they are not what you intended, you only meant well. You tried, but it didn't happen. I'd like to leave you with wise words from a fictitious, diminutive sage: "Do or do not. There is no try." Yoda showed us what it looks like to lead and act with intentionality.

Janet Gonzalez-Mena

Finding My Intention

When I look back at my own life, the words *wonder* and *wander* jump up at me instead of *intention*. I didn't really have intent, which as Debra said is simply what one wants to do or achieve. But what counts is having the mind and will focused on a specific purpose, ambition, objective, point, purpose, or target. As a child and a young person, I always thought I should have a purpose, but I didn't. I remember asking myself, why am I here? For what purpose was I born? I didn't have an answer, and I used to worry about that.

I suppose I did have the intention to finish high school, but it wasn't a clear intention. I just kept going until graduation day came along. Luckily for me, I liked to get good grades, so I had some intention there, but I had no intention of going to college. A job came along, and I went to work in the office of a very small telephone company in the tiny town where I lived (a town that had only one stop sign and no traffic light). I knew how to type, and that was about all. I learned to file and got along okay, but my paycheck was so small it was hard to see how I would ever be able to leave home and get out on my own.

In September when the school bus drove by the window where my desk was located, I had a pang—but not enough to consider continuing my education. By November I had received several letters from a high school friend who was at the University of California in Davis, which at that time was a small school. My friend was having a lot of fun. She invited me to come visit her. I did, and I was hooked! Luckily I qualified to get in, so I applied to start in the spring semester. I guess I had some intention there. I was accepted, and that was the beginning of my college career. My friend was a home economics major, so that's what I chose too. It didn't take me long to see that the course work was tremendously challenging; almost all the requirements involved hard science classes. That made me nervous, but then I met some English majors. The requirements for an English degree seemed a whole lot easier, so I changed majors before the first day of class.

I should explain that I was born during the Depression when few babies were born. So in a big contrast to the boomer generation, there weren't many in my generation. Getting into the University of California wasn't nearly as hard then as it is now. All I needed was a good grade point average in high school. That's why I was able to wander in instead of preparing for four years and competing with lots of other people. The university was also much less expensive than it is now. The fees were almost laughably low. At that time, the state of California had a goal of offering a free college education to California residents. (Times have changed.)

Anyway, you can see that I had some intention, but mostly I was just wondering and wandering. I liked going to college and I did well. When the end came near, again I needed some intention. Again I wondered what I should do, until I discovered I was qualified to be a high school English teacher and I wandered into a credential program that allowed me to teach while working toward my credential. I got a job teaching high school junior English in the town next to Davis, and I was set. Lucky me!

But I never did teach high school. Instead, I wandered into marriage after graduation and went to Europe where my new husband had a job for a year on an American base. I got bored while he was working and wandered into the German city where we lived. There I discovered something called the America House where they just happened to need an English-as-a-second-language teacher. With my new bachelor's degree in English, I was qualified.

Well, enough wandering—let's get to where I finally had some intention. I got talked into the first baby, but then I got hooked on motherhood and didn't want to stop. My intention was to have six children. I never intended to send my brood to preschool, but when a neighbor saw me on the floor scraping playdough out of the rug, she convinced me to try out the parent co-op she belonged to. I did, and that turned out to be a significant milestone in my life. Once I got involved, I didn't want to go home when it wasn't my day to participate, so I signed up with a new Head Start program as a volunteer. I ended up volunteering in two preschools and also volunteering one day a week teaching English as a second language to adults.

Aha, finally I had a goal and some intention—get qualified as a preschool teacher. The local community college welcomed me, and I took the classes I needed to satisfy the requirements. You don't need the blow-by-blow description of where I went from there to finally get some real intention. I think of it as finding my purpose in life, which was a very important step forward in a life of wondering and wandering.

It happened when I got exposed to people who were not like me culturally and racially. Economically I had been raised in a low-income, single-parent family but eventually ended up in a middle-income bracket, although I never quite felt like a middle-class person. The change in my life began with the Head Start program, which was focused on serving low-income immigrant families from Mexico. No one in the 1960s, to my knowledge, cared if anyone in the family had papers or not. These were the times of the war on poverty, and advocate groups were forming to do something about equity and social justice. I don't think I used those words at the time, but they are the ones that finally became attached to my purpose.

My second husband was a serious advocate and spent time demonstrating at sit-ins, stand-ins, and even a pray-in or two. Together we decided to open our own school for Spanish-speaking families, and through using volunteers from the Mexican community, we ran it for a year with no funding. Our goal—we had intention—was to teach people of the culture who were fluent in the language to be preschool teachers. The original school where I worked took the opposite approach and hired women from the Spanish-speaking community to be aides while trying to get the Anglo teachers up to par in learning Spanish and understanding the culture. Luckily we met some important people in the local county office of education who helped us write a grant for federal funding. We got it! We had to train the teachers, and I was the only one qualified to get a community college vocational credential, so I did that. Again, without ever intending to teach college. The opportunity presented itself, and I grabbed it. The school, called Escuela Cuauhtemoc, ran as a demonstration program for three years and then was incorporated into an existing state-funded preschool program.

Fast-forward again to the time when I got involved with babies by meeting Magda Gerber, a baby guru originally from Hungary. I learned more about intention from Magda when it comes to babies. She taught that adult intention comes into play during the times when a baby needs something. Then it is appropriate for the adult to have, as Debra said, "the mind and will focused on a specific purpose." Diapering, feeding, washing—those are all times for the adult to be goal oriented. When the baby's needs are met, that is when the adult's attention focuses on the baby's intention. The goal in the free-play periods is to observe and understand the baby's intention but not to interfere. That was very different from the infant-stimulation approach that was prevalent in the new field of infant-toddler education.

You may ask, when did I intend to become a writer? I never did. I just started doing it. I was surprised to get published. That's another aspect of my wandering life. But it fits in very well with my purpose, which is to do what I can to make the world a better place through working to increase equity and social justice. Writing is one way I do that and reach a larger audience than just the people around me.

Now that I have come to the end of my story, I just had a new thought. It's a question, actually. Was I such a wanderer because I fear failure? Setting out to do something—having a clear goal—and working toward it means you might not be successful. I found a lot of success by not setting clear goals. Does that explain something about me? I'm not sure. I haven't veered from my purpose of equity and social justice, but I haven't set definite objectives either. I still just wander and look for places where I can make changes, partly by merely understanding myself at a deeper level. For example, once

I discovered that society grants me power and privilege by the very fact of my white skin, I had to quit feeling guilty and learn how to use my privilege to work on undoing racism. Speaking up in the face of discrimination is one way. My priority is to spread equity and help others see how much better off we would all be if there were no more racism, sexism, classism, heterosexism, ageism, ableism, or any other isms in the world in which we live.

Holly Elissa Bruno

It's Me: Take It or Leave It

These tidbits from Abrahamson and Freedman (2006) delight me: People (like me) who organize by piles find things more quickly than do meticulously organized folk. In fact, many innovations were discovered by accident and as a result of "messy" thinking, suggesting that "our minds are prepared to do some of their best work when they're diverted, one way or another, from what we intend to focus them on" (250).

Why do I find these delightful? Because I am one of the most go-with-the-flow, don't-worry-be-happy, and least organized people I know. Do I drive fastidious people bonkers? You bet. Do I intend to have that effect? No. Am I okay with being the loosey-goosey, last-minute, laughing-all-the-way poster adult? For sure.

Why is this important enough for me to write about? Ah, there's the rub. Many people feel morally correct when they roll their eyes, repeatedly look at their watches in disgust, or otherwise judge my behavior as inappropriate. My last-minute behavior is frequently labeled disrespectful, irresponsible, thoughtless, and self-centered. Ouch. That is not my intention.

Of course, I fully understand why my laid-back ways are troublesome. Trains need to run on time. Meetings start on time for a reason. Predictability and timeliness are required by most organizations. The NAEYC accreditation process rewards the most organized, timely, and highly documented programs. Order must prevail over chaos. Otherwise, what would the world be like?

Majority Rules

My issue is not that organized people are in the wrong. My issue is that in their entitlement to being right, my behavior appears wrong. Being wrong means I am fair game for condescending remarks, personal put-downs, and outright (and often righteous) anger. What gives organized people the right to make these judgments so freely and with conviction? They are the majority. Fifty-five percent of Americans prefer to be organized, to be neat, and to follow the rules (Myers et al. 1998, 157–58). Of course, being in the majority, they make the rules. Being in the majority gives them the right to determine how the rest of us should behave.

Are you getting the picture? Majority rules: the majority's behavior is right, and the minority's behavior is wrong. We slothful people must clean up our act! But wait a minute. In our field, we respect differences. Our NAEYC *Code of Ethical Conduct and Statement of Commitment* centers on respect for differences, particularly cultural and ethnic differences. What about behavioral differences, like waiting until the last minute to complete a task? Is that a difference that warrants respect, even if it offends many?

Core Value: Respect for Differences

When it comes to accepting "inappropriate" behaviors, respect for differences flies out the window. Inappropriate behavior must be changed. Standards must be met. Being late is inappropriate. End of story. On this difference, we do not live in an accepting both/and world. We live in an either/or world. My behavior, natural and instinctive as it is, is inappropriate. I am a troublemaker.

My BAM radio colleague Errol St. Clair Smith says, "Identify the pain people feel and find ways to help; name the difficult-to-discuss issues, bring these issues out in the open, and offer honest relief." In other words, tell the truth and open the door to reflection and new understandings may result.

So here's the truth: The majority make the rules, follow the rules, and make sure others follow the rules. Folk in the majority feel entitled to demand that others meet their standards. When people make judgments about whose way is superior and whose is unacceptable, people in the majority usually prevail. Those in the minority are labeled inappropriate, unacceptable, unreliable, irresponsible, and just plain wrong.

Intentionality and the Brain

Maybe someday research will reveal that an organized, on-time person's brain is wired to perceive and deal with time differently than mine. It sure feels that way. I have to turn an eggbeater on inside myself and stir everything into a froth so that I can be ahead of time. I don't like that feeling. I tense up, get prickly with anxiety, and get headachy. I don't like being judged as lazy, irresponsible, or unreliable for something I rarely can change.

So, about being intentional? Deb, I have tried my heart out to intentionally show up on time. All that good intention added up instead to a tanker full of guilt and self-degradation. Since I am hardwired to live in the moment, I would like to enjoy that more and see it as a strength, not as a shortcoming. I love my innate capacity to drop everything around me and fully listen to a person who needs to be seen and heard. I love the fun of spontaneity and revel in the endless potential in each moment. When I cut flowers from my garden, I never plan what vase or what arrangement. I let the flowers tell me. Okay, so now you are convinced I am whacko? In my world, flowers sort themselves and select their right vase.

Now I need to level with you about something else: I have attention deficit disorder (ADD). As soon as I say that, I am quick to also say, "I don't want to use that as an excuse." However, if you want to get a picture of how my mind works, picture the Brownian movement of Ping-Pong balls bouncing and rebounding off the walls in a small room. Imagine fireworks continuously popping into magical lights and just as easily disappearing. If you have seen Salvador Dali's painting *The Persistence of Memory*, you have seen the face of a clock lying melted like a pancake over the edge of a wall. That's my internal clock. My brain does not "do time." Is my brain wrong? Dysfunctional? Sick? Or is my brain different, as are the brains of the 45 percent of us who get the job done, even if we wait until the last minute?

The Cost of Being Who We Are Not

My intentionality comes at a price: anxiety, exhaustion, and potential burnout. Janet is right in mentioning the shadow, Carl Jung's theory that we have our opposite within us. Within me is an organized, on-time person. Jung's other point about our shadow is that we feel physically stressed, emotionally ill at ease, and beside ourselves when we enter our shadow. Those of us whose work requires us to be our opposite (our shadow self) quickly burn out. In other words, living our shadow self is like wearing a hair shirt or walking on nails. I do it, but I can't sustain it without losing my true self.

If your job requires you to be objective and analytical and your preference is to be compassionate and nurturing, you likely live in your shadow at work. If you are a visionary leader and your work requires you to document everything in great detail, you enter into your shadow. Do you see how exhausting that can be?

How easy is it for a tiger to change its stripes? Tell an organized person to lighten up and take it easy, and you tell that person, "Become your shadow." Lightening up does not come easily to the highly organized; their feelings are hurt when they are told to go with the flow and to stop being so rigid. Highly organized colleagues have repeatedly told me they wish they could be more like me: relaxed and spontaneous.

What If Spontaneity and Playfulness Were as Valued as Being Organized and Planful?

What if instead of requiring everyone to be like the majority, we allowed space for differences in behavior? Eric Abrahamson's and David H. Freedman's (2006) *A Perfect Mess* makes a case for us less-than-organized folk. Can we as educators make room for people to be true to themselves without labeling one another wrong?

An organized person is not an uptight person. A spontaneous person is not an unreliable person. A quiet person is not stuck up. A friendly person isn't a bulldozer. We are born different. We bring different strengths to the workplace. Children need us to model both behaviors because children, like us, are somewhere on the continuum from ultraorganized to ultraspontaneous. Oh my, think of what the workplace would be like! Wouldn't chaos spread like kudzu and destroy our programs? Would NAEYC evaluators approve a program that wasn't uber-organized? I believe we can find a third path.

We can make space in our programs for spontaneity, just as we make space for emergent curriculum. We can make space in staff meetings for play and for open discussion of what's working and how we can create something better together. Workplaces where spontaneity is honored can be some of the most creative and productive workplaces (Abrahamson, Rutledge, and Bloomfield 2012).

Deb, when you described intentionality as one of your favorite topics, I thought, "I'm in trouble now!" If intentionality means to set goals and objectives and carry those out to a T, I am in trouble. If intentionality means to accept differences, including differences in how our brains work, then I am intentional. I intentionally want to help create a world where differences, including those determined by brain structure, are respected.

Perhaps the law will make these changes inevitable. Given the amendments to the Americans with Disabilities Act that took effect January 1, 2009, ADD is likely to be considered a disability. Attorney Linda Batiste (2011), a guest on my radio program, confirms that just about anything that is not a temporary condition—like a broken leg, the flu, or pregnancy—will likely qualify as a disability. What reasonable accommodations will the workplace need to make to allow us to bring our strengths to the job?

When going with the flow is seen as a strength rather than as a sign of a disorganized mind, I will feel more at home in this world. As Einstein, one of those spontaneous innovators who likely had ADD or ADHD, queried, "If a cluttered desk is a sign of a cluttered mind, of what then is an empty desk a sign?"

Luis Antonio Hernandez

Intentionality Defines Our Work

After pondering the comments of my colleagues Debra, Janet, and Holly, I am cherishing all their wisdom, stories, and challenging thoughts. I especially like Janet's observation of wondering and wandering since it reminds me of an old slogan from the *National Enquirer* (yes, the supermarket tabloid)—"Enquiring minds want to know." It fed my juvenile curiosity, and it left me with unanswered questions, such as whether the next-door neighbors were aliens from another planet or whether the dog that walked across the country found his owners. This takes me to a wider conversation on multiple meanings of intentionality and the willingness to go deeper than just glancing at a newspaper tabloid. The challenge with intentionality is to experience the wonder of living with purpose and the freedom to wander with or without direction. For now, I add to my colleagues' deep personal and professional analysis on the call of arms: "Intentionality or perish!"

Best to start right, as your dreams fade away in the early morning light, waking to a new day. I very much doubt we start with "What's my intention today?" Rather, we most likely follow a routine that gives security and order to the body and mind. We greet those around us, pet the cat, get the water boiling, consider breakfast but first feed the cat, go out and get the newspaper, look up to the sky. Looks like a nice day or a cold day or another day. I am up and ready to begin the flow of the next twenty-four hours. The hardwire that Holly Elissa describes predicts how each of us starts and ends each day, from lazy beginnings to rushed starts. Each of us comes with a sense of individual direction and predictable steps. Whether ordered or chaotic, these behaviors define our style and sense of life. Intentionality may be as ingrained as nails in our fingers and the sparkle in our eyes. And yet the universe, without our knowledge or approval, has placed us to wander at a time and place and to be one of wonder for self and others. Consciously or unconsciously, we know we have intentionality, or, in complete bliss, forget we have it.

It seems everywhere I turn intentionality follows. I was at a yoga class recently when the teacher softly asked us to close our eyes and to breathe in and out. Soon I was feeling calmer and more relaxed than I had in the previous ten minutes. Then she asked us to think of our intentions for the next hour and a half of yoga poses and meditation. "Geez." My head spun. "Do I want strength? Can I work some of the kinks out of my neck? Is it possible to lose five pounds? Can this class lead to world peace?" Then, no longer in bliss, I considered how the word *intentionality* has become generic, a common jargon overused in so many settings. Officer: "What was your intention going ninety miles per hour?" Spouse: "What's your intention painting this room orange?" Drive-up cashier: "Is your intention to order #5 with or without fries?"

Back to basics: let's consider how intentionality defines and impacts the work we do. At its foundation, the research and practices on intentionality point to the positive forces on how words and actions define relationships with children as learning experiences occur. At its core, intentionality is a methodology that recognizes and embraces best teaching and learning practices. It is about teachers working with purpose and direction—the embodiment of joyful engagement. And we want that in every classroom!

On the other hand, intentionality has become part of a jargon stew—a watery soup of semantics—blending with other ECE ingredients: appropriate spices, scaffolding juices, engagement veggies, and a dash of questionable quality. Unfortunately, the word *intentionality* has been sullied by making it a requirement, an item to be observed, monitored, and checked. "My, that teacher has a level five in intentionality!" Oops, is that good or bad? Even scarier is when quality indicators become Big Brother monitoring intentional practices. Yikes! Let's get back to a more natural and fluid process.

Intentionality should be a savory jambalaya of individual, unique, joyful, smart, and energetic ingredients. For teachers, it simmers at the start and end of each day with children. Those welcoming morning greetings and the afternoon departure hugs genuinely derive from a natural place, the intersection of heart, mind, and spirit. Those warm "Good mornings" and the sweet "See you tomorrows" are centered on a direct personal response to each child or parent. Intentionality defines a teacher who communicates, "I want to do this, I like doing this, and I am meant to do this."

Once intentionality is performed as a job requirement or done to satisfy a monitoring tool, it plainly becomes an insincere or artificial action. Time to gather your things and leave the premises quickly. A lack of consistent intentionality (yes, we can all have a bad day) says much about one's attitude and interest in the work. And if children had the language, they may say, "Lady, take two aspirin and go home." Remember: you have choices that can lead to other professional horizons. Changing our minds for alternate purposes and new places more aligned with our dreams and hopes is intentional.

The process of intentionality starts with a sense of passion for work decisively chosen. For some of us, we've known the path from very early on: "I always knew I wanted to be a teacher." Or perhaps the universe created this journey and somehow we ended up working with children. It is still a choice with purpose, resulting in a conscious decision to work with children and families. The clarity and decisiveness defines individual professional success and the steps for leadership to take place. But right now, at this moment, this is what is expected—a natural response full of wonder and wander.

Summary...

Debra Ren-Etta Sullivan

There were certainly a number of different takes and perspectives on the topic of intentionality. I like that. It results in the engaging conversations we should all be having about leadership. Janet's take on intentionality has all of us thinking about prominent questions that have been pondered throughout time: Why am I here? What is my purpose? In order to answer those questions, Janet has spent a lifetime wondering and wandering. The result is the Janet we know and love today: the social activist and babies' advocate who strives to understand cultural and racial differences and her role in helping others do the same. I would say Janet acts with great intentionality as a lifelong learner and a lifelong teacher. She does not think she knows it all, so she continues to learn. She knows that others may not have learned enough about diversity, social justice, and the rights of babies, so she continues to teach. She learns and teaches on purpose, with intentionality. "The opportunity presented itself, and I grabbed it." Sometimes it's the "grabbing it" that is needed in our leadership.

On the other hand, Holly Elissa saw intentionality as something that could become oppressive (even abusive) if used in the wrong way. She is right that there are those who will use the word to claim superiority and self-righteousness and who create environments where everyone else feels bad about themselves, doubts the very core of who they are, and perhaps even engages in nullifying activities trying to be someone they are not. The majority should not always rule. History is replete with examples of a whole lot of people implementing a really bad idea. And there are lots and lots of people (maybe even a majority) who are just like Holly Elissa, those who go with the flow, those who give life to their spontaneity, those who prefer to spend their time engaged in a meaningful conversation with others rather than spending time organizing files and being on time. I would say that Holly Elissa is intentional. She is intentional about being true to herself. She is intentional about responding in the moment to what that moment needs. She is intentional about enjoying life and all of the wonderful people who come into it because of her willingness to make room for the delights of the unexpected. Are there those who wish she would be intentional about other things? Probably, but that is not why she is here. That is not her purpose. Our leadership task is to know why we are here and to do that on purpose.

It comes down to Luis's challenge that we "experience the wonder of living with purpose and the freedom to wander with or without direction." Some want us all to be bees. Others choose to be butterflies. I'm not sure I can imagine our planet without both. Maybe it's about finding balance in our individual truths. I do not want my actions to result in my sister being hurt, so I need to pay attention to the consequences of my own intentions. However, that does not mean that everyone has to be like me and care passionately about my passions. That's how we find Luis's description of a sense of individual direction. Then we can have joyful engagement, we can value spontaneity and playfulness, and we can grab the opportunities that present themselves to us. Intentionality can hinder or it can help. It can propel us forward or keep us stuck in an organized, oppressive routine. It can support us in making the world a better place or making the world an unaccepting place where our unique qualities are not valued. It is a choice, and I believe we need to choose with intentionality—on purpose.

Discussion Questions ....

1. What has been your experience with intentionality? Have you used it to accomplish something that is important to you? Have you used it to judge others? Is it just a meaningless, "researchy" word? Does it help you in your work as a teacher and as a leader?

2. Why do you think you are here? What do you think is your purpose? What are you wondering about? What are you wandering into? What do you need to be intentional about, to do on purpose, to make that happen?

3. Who are you not? Are there boxes others want to put you in so you can fit in? How can you use intentionality to be who you are?

References ....

Abrahamson, Eric, and David H. Freedman. 2006. *A Perfect Mess: The Hidden Benefits of Disorder*. New York: Little, Brown and Company.

Abrahamson, Eric, Hile Rutledge, and David Bloomfield. 2012. "Free Spirited versus Highly Structured Leadership: Which Is Better for Education Leaders?" Podcast interview by Holly Elissa Bruno. *Heart to Heart Conversations on Leadership*, June 27. www.bamradionetwork.com/index .php?option=com_content&view=article&id=862:leadr&catid=36 :administrators-channel&Itemid=90.

Batiste, Linda. 2011. "Sweeping New Definitions of Disabilities, What You Need to Know." Podcast interview by Holly Elissa Bruno. *Heart to Heart Conversations on Leadership*, February 27. www.bamradionetwork.com /index.php?option=com_content&view=article&id=580:jackstreet54& catid=36:administrators-channel&Itemid=90.

Myers, Isabel Briggs, Mary H. McCaulley, Naomi L. Quenk, and Allen L. Hammer. 1998. *MBTI Manual: A Guide to the Development and Use of the Myers-Briggs Type Indicator*. 3rd ed. Palo Alto, CA: Consulting Psychologists Press.

Paddleford, Clementine. 1958. *A Flower for My Mother*. New York: Holt.

12

Lessons Learned from the Bumps in the Road

Holly Elissa Bruno

I don't know about you, but I can be really silly. I can picture my silly self, standing on the edge of a dock at a lakeside poised to dive, yearning for the soft, cool, sparkling elegance. I yearn, my leg muscles twitching to spring, but I hold myself back. I deny myself what I want because I dread the shock of the chilling waters.

Exasperated with myself, I either skulk back to shore to gradually walk in, cowardly acclimating myself to the cold, or I finally just do it! I dive, feel my lungs tighten and my skin brace, telling myself I need eleven seconds. That's what my sister Lynne, a doctor, told me: our bodies need eleven seconds to adapt to the cold. After that, the water is my gentle ally.

Eleven seconds. Sometimes I count the seconds to distract myself from the shock. Eleven seconds until I can suspend time. I dive under to explore, swim out to a float, or just float, arms and legs splayed to the sun's warmth. My soul is uplifted by my dive, my swim, the water and the sun, and that indescribable perfume of a freshwater lake in summer. I love the liberation; I fear the entry.

Everything Was Beautiful and Nothing Hurt

Do I desire a life free from shock, unencumbered by pain and upheaval, untainted by failure or loss? I hate to admit that is true because I fancy myself a risk taker. But at some level, I crave quiet and stability. Security. Nothing ugly: all things beautiful. Who chooses pain? "Suffering is optional," self-help experts say. In *Slaughterhouse-Five*, novelist Kurt Vonnegut describes the vision of a pain- and trouble-free life in this way: "Everything is beautiful and nothing hurts at all." We have such everything-is-beautiful moments when time holds still and our hearts ache with gratitude. We savor memories of these moments. We want life to always burst with such shimmering and enduring light.

I remember the moment my son, Nick, completed his rigorous program for adolescents with severe behavior disorders. Nick made great strides away from being an angry, surly, and sometimes threateningly violent teen into a young man who began to take responsibility for himself. I could barely speak over the tears as I told Nick he was my hero. I remember the moment my father—at age one hundred years, six months—died peacefully in his sleep. His trials were over. He was released. I remember the moment when, despite my sometimes crippling fear of heights, I leaped from a platform high above the Guatemalan jungle, and soared, without a fear in the world, over the treetops to the next zip line platform. After that, every leap was toward freedom and away from suffering. And I remember when I witnessed my precious daughter, Lily JinHee, get engaged to Jefferson, the young man who loves her to Mars and back.

When everything is beautiful and nothing hurts, we live in heaven on earth. These experiences are so rapturous that they set a near impossible standard for the rest of our days. Can you recall a moment in your life when everything came together perfectly, life was a splendid journey, and your heart was full of joy? As early childhood professionals, we have many of these moments with children. The world holds its breath as Emily takes her first step. Ezra forms his first word. Miranda, her tiny hands dripping with fingerpaint, hugs our necks.

We also can have timeless and wondrous moments with adults. When my coauthors present with me at NAEYC conferences, Luis, Debra, and Janet tell their truths and, in so doing, uplift participants into moments of deep and freeing understanding. I luxuriate in the grace of those moments. When Delechia, once unsure she could present to a large crowd at a national conference, finds her groove and engages her audience, I sit back, warmed by her smiling success. When director Lori crosses the stage to receive her baccalaureate degree, ten years in the making, we jump up and applaud her courage.

As you recall moments of timeless joy in your life, do you yearn for more sacred moments? Perhaps because we have experienced heaven on earth—we have seen loveliness—we tend to avoid or fear disastrous moments when the bottom falls out.

Pain, Loss, and Suffering: Who Needs Those Bumps in the Road?

When the road is clear, the horizon is alluring, and the moment is breath-taking, we feel as if we could drive on and on. Life is good. Then, without warning: a bump! A pothole appears out of nowhere. Thump! Our tire goes flat. Jump! An approaching car swerves into our lane. Bump! Our brakes fail. Crumple! A crashing thunderstorm obliterates our visibility.

Our serenity is shattered into tiny shards. Our safety is threatened. Our confidence is knee-capped. Our happiness is obscured by fear. We didn't choose those bumps. They chose us. Why on earth would anyone choose pain, loss, or suffering? The desire to avoid pain is human. We teach children to keep their little fingers from the flame. We bundle ourselves up against desperate weather. We get our teeth cleaned every six months as insurance against cavities and gum disease.

In fact, our bodies are on continuous alert for threats to our serenity. Our neurons screech loudly when a threat is perceived. Pain is our early warning of worse things to come. Our entire system snaps to attention at the call of the amygdala gland (Cozolino 2006). Pain and threat are the same: harbingers of unwanted events. We summon all our resources to avoid pain and disruption.

The Shadow Knows

Psychologist and psychiatrist Carl Jung, who long studied human nature, can still teach us about ourselves. Jung noticed that we all have a preferred way of being—our *preference*—and a hidden way of being. He named the hidden or lesser known part of our self "the shadow."

Whichever hand you write with, you have a preference for using that hand. If you had to sign your name with your opposite hand, could you? Of course you could. However, it will likely feel uncomfortable, and you may not want anyone else to see your effort. Our shadow is like our opposite hand. The shadow is always with us, is a part of us, but not the part we prefer to pay attention to and certainly not the part we prefer to use. We all like to put our best foot forward (our preference). No one likes to feel she is beside herself (our shadow).

The shadow is made up of behaviors we prefer to keep secret because they aren't our strengths. The easygoing person becomes cranky when she has to meet deadlines. The analytical person's patience is frayed by having to talk about her feelings. The outgoing colleague looks ready to implode when she has to sit still silently and listen for any length of time. Our shadow takes over when we are under stress. In everyday terms, our shadow shows up as a bad hair day. When stressed, we become our opposite. Curiously, Jung (1964, 180) notes, "Whether the shadow becomes our friend or enemy depends largely upon ourselves." Why did Jung so revere the shadow, especially when the shadow can be a dark and scratchy place?

When we accept our shadow, we become whole. When we own our shortcomings, we are, in part, liberated from them. They are no longer a dirty secret; we can deal with them. As we grow to accept our own shortcomings, we become more tolerant of other people's shortcomings. It seems we all have our shadow, our out-of-character behaviors. Understanding that we all have a shadow helps us accept one another, warts and all.

That uncomfortable part of our self is the portal to reverence because, as we pass through it, we begin to forgive ourselves for our weaknesses. We begin to accept our perfectly imperfect self. We join humanity and gain respect for the trials we all face, sometimes in private, sometimes in front of everyone. The shadow is our internal bump in the road. We can't predict when it will show up. We can't control it. If we pay attention to it, we learn humility and acceptance. We see that we always have more to learn. We see that we make mistakes we thought we would never make. We see that having a sense of humor about ourselves is our saving grace. We learn to ask for help. So it is with the bumps in our road. We don't invite them. We aim to avoid them. Yet they trip us up anyway. We pick ourselves up and keep going. No one else can do this for us. We each have our own lessons to learn.

What are the lessons we learn from the bumps in the road? What is one of the greatest life lessons you learned from a bump in the road? Therein lies the secret of leadership: When we make a mistake, that mistake does not define us if we define ourselves by what we do next. When we fail, we define ourselves by what we learn. We are not a failure as long as we stay passionately curious about what we can learn. The bumps in the road do not define us. Our mistakes and failures give us the opportunity to discover who we are and who we can become. Let's look at some ways we can benefit from the bumps in our road.

Forgive and Remember

Why keep talking about bumps in the road? Who wants to conjure up painful memories? Shouldn't we just move on after we hit a bump and try to put it behind us, let bygones be bygones, and forget what happened? Researcher Britta Larsen (Larsen and Offutt 2012) offers new insight on how to process painful experiences, especially when other people hurt us. Larsen challenges the conventional approach of forgive and forget. Larsen's point instead is forgive and remember.

But, if we remember the pain, aren't we setting ourselves up for more pain? It's easy to think that denial works by helping us forget. However, that's not the case. We might assume that distracting ourselves from perseverating or ruminating on the bumps in the road is an intelligent approach. As my father exhorted, "Rise above it!" To analyze the effects of forgiving, forgetting, or perseverating, participants in Larsen's study (Larsen and Offutt 2012) were asked to either recall hurtful events or distract themselves to avoid painful memories. Larsen divided the participants into three groups:

- People who did not forgive the offender and ruminated on the event.

- People who forgave the offender and tried to forget the event.

- People who forgave the offender and remembered the event.

She tracked their blood pressure and determined that attempting to deny or distract ourselves from what really happened is as bad (or worse!) for our blood pressure as holding on to the hurt. The people whose blood pressure stayed at or dropped to the healthiest level were the people who could both forgive and remember. When we are hurt from a bump in the road, our healthiest response is to forgive and remember. We are unwise to deny that the bump happened or tell ourselves, "I'm so over that." Instead, we need to be honest about the painful event while forgiving the person who caused the pain. Forgiving without denial of the event is the most healing choice of all. Fred Rogers (1994) said it well: "The toughest thing is to love somebody who has done something mean to you, especially when that person has been yourself."

Somehow, we need to find a way to live with the paradox of forgiving yet remembering. Without perseverating over the wrongdoing, we have to level with ourselves about the pain, forgive, and move on. Learning from the experience before putting it behind us is essential to our serenity. Here's what the process looks like:

1. Acknowledge that the bump occurred.

2. Hold people accountable, ourselves included.

3. Don't attempt to forget the event.

4. Forgive the person for the wrongdoing.

5. Learn from the bump by *not* pretending it didn't happen.

Sweeping the mess under the rug sets us up for another tumble. In fact, being in denial that something untoward happened eats away at our inner peace. Being too quick to move on and forgive without processing our emotions can also hurt more than help us. Want to hear more about this research? Listen to my interview with Dr. Britta Larsen and early childhood practitioner Susan Offutt on my podcast "Get Over It! Managing Grudges in Education Settings" (Larsen and Offutt 2012).

Disrupt Thyself

Okay, so one lesson from the bumps in the road is forgive and remember. Are you ready for another lesson? Lesson 2 is disrupt yourself.

What? Why would anyone want to disrupt her life or her career? Given all the challenges we have to deal with, why introduce more calamity and pain? Is Whitney Johnson (2012), author of *Dare, Dream, Do*, really urging us to create bumps in our road so we can tumble and find new ways to get up again? She is clear that "the status quo has a powerful undertow, no doubt" (147). She is equally clear that disruption stands a good chance of "dramatically improving your chances of finding financial, social and emotional success" (147). What is she talking about, and just how much counterintuitive advice can a body take?

According to Johnson, change for change's sake works. She maintains that disruptive thinking improves the odds of success for products, companies, and even countries. The world is changing too fast for those of us on it to try to hold still. If we do things the way we have always done them, we will do things the way we have always done them. Where's the learning, the innovation, the discovery? Especially as we work with children who grow every minute, we adults cannot stop growing and learning either. Convinced? Here are the four principles of self-disruption as outlined by Johnson (2012):

- Target a need that can be met more effectively: Consider what is obvious to you that needs changing that may be invisible to others.

- Identify your disruptive strengths: What do you do well that most others can't?

- Step back (or sideways) in order to grow: Career and life paths that zigzag can actually be more successful than those that follow a straight, predictable line.

- Let your strategy emerge: Take a step out of the box, gather data, and take another step.

Our true selves are forged in adversity. How we deal with injustice defines us. How we face failure defines us. Without those bumps and, more importantly, how we dealt with those bumps, we wouldn't be who we are. Character isn't defined by the mistakes we make; it's defined by what we do next. As John D. Rockefeller is reported to have said, "If you want to succeed, you should strike out on new paths, rather than travel worn paths of accepted success."

Knowing or Discovering Your Path: Which Works Better?

Do we stand a better chance of learning from the bumps in the road if we know what our path is? Does clarity about our purpose and our life's direction help or hinder us in dealing with the bumps? Do the people who don't have a clear sense of where they are headed have more resilience, or do they crumble under pressure? Which describes you: Did you always know who you were meant to be and where you were meant to go? Did your life unfold exactly as it was meant to unfold? Or are you still a work in progress, finding out who you are and what your purpose is by putting one foot in front of the other?

If You Always Knew What You Would Do

How remarkable to know your path and to stay on it. So many early childhood colleagues tell me they knew they always wanted to teach. As children themselves, they organized neighborhood kids into impromptu classrooms where they were in charge. They loved "teaching lessons" and seeing children raising and waving their hands: "Call on me, teacher. Call on me!"

My law school classmates who always knew they would follow in their fathers' (in 1973 only 3 percent of attorneys were women) footsteps also amazed me. They knew what type of law they would practice (from estate planning to general practice). Their fathers were at the ready to add "& Son" to the firm's letterhead. Silly me! Perry Mason and Atticus Finch were the only lawyers I had ever known. In my experience and observation, a tort was a many-layered chocolate cake lavished with raspberry ganache filling. Courtroom cases were most often settled by deus ex machina miraculous events: sobbing confessions of guilt on the witness stand or police officers loudly crashing through the doors of the courtroom brandishing missing evidence. My classmates knew better. They knew the ins and outs of everyday practice of law. Their path was clear and they were clearly on their path.

If Your Path Emerges One Step at a Time

I did not foresee my life's path. I wasn't like that. I did know, however, the path my parents established for their daughters to take. That path had one option: Go to college to become a teacher so you will have something to fall back on if anything happens to your husband. The message was, stay home and be a mother; having a career beyond being a teacher will not be tolerated. My sister Karen always knew who she would be and what she would do. She majored in home economics following my parents' dictate: Karen married, had two lovely daughters, and taught home economics. When my sister Lynne wanted to become a doctor, my father announced, "Daughter, you're on your own." I got the message: my parents always knew who I was supposed to be, but they didn't know me. The cost of striking out on my own path would be high. I could not fit into my parents' definition of a good daughter. I felt hounded to take one step at a time into a future that although uncharted, would reveal—I trusted—what I was meant to do. I gazed out my second-floor bedroom window, scanning the hilltops, believing that my future would begin on the other side of those hills.

Sometimes we are called by a deeper and more invisible purpose than what we consciously see or understand. That purpose reveals itself in a zigzagging way that requires us to take stock of what we are learning about our unfolding direction. I knew I was powerfully driven toward righting wrongs, but I did not know how I would do that. I did not know then that I was a statistic, one out of four girls who are beaten and abused by a family member. Most of my childhood, I felt unworthy of becoming anything special. My self-esteem had been regularly beaten out of me. Early attempts to walk my own path didn't work out: I failed at running away. Although my plans were elaborate and diagramed, I was unskilled in basic self-care and didn't take enough food. I thought I was invisible and would not be discovered. I imagined a loving family would pick me up and adopt me on the spot.

At least I knew what I did not want: a life destroyed by no self-confidence, buried anger, and resentment. I did not want my dreams silenced before I ever had the chance to discover them and say them out loud. At sixteen, I was accepted into an affordable college far enough from home that I could begin my life. I took heart from poet Robert Frost (1916, 9):

> Two roads diverged in a yellow wood
> And sorry I could not take both
> And be one traveler, long I stood
> And looked down one as far as I could
> To where it bent in the undergrowth . . .

Two roads diverged in a wood, and I—
I took the one less traveled by,
And that has made all the difference.

Although I had much sadness in my heart, I lived on hope. I found my way around campus greeting everyone with a smile and a wave. I acted as if I were confident and worthy. I dived deep into university life and began to see who I might be. As a consequence of choosing to find my own path, I was disowned and labeled a sinner. I gathered a family of friends who were equally unwelcome at their homes. I moved, explored, spoke up, stepped out, and stepped up to do and become what I had never imagined I could do. In the process, I discovered what I yearned for: I wanted to give what I did not receive.

I wanted to support people in finding their paths, accepting their gifts, and doing what they alone could do. The rest of my life has been the gradual discovery, one step at a time, of how I could fulfill that purpose. With each bump, I seem to recover more quickly. Some days I see or even anticipate the bumps. I have even learned how not to trip myself up as much as I used to. When I allow my ego to distract me, such as when I think I can get everything done at the last minute, I have to laugh. Scattering myself all over the place at the midnight hour is a sure way to trip and fall. I have to remember that I can choose to walk around the bumps as I encounter them or even move over to a whole new road.

In truth, I am grateful to my parents and for my early childhood experiences. My parents did the best they could, given what they faced as they were coming of age. At the time, my early potholes felt like abysses. Today I understand that those seemingly bottomless pits gave me the opportunity to learn lessons as deep as those pits were. I take heart from the wisdom of author Henri J. M. Nouwen, whose words taught me self-compassion and even gratitude. Nouwen helps me see that we are the most spiritual in the places where we are the most broken. We are all, in our own way, wounded healers.

All Roads Have Potholes

No one said the lessons of leadership would fall gently into our hands with the grace of a shooting star. Life demands to be taken on life's terms, not on our terms. The reward for learning to dig our way out of the holes is the strength in our souls and the vista around the next bend. If you have watched the sun rise or set from a new place, you know the joy of seeing the world anew.

This book is for all of us: for those who know who they are and what they are meant to be, for those who took the path less traveled, and for those who are still on the road to discovery. Bumps await all of us. What we learn from those bumps and how we keep going regardless is what defines us.

Janet Gonzalez-Mena

Lessons Learned from Taking Risks

Holly Elissa touched me from the very first paragraph when she writes about being poised on a dock ready to dive into a freezing cold lake. It was hard for me to think of anything else as I read along because I felt that I was the one on the dock. I got stuck on her statement that she fancies herself a risk taker, and when she went ahead and dove in, I totally forgot that she also said, "But at some level, I crave quiet and stability. Security. Nothing ugly: all things beautiful." Because I skipped that sentence the first time, it was hard for me to remember that her message is also, "Humans are hardwired to avoid conflicts and difficulties; yet only through facing difficulties do we find who we are."

The idea of facing physical risks is what made me look at myself. I've avoided them all my life. I have absolutely no desire to find out who I am by taking physical risks. Going over the speed limit on the freeway is enough for me. I have never dived into water—cold or otherwise. I'm terrified of water; it's in my DNA, or maybe I learned that from my elders who had the same problem. I've watched several members of my family work through their fear, but not me. I gave up working on it after four years of beginning swimming lessons in high school and more swimming lessons in my midthirties. My children all became good swimmers early in their lives—I saw to that. But at this point in my life, I have more pressing issues than my fear of water.

Once, on a ropes course, I came to understand more about myself. Nope, I didn't climb to dizzying heights, balance in scary places, or jump off of something that took courage. My breakthrough came while I was sitting on the ground watching women I knew doing those things. Just as a side note, I looked up "ropes courses" before I wrote this and discovered that, at the time I was there on the ground, ropes courses weren't nearly as safe as they are now. That was an interesting revelation by itself!

Anyway, I was on the ground because I just said no when told to join in. At first I was feeling guilty that I'm such a coward when it comes to taking chances with my body. My body is in good working condition, and I want it to stay that way. I guess I would say that my bumps in the road—the ones that stop me from proceeding or make me take a different road—often involve physical risks. I refuse to negotiate most of those bumps. There is a reason for that. I decided to be a mother in my early twenties, and my five children were well spread out. At the time of my ropes course experience, I still had a child at home. But as I sat there on the ground by myself, I had a revelation. I suddenly realized that I *am* a risk taker. I take risks every day of my life—it's just that they aren't physical risks. I negotiate multiple bumps in my road, but nobody knows when I'm doing something daring.

It has taken me many years to see myself in this light and even longer to state the reason, even to myself, that I'm constantly taking risks. I'll say it now: I'm shy. Nobody ever told me I was shy; I must have been good at hiding it. I'm definitely not one of the people who got labeled shy as a child. In fact, I was labeled a good girl, and in some situations, when I was comfortable enough, I ended up a leader. Maybe shyness made me a good girl—afraid to get into trouble. I'm not sure what put me in a leadership position. I don't remember ever putting myself forward to be a leader.

As I stood there that day watching my friends and colleagues risk life and limb in exchange for thrills and the satisfaction of facing fears, I realized that I'm quite practiced at that. All it takes is a new situation, a new person, or some kind of meeting or gathering where I don't know everybody well. When I stand up to talk in a group, I'm taking a risk. I take a huge risk when disagreeing with someone. I'm even taking a risk writing this.

What a risk I'm taking whenever I step into the spotlight to speak in public. Maybe I never learned to swim, but I did learn to write proposals for workshops, which, when accepted, put me in the same position Holly Elissa was in when she poised on the dock. You have to understand how risky speech making is for me. In college when I discovered I was required to take a speech class, I changed my major. As an English major, all I had to do was read and write—no speeches!

As I write this, I'm remembering that I was in a number of school plays as a child. That didn't feel scary, even though I was in the spotlight. All I had to do was remember my lines. I wasn't being myself. Maybe even today I use that same technique—I pretend that I am somebody else in tough situations. I have to think about that idea some more.

I don't mean to minimize Holly Elissa's message by focusing only on rather trivial bumps in my road. Of course, I have had life-changing bumps in my family of origin and my present-day family. Divorce, poverty, mental illness, deaths—I've experienced them all and hopefully have grown stronger from them. But I'm not ready to write about that. Instead, I choose to focus on how I have grown from taking less significant risks and learning about who I am from them. One set of experiences I've been working with for the last forty years relates to my work across cultures and my involvement in the struggle to increase equity and social justice in our country. As a person experiencing shyness, I've bravely put up with discomfort when speaking out for equity and when communicating across cultures with people who are different from myself. I can testify to how much those challenges in my life have helped me grow stronger and wiser. Though I said no to the ropes course, I have willingly put myself in other situations that were scary or at least difficult and uncomfortable. So to conclude, I agree with Holly Elissa that the bumps in the road are positive and growth producing.

Oh, and by the way, very recently when my six-year-old granddaughter asked me to go roller skating with her, I said yes. I haven't roller skated since I was nine years old. I was at least fifty years older than every other skater. Yet there I was in the spotlight in the roller rink, my knees shaking and my feet trying to slide out from under me. I'm still congratulating myself.

Luis Antonio Hernandez

Learning Lessons Forever

The wisdom, grace, and good thoughts of my colleagues Holly Elissa and Janet are the affirmation and continuity on the theme of personal and professional growth. Both detail opportunities and challenges in taking risks, ways to seek freedom, exercises to gain confidence, and the discovery of personal paths. I'll attempt to plunge into the cold waters of my own risks by shattering the calm waters of my comfort zones. How can I as an individual, a leader, and a teacher continually examine the layers of my social and emotional life that produce words, actions, and behaviors? It is not easy to peel this personal onion, for it will produce involuntary tears, hidden memories, and forgotten resolutions of good intentions. The work on oneself takes many turns. It is a lifelong learning process, full of risks. This process is part of being a leader in whatever location, time, or life stage. Learning is forever.

Paula Jorde Bloom (2000) has dedicated her life to leadership development in early childhood education settings. She challenges novice and seasoned trainers in the field to ignite their passion for learning and to be passionate, inspired, and confident. For learning to take place, it needs to be uncomfortable. I've always been struck by the power of this statement, for it frames learning as a rigorous and sweaty enterprise. A participant in one of my classes mentioned how true it was for her; she said that for her to learn how to ride a bicycle, there was always the risk and lesson of falling off the bike at some point. How true! Basically, you cannot learn how to ride a bike, ski down a huge mountain, or roller skate like Janet without falling at some point. And it also applies to other aspects of life: learning how to use a smartphone, making bread from scratch, sewing a button on a shirt, learning geometry, or swimming in the ocean. The initial uncertainty of something new or foreign either thrills, repulses, or enchants us. It is a risk that we learn how to conquer, accept, own, and move on from. It also builds the attitude of confidence to be fearless in various uncomfortable situations—translate falling off the bike to running a center, presenting at a conference, writing an article, or taking a difficult course.

As the title of the chapter suggests, we will face many bumps in the road of life as well as a multitude of potholes. We can have the confidence to see bumps as minor obstacles, but if we don't have that confidence, those bumps become insurmountable mountains never to be conquered. Or we can sidestep potholes and continue with the fear that the holes are deeper than a water well. As leaders, the stronger our sense of forward direction and confidence, the smoother the path will become.

For those bumps in the road, a sense of confidence gives us the power to surmount them. For that Everest peak to become an anthill, we'll need to peer beyond that huge mountain we have created. We tend to create our sense of reality, and the bumps in the road are products of our experiences and imaginations. We make things more awful or difficult than they really are. We set expectations way too high or create a situation that in our heads will surely not work out. "Why submit this proposal when I know they will turn it down?" And before you know it, it has been rejected and you are victorious in your own dark expectation—I told you so. Gosh, we are our own worst enemies. We engineer gigantic bumps and potholes in the road of life, a highway littered with one roadblock after another. It may be time to leave the mind-set of a bump engineer and concentrate on a more agreeable life road planner.

I suggest we start with building a superhighway of confidence. In a leadership development reflection exercise, one can look back on how adversity, difficult times, and bumps in the road help build confidence. Biographies are full of ordinary and extraordinary people conquering incredible obstacles—think of Gandhi, Martin Luther King Jr., and Maria Montessori. In many families, we still talk about how life was difficult during the Depression, how grandparents made do with less, and how the lessons of dire economic times provided a drive to survive and move ahead. Or, if you ever had the opportunity to talk to African American friends who experienced the days of segregation in our country, you will find a spirit of resiliency and confidence—we shall overcome. Or if you have met new immigrants willing to share their journey to our country as refugees from around the world, you will find in their stories incredible hurdles and bumps before they could settle and eventually thrive in the United States. None of their stories are easy or full of joy. The simpler lesson is how adversity and difficult circumstances can propel individuals and families to forge ahead by taking incredible risks, and how confidence is earned human capital—all through difficult times and forward determination.

Next time one of those pesky bumps in the road appears before you, challenge yourself to be a road builder. Be ready to pour asphalt on the potholes and step right over them. After all, it is your road of life full of risks—you own it.

Debra Ren-Etta Sullivan

Life without Bumps Would Pass Us By

What a nuisance all those pesky bumps in the road are! To live a bump-free life may seem appealing, but it must be boring as heck, and I doubt it is even realistically possible to achieve. It means being perfect and perfectly happy. Most people are neither, and those who claim to be are probably lying. They should read our chapter about self-doubts. Like Holly Elissa, I knew early on that there would be a number of bumps in my road and that I would have to strike out on new paths rather than travel worn paths of accepted success like others. Most worn paths have lost all of their bumps. Years of sameness have smoothed them out so much that we almost have to create bumps ourselves to avoid complacency and the danger of having real life pass us by unnoticed. What Luis wrote about learning to be uncomfortable really resonated with me. A worn path can be very comfortable, but there is nothing new, nothing to learn. We want children to appreciate lifelong learning, which is pretty impossible if they are to avoid discomfort! Bumps allow us to take the scenic route of life, a life filled with unexpected opportunities for growth and learning.

My Bumps

We were asked to consider if we always knew who we were or if we are a work in progress. Being the Libra that I am, I like to think I am both. There are aspects of who I am that I always was. From a very young age, I felt strongly about justice, equity, and fairness, and I spoke up about them. I got into a lot of trouble for that. For example, in chapter 9, I talked about how unfair I felt it was (when I was a child) that I had to eat peas but my father did not. I demanded an answer. I was sent to my room. On the other hand, I find myself regularly questioning if I really know where this life is taking me. Am I misreading signs of what I'm supposed to be doing? Am I missing opportunities to do what I'm really supposed to be doing? If I'm really heading the right way, why are there so many obstacles and challenges? What does it mean when there seems to be an inordinate number of bumps?

I certainly did not fit in with my father's definition of a "good" daughter. I was about thirteen when I figured out that I would never fit his definition of good wife material: submissive, unquestioning, deferential. I was momentarily saddened when I realized that I was going to grow up to be the kind of woman my father never would have chosen for a wife. I got over the saddened part, but I could see many bumps unfolding right before my eyes. Holly Elissa says go around the bumps, and Janet, in her example about her fear of water, suggests that we just let some of the bumps go. Feeling guilty about not being the kind of woman my father thought I should be was one bump I had to let go of because I couldn't see myself becoming my mother. I decided I would not feel guilty about being smart, having opinions, and taking stances against injustice, inequity, and unfairness. And, I will not be sent to my room for asking questions and expecting answers.

I did foresee a life full of bumps early on, but there are also those big bumps that I never saw coming. Most of us experience life-changing events in our journeys, events that change who we are and how we view life. Losing loved ones is such an event. Such losses redefine who we are and how we are. I learned a lot about myself through losing loved ones. I learned that I do not have complete control over all aspects of my life. I learned that losing someone does not mean I have lost everyone. I learned that I never know when my road may change direction. I learned that I can't make assumptions about who I am or that I will never change. I learned that there are still reasons to continue on the path after experiencing a big bump and that, yes, more bumps may be coming. I learned that I am not the "boss of everything" but I can be the boss of deciding that I can "strike out on new paths" and continue to grow and learn.

Summary ....

Holly Elissa Bruno

I once hitchhiked down the East Coast. I was twenty-two. At the time, I thought of my hitchhiking as unremarkable. Hitchhiking was an accepted way to travel distances. Drivers weren't warned about the dangers of picking up strangers. Hitchhikers didn't fear that a serial killer was trolling the highways to pick up innocents. The man who gave me a ride was a devotee of Ernest Hemingway. As an American literature major, I had read Hemingway's books. We talked Hemingway all the way through the Pennsylvania mountains, following the Susquehanna River from upstate New York toward Baltimore. My fellow hitchhiker, a young woman from England, dozed gratefully in the backseat. When we arrived at our destination, we thanked our generous driver and he thanked us. To this day, I recall the ease of our conversation and the freedom of "riding my thumb." I felt like an explorer, open to the unknown, willing to take the risk.

I was crazy! Today I would never hitchhike. What a dangerous, foolhardy, and naive choice, especially for a young woman. I had no control over the outcome. I put myself in danger. Trust me, you were likely far more mature in your early twenties than I was. However, I didn't hit a bump in that road. I wasn't harmed. In fact, I felt free and happy as if I were protected by a guardian angel. Sister Madeline Birmingham, my spiritual director, advised, "No decision is a mistake unless you harm others or yourself. Learn from each decision." I learned.

Some folk believe in karma, that we are given challenges to learn necessary life lessons so we can move on. Until we learn the lesson, we are given one bump after another until we get the point. Whether we bound over the bumps, fall into them and pick ourselves up, create our own bumps, or pretend there are no bumps, we make a choice. Each choice takes us closer to or further away from our true self. What matters to me is that I keep learning.

Discussion Questions ....

1. Have you ever felt you have been protected or guided by an invisible force through a hard time? How do you understand or explain that experience?

2. What bump has taught you an essential and life-changing lesson? What are the lessons you know you need to learn but are avoiding?

3. What's your current bump? What holds you back from taking action?

References ....

Bloom, Paula Jorde. 2000. *Workshop Essentials: Planning and Presenting Dynamic Workshops*. Far Hills, NJ: New Horizons Press.

Cozolino, Louis. 2006. *The Neuroscience of Human Relationships: Attachment and the Developing Social Brain*. New York: W. W. Norton and Company.

Frost, Robert. 1916. "The Road Not Taken." In *Mountain Interval*. New York: Henry Holt.

Johnson, Whitney. 2012. "Disrupt Yourself." *Harvard Business Review* (July–August): 147. http://hbr.org/2012/07/disrupt-yourself/ar/1.

Jung, Carl Gustav. 1964. *Man and His Symbols*. New York: Dell Publishing.

Larson, Britta, and Susan Offutt. 2012. "Get Over It! Managing Grudges in Education Settings." Podcast interview by Holly Elissa Bruno. *Heart to Heart Conversations on Leadership*, September 1. www.bamradionetwork.com/index.php?option=com_content&view=article&id=884:leadr&catid=69:infobamradionetworkcom&Itemid=144.

Rogers, Fred. 1994. *You Are Special: Words of Wisdom for All Ages from a Beloved Neighbor*. New York: Penguin.

About the Authors

Holly Elissa Bruno

A question Holly Elissa hears often is, "Hey, you're an attorney. Why did you come over to early childhood education?" Her short answer is that she learned from the bumps in her road:

- Practicing law wasn't much fun (imagine criminal law and copyright law).

- Her approach to life isn't adversarial.

- She missed being with people devoted to teaching and learning (Holly Elissa started out as a teacher).

- She didn't feel she was making a difference.

So Holly Elissa did what she does best when she hits a bump: put one foot in front of the other and kept walking until she found a home. Wheelock College early childhood leaders Gwen Morgan and Andi Genser asked if she would work with them. The rest, she says, is (joyous) history.

Today Holly Elissa Bruno, MA, JD, is an author, attorney, and acclaimed international keynote speaker. You can listen to podcast interviews with Holly Elissa on NAEYC Radio, National Head Start Association Radio, and National Association of School Principals Radio. Tune in to Holly Elissa's online radio program, *Heart to Heart Conversations on Leadership: Your Guide to Making a Difference* at BAMradionetwork.com or via her website hollyelissabruno.com.

Janet Gonzalez-Mena

Janet fell into the early childhood field by being a parent in a co-op preschool. She never left the field after that. As a reentry student-mom with a bachelor's degree in English, she got her California teaching credential followed by a master's degree in human development from Pacific Oaks College. Her ECE career includes preschool teacher, home visitor, director of child care services (which included opening an infant center), plus coordinator of a pilot program of therapeutic child care for abused and neglected children. She eventually went on to teach at Napa Valley College in child and family studies until she retired.

Author of many books and articles, her favorite is fondly called "The little yellow book" by many in the field. The real title is *Diversity in Early Care and Education: Honoring Differences*. Janet has an interest in negotiating conflicts with a focus on equity and social justice. She has worked in Head Start as a teacher and trainer. She now serves as adjunct faculty for WestEd's Program for Infant/Toddler Care.

Nobody was having many children during the Depression when Janet was born. When World War II came along, even fewer children were born. Janet's dream was to grow up and have lots of children. She aimed for six but stopped at five. In a way, she never left early childhood—at work and at home. Now she is slowly becoming surrounded by grandchildren, so she can still use the skills at home that she learned long ago.

 Luis Antonio Hernandez

Talk about turns and bumps on the road: while studying architecture, Luis worked as a teacher's assistant in a kindergarten classroom and fell in love with the wonderment of learning in the young years. He was hooked. He eventually received a master's degree in bilingual/multicultural early education, and to his parents' delight, he also completed his degree in planning and architecture. He became a teacher in the public schools of San Francisco—a defining life experience. From there, he worked with Migrant Head Start programs throughout the West, learning about the dreams and aspirations of families and the hard work of teachers. This led to opportunities to train teachers and staff. The work also led to active advocacy with organizations that support children and families as well as the ECE profession.

Today Luis provides training to a variety of programs across the country on topics close to the heart of those in the ECE field. For Luis, the best part of that work is meeting and interacting with participants during conference presentations. And together with his friends Janet, Debra, and Holly Elissa, he works to design a learning experience with a high level of motivation, challenging thoughts, and energy. "Never boring" can be their motto!

While it may seem that Luis lives in airport terminals due to his extensive travels, he loves living in Miami with its hot summers and delicious winters. And kayaking and yoga are some of his favorite activities wherever he is: both are sure ways to ease some of the bumps in the road.

Debra Ren-Etta Sullivan

The path to our present is always filled with twists, turns, detours, and scenic sites. Debra's path to leadership and early childhood education began in the fifth grade when she decided that one day she would open her own school where every possible aspect of diversity would be represented in the faces and lives of all the children, where all children learned one signed language and two voiced ones, and where children and their families found their voice around equity and advocacy. Twenty-seven years later, Debra has studied five languages, completed a bachelor's degree in cultural anthropology, a master's degree in curriculum and instruction, and a doctorate in educational leadership.

Then came a twist: Debra became the dean of a small early childhood and K–8 teacher preparation college in Seattle with a focus on preparing teachers for successful work with children from low-income communities, with children of color, and with children learning English. She immersed herself in the study of young children's education, growth, and development and increased her commitment to work with underserved and underrepresented families and communities in developing the critical skills needed for them to be strong, effective advocates for their children.

In 2002, Debra cofounded and became the president of The Praxis Institute for Early Childhood Education, a nonprofit organization that provides professional development and continuing education for those who work with young children, their families, and their communities. She continues her advocacy on behalf of underserved children, families, and communities through her work with the Seattle Black Child Development Institute, the Coalition for Equal Education Rights, and the Cultural Reconnection Mission delegation. Her first Redleaf Press book, *Learning to Lead: Effective Leadership Skills for Teachers of Young Children*, is a self-directed guide to leadership development for early childhood teachers, aides, assistants, and care providers and is based on the premise that we are all leaders.

Index

decision making
  learning from, 216
  modes of, 45–46
Defense of Marriage Act, 88
Delany, Samuel R., 98
denial of events, 204–6
depression, as opposite of play, 129
Derman-Sparks, Louise, 82, 83
development
  cognitive, 99, 130, 134
  impact of technology on, 99, 103, 107
  language, 99
developmentally appropriate practice (DAP)
  bases for, 79
  as best practice, 110
  considering in goal writing and planning, 111, 136
  reactions to NAEYC position statement, 4, 73–74
Developmentally Appropriate Practice in Early Childhood Programs (1987; NAEYC), 4, 73
Developmentally Appropriate Practice in Early Childhood Programs (1997; Bredekamp and Copple), 4, 74
Developmentally Appropriate Practice in Early Childhood Programs (2009; Copple and Bredekamp), 74, 140
disasters, affirmation of civility and, 13–15
discipline
  aggression and, 151
  diversity in approaches to, 72–73
disruptive thinking, benefits of, 206–7
diversity
  acknowledging, 79–80
  conflict resulting from, 2–4
  consistent care in ECE, 69–70
  cultural bumps, 3
  discipline, approaches to, 72–73

discomfort with, 90–92, 93
effects of, 69
global influences, 68–69
misunderstandings based on assumptions, 19
multicultural readiness, 80–87
pluralism and, 74–76
social justice and equity, 33–36, 79, 85
third space perspective, 3, 4, 15
we versus I perspectives, 72–73
See also uniformity; universal principles
documentation of assessment and observations, 115
dominance. *See* oppression and dominance
Don't Be So Defensive! (Ellison), 150
dualistic thinking
  dichotomous judgments, 11
  versus holistic thinking, 4

E
early childhood education (ECE)
  consistent care, 69–70
  curriculum considerations, 109–18
  infants and toddlers, 122–24
  Reconceptualizing Early Childhood Education (RECE), 73–74
  values and ethics, 67–68, 116–17
  See also educators; National Association for the Education of Young Children (NAEYC)
Education of Man, The (Froebel), 130
educators
  characteristics of excellent teachers, 116–17
  compared to other professionals, 116
  desired characteristics of, 65
  flexibility, need for, 112, 175
  as learners, 120–21

lifelong learning, 67, 75–76, 165, 197, 212

passion of, 65, 75–76, 116, 158, 197

self-doubts and professional insecurities, 165–71, 173–74

sensitivity and responsiveness, suggestions for, 6

See also leadership skills

Edwards, Julie Olsen, 83

egocentrism, 53

Einstein, Albert, 195

Ellison, Sharon, 150

emergent curriculum, 72, 121

emotional intelligence (EQ), 105, 130, 161

employment, power dynamics and, 34

endorphins, release through laughter, 132

English, as dominant language, 82

EQ. *See* emotional intelligence (EQ)

equity issues, 13–15, 32–36, 37

See also power dynamics; social justice and equity

Escuela Cuauhtemoc, 58, 190

ethics

NAEYC code of ethical conduct, 86, 192

See also values and principles

evaluation of learning environments, 112

executive function, 127

expectations

about technology, 97

consequences of, 20–21, 26

of effective leaders, 175

extroverts, 49, 177

F

fairness. *See* social justice and equity

families

teacher-family relationships, 3, 113–14, 119

See also parents

fear

amygdala and, 133, 134

of change, 77, 105

of emotional expression, 11

of "not the same," 60

steps for diminishing, 133–34

of unknown, 60

See also risk-taking

feelings

exploring, 144–45

self-regulation, 149

showing, 145–46, 153, 155, 157–58, 161

See also social-emotional competence

"Filling the Shoes of the Founder" (McLaughlin and Offutt), 22

flattery, 174

flexibility, need for, 112, 175

forgiving and remembering, 204–6

Freedman, David H., 191, 194

Froebel, Friedrich, 130

Frost, Robert, 23, 208–9

Fulghum, Robert, 70–71

G

Gardner, Howard, 130, 160

gender

gender fluidity, 89–90

power dynamics and, 34

See also sexual orientation

Gerber, Magda, 103, 124, 150, 151, 190

"Get Over It! Managing Grudges in Education Settings" (Larsen and Offutt), 206

Goleman, Daniel, 130, 161

Gonta, Michael, 178

good intentions. *See* intent/intention

"Great Pretender, The," 165

ground rules, in teambuilding, 28–30

marginalization, 80
power dynamics and, 31–36
understanding through self-
    assessment of, 84–85
See also social justice and equity
organized people
    characteristics of, 194
    as majority, 191–92

P

Paddleford, Clementine, 186–87
pain, 203
Panksepp, Jaak, 127
parents
    as child's first teacher, 113, 119
    as partners, 113–14
    views of play, 131–32, 136
    See also families
passion
    of educators, 65, 75–76, 116, 158,
        197
    expressing, 157–58
patriarchy, 37
Perfect Mess, A (Abrahamson and
    Freedman), 191, 194
Persistence of Memory (Dali), 193
personal power, 37–40
personas, 171–72
physical ability, power dynamics and,
    35
physical security, 123
Piaget, Jean, 130
Pikler, Emmi, 130, 150
Platters (musical group), 165
play
    of adults, 127, 128–29, 136–38,
        139–40
    characteristics of, 127–28, 135
    children's need for, 130–31
    definition of, 138
    parents' views of, 131–32, 136
    pretend/make-believe, 135, 137

sports and, 131
work and responsibility versus, 128,
    129, 135–36
*Play: How It Shapes the Brain, Opens the
    Imagination, and Invigorates the
    Soul* (Brown), 128
Plessy v. Ferguson, 88
pluralism, power of, 74–76
policies and procedures, importance
    of, 31–32, 64
power dynamics
    assumptions about, 19–23
    impact on children, 31–32, 40
    knowledge and, 75
    oppression, dominance, and privi-
        lege, 32–36, 37, 38–39
    organizational dynamics, 19–23,
        31–32
    personal power, 37–40
    shared power, teaching about,
        82–83
    social contracts, 24–26
    in teambuilding, 51, 59
    understanding through self-
        assessment of, 84–85
praxis, 119
prefrontal cortex, 133
prejudice and discrimination
    marginalization, 80
    power dynamics and, 35, 82–83
    self-assessment of, 84
    See also social justice and equity
pretending. *See* imposter syndrome
pretend play, 135, 137
privilege
    power dynamics and, 32–36, 37
    understanding through self-
        assessment of, 84–85
    See also oppression and dominance;
        social justice and equity
problem solving
    leadership and, 150–51

RERUN approach, 5–6

procrastination, 184

promissory estoppel, 24

protective instincts, recognizing, 149, 155, 156, 159, 162–63

psychosynthesis, 138, 172–73

public speaking, 211

purpose

versus intent, 184

seeking, personal accounts, 188–91, 198, 207–10

See also intentionality

R

race, power dynamics and, 35

Reconceptualizing Early Childhood Education (RECE), 73–74

reflection, 5, 112, 119, 175

relationships

authenticity in, 76, 100, 101

continuity of care/consistent care, 69–70, 123

creating with children and families, 6, 113–14, 119

importance of, 64

with infants and toddlers, 122

pluralism and, 74–76

role in language and cognitive development, 99

synergy in, 4–5

workplace, 26–30

See also teambuilding; villages, hypothetical

religion, power dynamics and, 35

RERUN approach to problem solving, 5–6

resiliency, 112, 175

respect

for behavioral differences, 192

importance of, 52–53

responsibility, need for, 54–55, 57

Reyes, Luis-Vicente, 7

risk-taking

building confidence, 214

learning and, 212–13

personal accounts, 210–12, 216

"Road Not Taken, The" (Frost), 208–9

Rogers, Fred, 54, 130

ropes courses, 210

Rosenberg, Marshall B., 150

Rumi, 4

S

Sandy, Superstorm, 13–15

secrets, keeping, 176–78

self-assessment

discomfort of, 90–92

of multicultural readiness, 80–81, 83–85, 86–87

self-compassion, 53, 209

self-disruption, 206–7

self-doubts, 165–71, 173–74

See also imposter syndrome

self-esteem, 147

self-reflection, 5, 112, 119, 175

self-regulation, 149

self-respect, 53

sensitivity and responsiveness, suggestions for, 6

sexual orientation

gender fluidity, 89–90

legal issues, 88–89

power dynamics and, 36

shadow concept, 83–84, 193–94, 203–4

shyness. *See* introverts

Sisters of Charity, 51, 59

Slaughterhouse-Five (Vonnegut), 202

slavery, 38–39

Smith, Errol St. Clair, 192

social change, early childhood education and, 110, 118

social contracts, 24–26

social-emotional competence

expressing caring, 145–46, 153, 157–58, 161

having confidence in abilities, 146–49, 154, 155, 159, 162

knowing what you want/don't want, 144–45, 152–53, 155, 156–57, 161

recognizing protective instincts, 149, 155, 156, 159, 162–63

saying no, 146, 154, 155, 158–59, 161–62

self-examination of, 143–44, 164

social justice and equity

in disaster situations, 13–15

goals and strategies, 86

issues of, 32–36, 37, 79, 85

legislation and, 88–89

as life's purpose, 190–91, 212, 215

social networking, 97–98

socioeconomic status

accentuation of by disaster, 14–15

in hypothetical village, 47

power dynamics and, 36

Southwest Airlines, 140

speeches, making, 211

spelling, texting and, 98, 103

spontaneity, valuing, 194, 198

See also play

sports play, 131

Starr, Alexandra, 7

Star Trek, 96–97, 100, 102

stress

physiologic responses, 132

shadow concept and, 203–4

workplace, 133

subpersonalities, 172–73

success

celebrating, 117–18

requirements for, 125

synergy, in relationships, 4–5

T

Taking the War Out of Our Words: The Art of Powerful Non-Defensive Communication (Ellison), 150–51

Tardos, Anna, 150

teacher-family relationships

conflict in, 3

establishing, 113–14, 119

teachers. *See* educators

teambuilding

celebrating success, 117–18

core values and principles, finding, 51–54

example exercises, 28–30

hypothetical villages, creating, 43–50, 53–54, 55–57

team members, 50

technology

changing nature of, 100–102

child development and, 99, 100, 103, 107

dependence on, 101, 103–4

impact of, 95–107

inequity and inequality of, 97

personalization of, 105–6, 107

Star Trek analogy, 96–97, 100, 102

Terrell, Ann, 53

texting, 98, 102–3, 106

third space perspective, 3, 4, 12, 15, 16

timeliness, 19, 191, 192–93

time-out approach to discipline, 73

toddlers. *See* infants and toddlers

tolerance. *See* civility

toys, impact on child development, 99, 100, 103

transparency, workplace issues and, 27

twelve-step programs, 132

Twombly, Sue, 69–70